Ahad Cobb has written a very compelling book that catalyzes each of us to search deeply into our own soul's history. His honesty and openness in telling his personal story are presented in a flowing poetic style with both humor and reflection. This is definitely a book that I would want to re-read and keep in my library!

> —Marcia Starck
> Author, *Medical Astrology and Healing for the 21st Century,*
> *Women's Medicine Ways, The Dark Goddess*

An audaciously revealing spiritual odyssey, rich in whimsy and insight.

> —Steven McFadden
> Author, *Legend of the Rainbow Warriors, Profiles in Wisdom*

A courageous effort!! Most writers of spiritual books are afraid to write the shadowside of their spiritual search.

> —Samara Christy
> Psychic and teacher of the *Be Your Own Psychic* workshop

Superconscious is more than just an interesting story about a unique and eccentric character. In the telling of Orayna's story, Ahad also reveals a valuable world-view template for healing into consciousness.

> —Karin Arielle
> Co-owner, The Ark Bookstore, Santa Fe NM

Ahad Cobb has written a lively and compelling account of the teachings of an eccentric, gifted, all-too-human spiritual teacher who refused to proclaim herself a spiritual teacher. Orayna's insights are pure and lovely, her personality thorny, her language direct and uncompromising. Her effect on one man's personal transformation will be an inspiration to any seekers who wish to integrate psychology with soul, wisdom traditions with iconoclasm, the personal with the universal.

> —Mirabai Starr
> Author of a new translation of *Dark Night of the Soul*
> by St. John of the Cross

SUPERCONSCIOUS
RELEASING PAST-LIFE RECORDINGS

Ahad Cobb

Frog, Ltd.
Berkeley, California

Published by Frog, Ltd

Frog, Ltd. books are distributed by
North Atlantic Books
P.O. Box 12327
Berkeley, CA 94712

Printed in the United States of America

Cover and book design © Jan Camp

North Atlantic Books' publications are available through most bookstores. For further information, call 800-337-2665 or visit our website at www.northatlanticbooks.com.

Substantial discounts on bulk quantities are available to corporations, professional associations, and other organizations. For details and discount information, contact our special sales department.

Library of Congress Cataloging-in-Publication Data
Cobb, Ahad.
Superconscious: Releasing Past-Life Recordings / by Ahad Cobb.
    p. cm.
ISBN 1-58394-064-2 (paper)
1. Ahad Cobb.   2. Spiritual biography — United States.   3. Past life readings.
I. Title.

BF1679.8.C63 A3 2002
133.9'3 — dc21

                                                          CIP
                                                  2002022190

1 2 3 4 5 6 7 8 9 / 06 05 04 03 02

To Orayna Orr (Joanna Walsh)
"the most beautiful and knowing woman in this or any other galaxy"

and to my mother Mary
whose constant love made all these adventures possible

PREAMBLE

This is the story of my relationship and inner work with Orayna Orr, who was my spiritual mentor and closest friend for a period of fifteen years. We met in 1983 when I was thirty-five and she was seventy-five, and our relationship continued until her death at age ninety.

Interwoven with this are some of the amazing events of Orayna's life, as told to me over the course of our friendship. Her life story is a teaching as much as her philosophy. Spiritual life is based on actual experiences, not on ideas or opinions.

Embedded in these two narratives are the philosophy of Totality as realized by Orayna and her husband, the Total Meditation which leads one to the awareness of being Superconscious, and the methodology for releasing past-life recordings through the use of the vortex energy.

"Superconscious" refers to that which is above and beyond our normal waking consciousness. An adjective used as a noun, "Superconscious" refers to an all-pervasive quality of existence, of awareness, rather than an entity, some thing. Superconscious is always present in our lives, although, as the name implies, we are usually not aware of its presence. Superconscious can be accessed through meditation and prayer. Superconscious comes to us in the form of intuition, inspiration, inner guidance, visions and lucid dreams. Superconscious is active, creative, loving, compassionate, and beyond the limitations of our personal self-identifications.

"Subconscious" refers to that which is below our normal waking consciousness. Subconscious is like a basement warehouse in which all the

1

experiences, sensations, and emotions of an individual are automatically recorded and stored in complex clusters. Subconscious is the reservoir of all our desire and fear, anger and sorrow. Most of our dreams are simply wanderings through the subconscious storehouse. Karma is held as recordings in subconscious, which can enhance and amplify our abilities, but all too often distorts and aberrates our intentions and actions with irrational perversion and aversion. Subconscious is automatically reactive and unique in each individual.

At times in life we may find that our ability to function in freedom, to create the kind of life we desire, is interfered with by irrational fears, rages, addictions, etc. The root of the aberrations can often be found in subconscious, in recorded memories of previous traumatic experiences that are coming to the surface, reacting out in present time, for instance, under the stress of immediate challenges, a new job, a new relationship, for instance. Bringing these traumatic memories to the light of consciousness can loosen their grip on us and allow us to function in a more normative manner.

These reactive imprints are often relieved by reliving the more traumatic events of our early years in life. However, we sometimes find that these subconscious traits present as memories that are not based in the current life experience, as if they were impressions from other life times in other time periods. Whether our belief system permits anything like reincarnation or not, nevertheless, "past-life recordings" do seem to be affecting us in present time.

This book presents my experience of the inner work of releasing past-life recordings. Whether or not there may be reincarnation leads to some philosophical reflections, but it is irrelevant to the effectiveness of this work in my life. Through guided meditation I came into touch with superconscious awareness and from that awareness cleared away some of the contents of my subconscious over a period of years. At the same time I became aware of the functioning of Superconscious in my daily life and became more open to superconscious inspiration and guidance.

The spiritual philosophy and technology Orayna and her husband arrived at through their inner journeys together has resonance with many spiritual traditions and yet is uniquely modern and American, innovative and idiosyncratic. I present it here as it was presented to me, making no claims that this is the ultimate truth, only that it was an effective approach to the great mystery for me at a certain time in my life.

A note about names.

During the period of our work together, Orayna's name was Joanna Walsh, and that is how her name will appear in most of these pages. Toward the end of her life, she had her name legally changed to her home-planet name Orayna Orr, which is how I remember her now.

She was born Blossom Cohen on December 21, 1907, in Syracuse, NY. She was married as Bluma Friedman in 1926, divorced in 1946, and married as Joanna Walsh in 1953. She legally changed her name to Orayna Orr in 1993. She died on June 17, 1998 in Santa Fe, NM.

Her husband was born Hardin D. Walsh, born on July 13, 1905, in Baltimore, MD. He died on October 23,1987 in Santa Fe, NM. In person, Joanna usually referred to her husband by his home-planet name, Hadron of Orr, although in telling her story she freely uses both names, Hardin more for the outer person, Hadron for the inner reality.

This is an oral history. I spoke this story into a hand-held cassette recorder during sunny afternoons while wandering paths through the mountains and by the streams of northern New Mexico, beginning in the spring of 1995. A quiet, clear voice deep within recited this story as I walked. You have it as I received it, with a little bit of editing.

In addition, I have incorporated three other sources.

Over the winter of 1993–1994, I made a series of recordings of Orayna telling her life story to me. Portions of these transcriptions are included here, under the chapter headings "Her Story."

I have included passages from her husband's unpublished masterwork, *Totality Concept* by Hardin D. Walsh, to give further direct flavor of the philosophy this couple pioneered and lived by. These ideas not only informed all the work that Joanna did with me, but they also stand alone as theory and practice.

Joanna kept longhand notes on sessions she did with people. I was able to recover her notes on some of the sessions she did with me. I have included a few brief comments from her session notes as a contrapuntal voice.

These three other sources are the property of Totality Research and Development Corporation of Santa Fe, NM, and are used by permission, as are Hardin's drawings and several personal photographs.

My stories inevitably involve relationships with other people who shared real-life time with me, who stimulated and shared in my inner work. Some of their names have been changed and some have not. Some of their individual realities about the experiences we shared might be quite different from mine. Though grounded in real people and actual events, the experiential reality I relate is mine alone.

The original title of this book was *Superconscious Comics & Stories*. This is the reason.

It is said that Western civilization views life as a tragedy and that Eastern civilization views life as a comedy.

Tragedy ends in death. There is only one life which ends in death, followed by eternal bliss in heaven or eternal damnation in hell. "It's never too late to believe, until death. Then it's too late."

Comedy ends in marriage. Reincarnation is the perpetual recycling of body stuff, mind stuff, soul stuff, karma and kama vasanas — sorrowful, joyful, deeply poignant — ultimately leading to release from the illusion of individuality and union (or marriage) with all that is.

Some elements in these stories can be seen as pathetic, if not tragic. She dies without having achieved her grandest ambitions, without a successor to carry on her life work. He does not marry his beloved and ride off into the sunset. No one achieves total enlightenment, at least not in these pages.

If you are expecting a lot of action, it might seem like hardly anything happens at all, except for two jokers hanging around in empty space philosophizing and telling old lives' tales.

But for those of you who might appreciate the subtleties of love, lover, and beloved, the delicate interweaving of knowing, pretending, and forgetting, the levity of karmic comeback, the thrill of karmic pay-back, the bliss of reunion and the sweet joy of release, and for all who enjoy the never-ending mystery of life, Orayna and I will rehearse our roles for your delight. For we are superconscious comics, and these are a few of our stories.

We begin with a little background music.

BEGINNING AT THE END OF THE LINE
1968–1969

Now here this

      this story

            one story:

                     1969: at the end of the
line . . .

      Just turned 22, grown-up blues, I'm at the end of the line,
at the end of the line . . .

            I keep hearing those words, *at the end of
the line,* standing on an empty railway platform, winter after
midnight, *at the end of the line,* seeing this image. . . .

                   *Snow drifting
down in the night, thick silent snow falling through the aureole of a single
light up high, bright snow angels swirling, sifting down through the trees,
filling the forest, covering the embankments and the railroad tracks in deep
cold white, "silence in the snowy fields". . . .*

               *I'm in a deserted way station
next to the rails, just a wooden bench against a board wall, peaked roof
overhead, half walls on three sides, a platform to pick up and discharge
passengers, barely a shelter, open to the snowy night drifting down, the
empty spaces beyond the light. . . .*

              *White upon white upon white, snow
drifting down, silence folding into silence. . . .*

                 *No where to go. No thing to
do. No one to come. Fear on the run. Run out of time. End of the line. . . .*

Fascinated with homelessness, fugitive status, life on the run, run out of time, driving miles without meaning in a rusted-out VW bus, counting the hours in dead heads of cigarettes sucked into the slipstream, driving up nameless country roads to crash out at dead ends beside streams, bogs in the road, no where to go, to escape, hopeless hitchhiking on wooded turnpikes as afternoon fades to dusk, and dusk to night, absorbing the headlights of hundreds of cars passing me by. . . .

Lingering at railway stations late at night long after the last commuter train has gone to bed, savoring abandonment, helplessness, hopelessness, homelessness, drifting snow descending. . . .

College graduation is the opening of the abyss, pure terror, no where to go, no thing to do with my life. My classmates, stoned on acid, see large silvery beings of light in the air presiding over the ceremonies. I refuse to go to the ceremonies, graduating, nevertheless, Phi Beta Kappa, Magna Cum Laude, totally unprepared for life outside the educational institutions that have sheltered me, whose limited games I have doggedly mastered for the last sixteen years. Having no idea what to do or where to go, I hit the road. . . .

Restless unblessed wanderings through glorious summer days in New England forests, green and gray mountains, mind spinning, whirring, buzzing, voices swarming like bees around a hive, mind opening, reaching, grasping, collecting thoughts, phrases, impressions, reflections, central switchboard swamped with calls from above, beyond, all around, red lights blinking, much noise, little signal, no direction known. . . .

Stop the car. Get out by the rushing river. Sunlight streaming down, wind flowing, sheets of clear water drinking in the light as it tumbles, gurgles, purls over its bed of stones sparkling and gleaming, pushes through decades of deadfall, wood stripped and bleached white, past–life forms becoming porous and transparent. . . .

Breathe in the oxygen and
the cool moist wind. Wash the mind with dancing colors, granite,
gypsum, slate, shale, rosy quartz, pale green moss, ash, pink, orange
lichen, submerged in the deep clear running water and bubbling
backwaters gulping in the *prana,* vitality of air, sunlight flooding the
cathedrals of pine, fir, spruce, and birch. . . .

Delight in time out of
time and then hustle back to the car, the cigarettes, the rushing
asphalt — seek refuge in the road. . . .

Robert Bly said that to learn
to be a poet one must be alone. Pursuing the muse, with only this
thought as a guide, I undertake the discipline of solitude, of isolating
myself in my aloneness, all oneness. The Ski Club at my college has
a cabin just outside Franconia, New Hampshire, so I drive to that
location, hoping no one will disturb me. It is an ungainly unfinished
structure up a steep dirt driveway, a large gray box that asks for
finishing work. I let myself in and begin my first hermitage. . . .

The thrill of the poem, music heard in the ethers materializing into
words, engraving white spaces on paper with structures of image and
sound, hearing writing and replaying fragments of the ceaseless song
of the angel fire. . . .

The thrill of the poem is something to live
for, but not for long. . . .

For it passes in flashes, *tajaliyyat,* flashes of
brilliance in the roiling clouds. . . .

But the fog remains, the vague
haze of obscuring, ongoing ignorance, not knowing. . . .

Words,
ideas, feelings exploding like popcorn in the smoky kitchen,
glow-worms of lightning rolling, flashing within the clouds, but
never grounding, brief and unpredictable streaks of particles in the
cloud chamber, sparkling, invisible laughter, charm. . . .

Scattering,
dissipation of attention, chasing fireflies in the smog, grasping at the

blinking lights, clutching at them, collecting them in a jar — to what end? Random activity, lack of motivation. . . .

Contrary to popular opinion, ignorance is *not* bliss, though not-knowing does buffer feeling true suffering, disperses in secondary symptoms: restlessness, instability, anxiety, paranoia, addiction, nameless fear. . . .

Deluding myself, pretending that I know what I'm doing, where I'm going, when deep down inside I'm terrified because I have no idea what the fuck I'm doing, where in the hell I'm going. This is incredibly painful, too painful to admit to myself. So I'll just maintain that these flashes of inspiration are what my life purpose is all about and stay in denial about ninety percent of the time. . . .

until the pain is too massive and elemental to deny, totally freaked out and I have no idea why. Why does it hurt so — no, cross that out, not ready to feel for real just yet — why am I so freaked out?

I've put in time at the Church of DSRR. (Drugs Sex and Rock 'n Roll — pronounced "deseyeyerrrr.") But that has brought no peace of mind. Far from becoming fulfilled, desire only gets greater, more aggravating and irritating the more I feed the flames with my lust and greed for sensation. The more I want, the more intensely I desire, the less I have and the less satisfaction comes to me. Earthly Taurean desire. It's all the same old bull: desire a bull, adore a bull, love a bull, forget a bull. . . .

Actually I feel like I have been thrown out of the Church and am not permitted to come back in. And this really rankles. Even though I don't want it, deep down inside I still want it, and I know no peace inside or outside. . . .

1

PLUTO ENTERS SCORPIO
November 5, 1983

The day that Pluto entered Scorpio, MTV sucked my brains out.

It wasn't that hard to do.

I had been living outside electronic civilization for the past fourteen years at Lama Foundation in the mountains of northern New Mexico. All of the great music, movies, TV, and most of the news of the seventies totally escaped my attention. I had just moved back into Babylon (Santa Fe) the week before. My mind was almost as fresh and naive as a cloistered virgin. A good deal of mental and emotional purification took place during my years in the wilderness.

Now I had gone from living in a sunny cabin alone in the forest with only birds and squirrels, woodpeckers and skunks, and the occasional bear to disturb me, to sleeping on the floor of a ground-level one-bedroom apartment with cars rushing by not ten feet from where my head lay.

I had moved from Lama to Santa Fe to be a closer to my five-year-old son, Abe. His mother, my former wife, Varda, had taken him from Lama to Santa Fe three years previously. Somehow it took me three years to figure out that Abe needed a full-time father.

My first night in Santa Fe, Jesus knocked on the door to my apartment. At least that's who he said he was. Where I had just come from, if someone told you he was Jesus you accepted that as being real for him in the moment. Of course, the next day he could be Krishna or Buddha.

The young man standing in my door had large eyes, clear olive skin, an oval face, and long crinkly black hair that fell below his shoulders. He looked like a Mexican Jesus. He said he lived across the street. He asked if he could come in and use my phone since the phone in his house was broken. It is a great honor to have Jesus come into your house and use your phone. Of course I let him in. As he walked across the one room of my apartment his eyes darted back and forth checking everything out, perhaps looking for what could be boosted. He got on the phone and began talking rapidly about an ounce of this and a gram of that, still looking nervously about. Jesus was making drug deals on my telephone! The next night when he showed up again, I asked him to go somewhere else to find a phone.

The day that Pluto entered Scorpio, I was sitting on the sun porch of a Territorial-style mansion on Canyon Road with my friend Dennis. He was house-sitting this beautiful home which belonged to a state senator from Deming, who was rarely in Santa Fe but liked to stay in style when he was there. That day Dennis wanted to turn me on to MTV. We turned on the tube and went out on the groove. Like a practiced twenty-four-hour hooker, MTV skillfully wrapped its electronic lips around my tender mind and sucked me into multiple psychic orgasms until all my juice was used up and gone. The intuitive, incessant interweaving of sight and sound, of video clips and rock music, struck me open with the force of a minor revelation. A segment of the mass mind of the future had developed while I was away from the world. One afternoon of MTV was sufficient sensory overkill for me. I didn't go back for more.

This incident lies like a bookmark at the opening of a new chapter in my life, a period of internal work, of digging deep inside, uncovering and releasing ancient psychic blocks. It was a period of having to deal with money, sexuality, and personal power in the so-called real world, a period of necessary transformation, all of which is signified by Pluto's transit through Scorpio.

MEETING JOANNA & HADRON
November 24, 1983

A few weeks later, Dennis invited me to Thanksgiving. His temporary home was an exquisite venue for entertaining. Spacious white rooms with gold trim, sparkling electric candelabras, cabinet work in deep red and dark green. The decor may have been Mandarin, but it seemed Tibetan to me. His Aquarian Moon brought an unusual group of people together around the table that night. Most of us were meeting each other for the first time.

The most extroverted and talkative person there was a older woman by the name of Joanna Walsh. She had a crown of white hair, a glowing face with smooth, youthful skin, and sparkling blue eyes. She was dressed in a gold wool suit and wore an amber necklace. Though in her seventies, she had the vivacity and enthusiasm of a much younger woman. She seemed delighted to get to know everyone who was present and was especially delighted with herself. She had an effervescent quality of joy that was in no way silly or giddy.

She and her husband Hadron had moved to Santa Fe from Los Angeles in the past year. The previous winter they had given what she called the Intergalactic Federation Ball. The theme was *'Come dressed as you are on your home planet.'* Her intention was to meet all the people in Santa Fe who had come from another planet. If I had been in town, I would have come as myself. My personal reality is strange enough. Why cover it over?

This seemed kind of kooky to me. I certainly would not have gone to such a ball. I never dress up in costume, not even for Halloween. I think my day-to-day personal reality is strange enough without having to put on make-up and assume an even deeper level of false identity. I had read about UFO abductions and that sort of thing, but I had never met anyone who embraced a reality about having come from another planet.

Sure enough, the next thing I knew she was asking me if I remembered having come from another planet and if I remembered what it was like on my home planet. I said as far as I knew my home planet was Earth. She thanked me for my knowing and continued merrily holding forth.

Her husband Hadron was sitting across the table from me. He had barely spoken a word all night, which later I would find out was due to advanced Alzheimer's disease. He had the husky build of a former athlete, a handsome face with a prominent forehead, thick bushy eyebrows, and shimmering green eyes. His face suggested love of beauty, refinement of thought, and nobility of spirit. I felt a little uncomfortable with him sitting across from me saying nothing. But he seemed content to be

15

sitting there next to his wife, probably out in space somewhere, hardly there at all.

Every now and then he would appear to focus into the present moment, pick up his head, look alert, and say something unexpected and humorous, such as: "This sure is a strange planet." Joanna would repeat what he said. Everyone would laugh. Then his head would droop and once again no one was at home.

At one point everyone was sounding off about politics, airing their opinions and feelings. Hadron picks up his head and says, "War is business. Business is war," which Joanna repeated and everyone laughed. "That is one of his Hadronisms, which everyone used to appreciate so much," she said.

Then a most unusual thing happened. Hadron raised his gaze, looked me straight in the eye, and said softly but very forcefully, "Sell DuPont stock now. Sell DuPont stock now." Then he nodded off again. That was the only thing he said directly to me that whole evening.

This shocked me. How could he know that my sole source of financial security was some DuPont stock which I had inherited from my grandfather almost twenty years previously? It had not occurred to me until that moment that my karma was to have homeopathic ownership in one of the vilest corporations on the face of the planet, a major contributor to warfare and armaments, chemical and nuclear pollution. But here it was, plain in my face: *"War is business. Business is war. Sell DuPont stock now."*

This was my first hint that something unusual was coming into my life.

Joanna said that Dennis had told her that I was an astrologer. I said indeed I was. She said she had always wanted to work with someone who was a good astrologer. Would I be interested? I said perhaps at a later date, being non-committal and evasive. I am wary when anyone says that they want to work with me. Usually it means that they want to do their work on me, like massage students who give free massages to up their learning curves.

Meanwhile I went out and sold the remainder of my DuPont stock. Financially it would have been wiser to wait four or five years until I absolutely had to sell it, for the price would have been much higher at a later time. But when a message comes spontaneously and hits the mark that accurately, whether it comes from within or without, I don't worry about it, I just do it.

That was the beginning of the burning of karmic ribbons under Pluto in Scorpio.

A little while later Joanna called and asked me if I wanted to work with her and share knowledge with her. But I was not ready for that yet. It would be almost a year before the necessity was on me to work with her.

2

FLASHBACK—DANCING WITH GLORY
July 16, 1982

Lama Foundation is a living experiment, a spiritual school, a mystery school, in the form of a community situated in meadow and forest on the western slopes of the Sangre de Cristo Mountains north of Taos. The community honors and learns from, receives teachers and practices from, all of the spiritual traditions of the world. A road-weary refugee from *koyanisquatsi* (lives out of balance, worlds out of whack), I had first arrived here in 1970 during Lama's initial building phase.

Being a forest dweller is much simpler than being a city dweller. The forest is a vast, peaceful, breathing green context for awareness in which deep, quiet, often formless thoughts can arise. Tension, anxiety and paranoia are far away.

Slowly cooking in the heart soup of the Lama beans, I had healed, matured, and recovered much of my wholeness. Grounded in emptiness through meditation and work in service, illumined by high-altitude sunlight and the companionship of joyful hearts, resonant with the subtle harmonics of consensual community, living close to nature, some essential qualities began to emerge from the shell shock of my adolescence.

You will note that I am speaking of the emergence of qualities from the essence, qualities like love, joy, and peace which are in the essence of each living being. This is not a fable of quantities, of how many poems I wrote, how many bricks I laid, how much money I didn't make, or how many times I just called to say I love you and you were or were not home. This is a "song of degrees" of the qualities of the beloved.

One Friday night I stepped outside my cabin in the woods at Lama. At 8,600 feet on the mountainside overlooking the upper Taos mesa, the summer nights are cool and restful. It was Shabbas, the last night of a Ram Dass retreat, and dance music throbbed from the Dome. Tall thickets of scrub oak were silhouetted against the salmon afterglow of sunset, which was rapidly fading to pale gold on the borderline of night. I walked through the oak grove, through the tall grass, past the wild rose bushes beside the kitchen, and down the broad stone stairway to the entrance of the Dome, which glowed with the only visible human light for hundreds of miles. Venus was gleaming in the deepening dark on the far horizon.

The interior of the Dome is a forty-foot-wide octagonal room, whose adobe walls are finished with a mud slip of *tierra amarilla,* which glowed golden in the soft solar electric light. The eight-foot octagonal west window was open to the dark night and cool breezes. I stood in the shadows and watched the party and the free dancers, intoxicated with love and a little wine, expanding into the space. No one dresses up much out in the country, so what one sees is the dance of souls, not the dance of clothes. There were maybe thirty people dancing, so there was no crush of bodies, just ample space in which to exult and exalt.

Fascinated, I watched Glory dancing as if for the first time. Her name was Gloria, but we called her Glory. We had lived in community for years, worked in adobe, accounting, and kitchen cleanup, and were part of a team of sacred dance leaders, but I had never seen *this* woman dancing wild and free as if the earth were a drum beneath her feet. Lithe limbs, long waves of blonde hair, fluid movement in a shimmering dress, she captured my total attention.

She took my hands and pulled me into the dance. To my surprise, I did not resist.

Never touching, our bodies flowed together in perfect harmony, pulsing in and out of an unseen center of unity, fragments of an ancient puzzle falling out of space and fitting together. Whirling among the moving lights, we seemed to be dancing among the stars in a timeless space before we were born, gliding, leaping, whirling, radiant. My body remembered its natural ecstasy, so long kept in secret. She summoned forth my blissful spirit and "increased the sounding joy" with rebounding gladness. That night I meet my soul mate, my twin flame.

Afterwards she said, "Let's go to your house. I want to tell you a bedtime story."

Her first kiss flooded my whole body with light.

HOW CAN SOMETHING SO RIGHT BE SO WRONG?

Like a white-hot ball of fire, Glory's love seared a path through my soul, like a firestorm consuming the dead wood of my personal realities and leaving a vast burn area to be seeded with new life. Everything I had always thought was real was stripped away so that everything I have always known is real could surface from the subliminal and come into fullness in my life. Glory and I exchanged essence recognition and validation on the deepest levels.

One of Glory's gifts to me was walking in the woods. My relationship with nature had been much more contemplative: walk into the woods a little, sit down under a tree, and meditate for a couple of hours, or climb up an easy ridge and take pictures of clouds, that kind of thing. My relationship with my body was also tenuous and variable. I enjoyed spending as much time outside of it as I could.

Glory had a passion for walking, hiking, climbing, sweating, breathing deeply — intense aerobic exercise. She had to go walking for at least an hour every day the way some people need coffee and cigarettes to wake up in the morning. If I wanted to hang out with her, I had to walk her walk so we could talk our talk. I began to learn the joy of sweating and breathing deeply, but not sexually. Our physical expression of love was limited by the fact that she was a married woman. Our mingling was mental and emotional, creative and spiritual.

We kept on walking, never stopping talking, opening our hearts, flowing out to each other, often saying *"I love you"* at the end of every other sentence. The feeling was that intense, and our time together was so short. Glory was the first woman who totally loved me. In this lifetime I have felt chronically unloved and, even more, unknown. Even with my best friends and longest lovers I felt I was a pretender, a stranger in this world, unknown and unknowable. With Glory I could say anything, feel anything. There was no need to hold anything back. I felt perfectly loved, even adored, and could allow the unknown, unloved parts of my being to come forth. She loved me so much I could allow myself to know myself and love myself as never before, which at the time was an invisible side effect, since I was totally focused on delighting in her joy, her beauty, her heart wisdom.

Glory's husband came to talk me out of this passion. He was a good, compassionate man. Though I had dreams of his towering wrath, he never said an unkind word to me.

"Look," he said, "I can understand being seduced by a beautiful woman like Glory. I certainly was. But we've been married for twenty years, and I have to ask you to promise not to see her alone again."

Although it was the right thing to do, I could not make that promise. In that moment he and I became very real to each other.

Glory had said to me that they had decided long ago to have an open marriage and that she was free to come and play with me. Now her husband was asking me to stay away from her. It was not my intention to interfere with their marriage. But when she kept coming to me, I found I could not refuse her love.

"Another thing that bugs me about you," he said, "is all those books you read about ghosts, possession, and UFOs. Why do you read this stuff?"

"Because I have experienced it!" I surprised myself by saying. I had not admitted all this was real to me until he confronted me.

My love for Glory was the reason I left Lama after thirteen years. I loved her too much. She loved me too much. And she was married.

When she first started playing around with me, she had no idea that she would fall so deeply in love. Nor did I. The unitive love, the blissful light, the intimate communion, the delicate play of thought and feeling was the answer to every dream of love, lover, and beloved. But our twin flames could not merge together on the Earth plane.

"How can something so right be so wrong?" we asked, in the midst of telling each other *"I love you"* thousands of times. Our love play was damaging her marriage and dividing our community. It was time for me to leave. And leave I did, in the fall of 1983.

However, my body, heart, and soul would remain dedicated to Glory in true-blue troubadour fashion for a period of seven years, nurtured by long phone calls and infrequent clandestine meetings. It was a full seven years until we both finally let go of believing that we could be together.

This devotion, this obsession, this burning, yearning longing which has never been quenched, this question *("When can I see you? When can I be with you? When can I touch you? When can I hold you?"* and most of all, *"Why can't we be together right now?")* provided the impetus and the passion to discover deeper levels of reality and further realizations of truth in the totality of all that is.

When love first touched me in my youth, I was preoccupied with being a poet, a romantic artist, and I took as much of that fine energy as I could into creating what I thought were expressions of beauty in image, word, and song.

When love finally found my heart twenty years later, I was no longer focused on the art mart of the lover's ego but on the beauty of the beloved.

We said *"I love you"* ten thousand times. I wrote long letters declaring eternal love in the most basic phrases that would be boring to anyone not burning in the same fire. This love, this koan *("Why can't we be together? How can something so right be so wrong?")* triggered my burning within and my desire to penetrate this mystery.

As it happened, before I began my work with Joanna, it was Glory who opened me to my first past-life recall.

REMEMBER WHAT IT WAS LIKE BEFORE YOU WERE BORN

At that time, when I was reading horoscopes, I would ask the person to close his or her eyes and do a brief meditation.

"Remember what it was like before you were born," I would say.

"Remember that impulse, that desire, to come to Earth this time, to choose your parents and your incarnations."

I wasn't doing research. I didn't ask for feedback. I just was asking everyone the same question I was asking myself at that time. I wanted to get in touch with that movement within my spirit that led to this unlikely incarnation. I had had enough of blaming my parents, rejecting the world, and raging against the universe and everything that is for just being the way that it is. I wanted to take responsibility for my entry into the Earth-plane game this time. Much of the time my personal reality seemed unbearably strange, estranged, and isolated to me. By knowing myself and accepting myself I could accept my choice of incarnation and everything that came along with it.

One day I asked Glory the same question. We had been climbing high in the forest above Lama and were sitting in a clearing under a certain tree known to Glory as her weeping tree, a place where she came to weep and pray.

"Close your eyes and remember what it was like before you were born," I said. "Remember your first desire, your first impulse to come to Earth this time."

We both closed our eyes and went within.

After a moment of silence she said, "I see a great light deep in space, a great light that is my home."

When she said that I began to see something too, a huge galaxy deep in space, millions of stars turning in a vortex with outflung spiral arms, slowly drawing closer in my vision.

"I didn't want to come," she cried. "I didn't want to come back here, but they asked me to come to be with them, and so I said OK I'll come." She was weeping freely, lamenting intensely. "I don't want to be here. This is not my home. I'm here because they asked me to come."

"Who are they?" I asked her.

"My family," she said. "My family wanted me to be with them."

This was no sob-sister pity party. This anguish came from deep within, contrasting with her normal personality, which was light and sunny, playful and delightful.

When we were processing and exploring inner realities, we never invalidated each other. We never questioned the reality of what the other one was getting. We accepted whatever came and asked for more.

This was her answer to my question. Somehow I touched on home with her. My own answer was yet to come.

TRUCHAS PEAK EXPERIENCE
September 11, 1984

Glory and I had decided to climb South Truchas Peak during one of those brief interludes when we actually spent time together. The Truchas Peaks are some of the highest, most remote and most sacred mountains in the Pecos Wilderness.

Starting out from the Santa Barbara Campground outside Peñasco, we backpacked into the wilderness, following the trail south along the West Branch of the Rio Santa Barbara, a wide, sparkling mountain stream. It was a long day's march under clear, deep, blue autumn skies. By late afternoon we reached the broad meadows in the upper part of the valley, sheltered in the arms of gentle, ancient peaks. There we made camp for the night in the forest by the river.

In the morning we began ascending the valley wall, crossing over many small streams, climbing through several climactic zones of vegetation, until at last we came out above timberline on a barren saddle below the peak. To the south we could see a pack trail etched along the head of the valley.

To the north, right in front of us, Truchas Peak loomed against the graying sky, like a huge pyramid worn down by time. The steep rock face displayed what appeared to be hieroglyphic markings meant to be seen from the air — dark, blood-hued lines of stone forming V's and W's, containing within them whiter fields of pebbles. The suggestion of a runic message was unmistakable and uninterpretable, blurred by several thousand years of weather.

We could see gentle banks of clouds coming in from the west and feel the moistness in the air. We moved among the squat green bushes, through a stretch of bleached wind-warped driftwood, and began the steep ascent up the face of the peak.

Though we had been close together and never stopped talking, we separated for the final ascent. I went straight up the steep slope in short spurts, climbing up and over the rocks until my heart was beating too fast and my lungs were gasping for the thin, high air. Glory used her walking stick to pick a slow, gentle trail switching back and forth across the face of the mountain, walking slowly, never stopping, like a mountain goat.

Halfway up, mist swept over the slope, the temperature dropped and it began raining, gently at first, then harder, steady streams of water blowing down diagonally in front of us. We put on our ponchos and continued climbing. We were wary of being caught on a high peak during a lightning storm, but we heard no thunder. We kept on climbing for over an hour and made it to the top at almost the same time, despite the different paths we were taking.

The rainstorm had moved on and the sky was beginning to clear. We were on the southernmost of the three Truchas Peaks, which was relatively accessible compared to the northern peaks, which we could see rising across from us, a sheer, dark, jagged alpine reef in the sea of the sky.

To be so high in the thin air on the top of a 12,000-foot sacred pyramidal mountain guarded by strange markings, rain, mist, and remoteness was an awesome experience. I was probably in an altered state already. I did what seemed to me to be the natural thing. I reached for my pouch of Bull Durham tobacco, rolled a cigarette, and began to smoke it.

"Ahad, what are you doing?" Glory exclaimed. "Here we are on top of this most sacred mountain — and you are smoking a cigarette!"

This was unusual, for never before had she complained about my smoking tobacco. It was masculine, reminded her of her father, she kind of liked it, she had said.

Now she said, "Put out that cigarette! Now! Come over here and sit next to me. Sit down and close your eyes."

I did what she asked without questioning why. That was the nature of our relationship. I sat down and closed my eyes.

"Now I want you to remember what it was like before you were born," she said, turning my own question back on me. "I want you to remember why you chose to come to Earth this time."

I let the question resonate within my being and opened to receive. I saw the face, the head, and shoulders of a European Jewish matriarch, her gray hair pulled back in a bun, her eyes large and piercing, stern and loving. I knew this was my grandmother. Now I was not born into a Jewish family, nor did this picture resemble my grandmother. But the information was very clear and I didn't question it. I told her what I saw.

"That's good," she said. "Go with it. What more do you get?"

I saw a dining room and my family seated around the table for Shabbas. It was an inner room, no windows, dark wooden paneling, big wooden table set with silver and brightly glowing candles. We had lit the candles of Shabbas. I remember feeling, "We are the Chosen People, illuminated by God's light." I was a young man with my grandmother, grandfather, mother, father, and sister at that table. It felt warm, safe, and secure.

"That's good. Go deeper. What more do you get?"

Then my body started shaking, sobbing from the deepest part of my being, weeping uncontrollably. This was unexpected and shocking. I rarely let emotions overcome my intellectual front, and such deep feelings were unknown to my conscious personality. But my body was overcome by the emergence of memories I could not yet articulate. This traumatic heaving went on for a long, long time. Glory put her arms around me and held me. I was unable to say anything for what seemed like an hour, overwhelmed by the release of grief and terror.

When I was finally able to verbalize what was written in my soul and released through my body, I said, "They destroyed my culture. They destroyed my family. And I lost my life."

This was the information I was given.

Immediately many strange things about my life became clear, which I discussed with Glory during our descent through the glorious afternoon and our long trek back into the world the next day.

In high school I had been very attracted to Jewish girls, despite my parents' disapproval. I was drawn to their families, which were warm, tactile, emotional, cultural, and intellectual, in contrast to my conservative WASP upbringing. These were not the girls I would fall deeply in love with but the kitchens I would love to sit around in, having open discussions about art, ideas, and politics. Later many of my closest friends, male and female, would be Jewish.

Ten years previously I had gone to Jerusalem with no real conscious intention or awareness about what that meant. I was just traveling with a group of friends. Our boat landed in Haifa and we took a taxi to Jerusalem. As we cruised down the Mediterranean coast, the landscape seemed a lot like Florida to me. From the outskirts, Tel Aviv seemed like a cut-rate Miami. Then we turned inland across the plain and began climbing through the hills to Jerusalem. As I caught my first sight of that ancient city, shivers of remembrance began to tingle throughout my whole body. I knew without a doubt that I had been here before. This was the first time I had had such an intuition.

In Jerusalem I met Varda, who was Jewish and would become my wife and the mother of my child, Abe, who also by birth was Jewish.

Back at Lama, engaged in intense Islamic Sufi studies and practices, I found that I could not accept Islam or become Muslim. I became very involved with the communal practice of Shabbas, the ceremony, the songs, the stories, and teachings.

This also explained the nightmares which had terrified me throughout my adult life, dreams in which I was a fugitive, a stranger in the everyday world, pursued by shadowy groups of men who were fascist thugs. My dreams did not depict them literally as Nazis with swastika armbands, but now it was clear just who they were.

Apparently I had been a young Jewish man in Europe in the thirties, seen my family and my culture destroyed by the Holocaust, had become a fugitive, and lost my life. Once out of the body, I had not returned to the spirit world but stayed around on the Earth plane until the war was over and then sought a new life in a new body with parents in America, which seemed to be a safe and secure place. This is why, when Glory asked me to remember choosing my birth when I came to Earth *this time* around, I remembered images of my family and my life in Europe, for I had not been away from the Earth since coming to birth in a Jewish family in Europe in the twenties.

Though I had read books about reincarnation and past lives and such, I had had no actual experience of past-life memories up to this point and was skeptical, that is open-minded, about the subject. Glory's belief system was fundamentally Christian. Her theology had no room for ideas about past lives. She was playing a game of inner imaging with me that I had played with her. There could be no question of her projecting her belief system on me and suggesting that I go into previous lives. This gave the experience a more objective quality. No one was doing a psychic reading for me. The images had arisen spontaneously. The power and depth of the emotional release left no doubt that these memories were real down in my soul, without answering the question of how they had gotten there and why they had remained buried for so long. The best working assumption was that these were deep memories of my immediate past life which now were ready to emerge.

We came down from Truchas Peak, back into the human world. Glory went home to her marriage, and I went home alone.

3

BEGINNING WORK WITH JOANNA
September 22, 1984

Joanna Walsh had indicated that her work involved helping people with their personal problems by releasing emotional blocks and guiding them to an awareness of their true nature. And did I have problems! Problems of the irresistible force (attraction) meets immovable object (separation) type, or so it seemed.

My presenting and pressing problem was lovesickness, obsessive pre-occupation with my beloved. The fact that she was equally obsessively preoccupied with me made the emotional stew all the richer and truer. Neither of us had ever experienced anything close to the unity and ecstasy of our being together. Nevertheless, the possibility of our union on the Earth plane seemed out of the question. Although we had had fantasies of running away to Mexico and leaving it all behind, it was by now evident that this was not going to happen. Her commitment to her marriage and her religion proved stronger than the firestorms of passion that swept through our hearts and clouded our minds.

Ten years later, I try to keep my hands gainfully employed and my heart and mind focused in spaciousness of the present moment. But at the time I could think of nothing else but Glory, as reams of my love-letter ravings bear witness.

So I called up Joanna and asked if I could come in and work with her. We made an appointment, and I showed up at her home on Maclovia Street. I stood on her porch and knocked on her door. She came to the door and opened it part way.

"Yes? Who are you? What do you want?" she said.

"I'm Ahad. We have an appointment to work together today."

"You're Ahad? My goodness, I didn't recognize you at all. You look just like a tramp. I wasn't sure if I should open the door. You looked so nice when we met at that Thanksgiving dinner. Now you look like another person entirely. Well, don't just stand there on the porch. Come on inside."

She welcomed me into her home.

She and Hadron lived in a small duplex. The front door opened right into the living room, which was densely yet tastefully furnished. Several generations of Hadron's artwork adorned the walls. House plants sat on the chest in front of the window. Greeting cards and pictures of family and friends sat on the tables. Correspondence and magazines were piled on the desk. The bookcase was crammed full of books on Scientology and metaphysics. A bust of Nefertiti sat under the lamp next to the telephone. All in all, a typical Earth-plane environment in which to find an elderly retired couple — who were not so typical at all.

Joanna appeared to me then as she had when I met her and as she would in the future, a Jewish grandmother with a crown of white hair, sparkling blue eyes, and the vivacity of a much younger woman.

She asked me to sit and went to get glasses of juice and water for us. She came back and sat on an olive-green love seat across the room from me, with Hadron sitting on her right-hand side. Hadron sat there the whole time, impassive, unmoving, like seated Buddha. He was so still I forgot he was there. And indeed, he probably wasn't.

She looked directly into my eyes and began to hold forth endlessly on Totality, Superconscious, Knowing, and Evolution.

When I say *hold forth endlessly,* I mean that Joanna could literally speak for hours on end with barely a pause, with no interruption, with forcefulness, enthusiasm, and humor. Her words did not darken the mind, stuffing it full of "useless and pointless information." Her words opened up in me areas of awareness and knowingness that had long been covered over. Being naturally receptive, I was an excellent socket for her strong outflow to plug in to.

Every now and then she would ask me for recognition and validation. Did I know what she was talking about? Did I agree with what she said? And then she would roll on in her discourse. At times my personality, which is mental, clever, and likes to use its tongue, felt like it was being browbeaten into submissiveness with no chance to exercise its own genius. Although she spoke of the subtlest of matters in the simplest of terms, I could find no argument with what she was saying. Indeed, her understanding was remarkably free of any religious mumbo-jumbo, that morass of incomprehensible subtleties we are asked to swallow with unquestioning belief.

A good deal of the time, Joanna would employ the Socratic method of questioning. *"What is your reality about this? What do you think about that? How does it seem to you?"* She would acknowledge and validate whatever my knowingness was and then proceed along the lines of the greatest agreement. With most clients presenting a problem, Joanna would get right down to work with them on releasing their inner blockages. But in my case she spoke with me for many days, transmitting the basic data of her understanding.

It is said that when the student is ready, the teacher appears. I would say that when necessity is all, help appears. After all my years of training and practice at Lama Foundation, after a wealth of teachers and teachings from many spiritual traditions, I had to come to Santa Fe to meet my teacher — a white-haired Jewish grandmother who came from another planet, from beyond outer space!

Joanna, however, refused to be identified as a spiritual teacher or a teacher at all.

"I don't use a spirit," she would say. "Only Earth beings need spirits. I function directly as Superconscious. I'm not a teacher. I'm a trigger. I trigger people to the awareness of being Superconscious. You Superconscious is who you really are."

In one metaphor, the student is like an empty cup which the teacher fills with the wine of wisdom. In another metaphor, the student is a cup full of egotism and vanity which the teacher empties.

Glory's love was like a firestorm that swept through my soul. Joanna's knowingness was like a controlled burn in a forest, sending in flame throwers to burn out the choked undergrowth of my mind and soul with precision and compassion.

Joanna would hold forth eloquently and unceasingly on abstract metaphysical matters with such enthusiasm and vigor that I would begin to wonder if she even knew I was in the room. But then she would focus right in on me with probing questions as to my own knowingness, experience, and opinions. Surprisingly, I found I was in agreement with her on most matters. And when she focused on my personal case, my emotional complexes and problems, she was extraordinarily perceptive, although her method was not to lay her perceptions directly on her clients but to guide the client into coming to new realizations for themselves.

It was almost as if Joanna was plugged into an unseen dynamo that supplied her with an endless abundance of high, white-light energy, night and day. This I now know is Superconscious, which she embodied to an extraordinary degree. Indeed, a psychic reading her aura perceived, along with all the other goodies, a column of white light extending out of the top of her head and continuing beyond the Earth plane.

She was always projecting positivity, self-confidence, enthusiasm, delight, knowingness, understanding, and compassion. In addition, she had a great deal of chutzpah. She had no use for modesty or humility and was not afraid to say anything to anyone. No matter what happened, she always seemed to maintain her equanimity and never got caught in negative emotional reactivity, which is the unconscious projecting of anger, fear, blame, or hatred onto other people or circumstances. She always had a strong creative vision and a knowingness that Superconscious was manifesting her vision in present time.

Joanna was totally dedicated to her work of triggering superconscious awareness and abilities in her clients. She never gave any consideration to time or money when she was working with me. When I came for a session, she would offer me a glass of juice with water and then sit with me in her living room holding forth endlessly on the wonders of Superconscious for two or three hours before we ever went back to her study to begin our formal session. When in session, she had endless patience to allow me to work through things and come to the realizations on my own. We were literally outside of time, though when we came back into time she would often complain of developing "sititis" from sitting so long.

Joanna enjoyed life to the max and found a constant source of delight and amusement in the most ordinary of circumstances. Often when I was walking up to her house, I would hear the sound of the TV playing some old sitcom, like "I Love Lucy," "I Dream of Jeannie," and so forth. And I would always hear gales of laughter pouring forth as she enjoyed the joy of the performers. Being a Hollywood woman, she always appreciated the talent and skill of the young people on TV, no matter how superficial they might seem to me.

She related to me how some Jehovah's Witnesses came to her door one day, talking to her about God. She answered them, "You want to talk about God. How about talking *with* God? I'm God—in person. What do you want to know?" Gales of laughter.

Joanna had no sense of modesty when it came to knowingness. This offended some people, who would exclaim, "You have no sense of modesty, no shame!" Joanna would reply, "I have no use for modesty or shame. I know that I know because I know that I know. What is there to be ashamed of?"

JOANNA AND HADRON

What I most appreciated about Joanna and Hadron was that they were self-realized beings. Their abilities and awarenesses came from direct experience of Totality and Superconscious. They had no use for faith, belief, or hope in things unseen. They worked together to gain direct experience of things unseen instead of hoping and wishing, theorizing and speculating, thinking and stinking. (As Joe Miller used to quip, "You can get more stinking from thinking than you can from drinking.")

Joanna had met Hardin Walsh in Los Angeles right after World War II. (By now she was calling him by his home-planet name, Hadron of Orr.) They found each other in the midst of mutual mid-life crises, divorces and, for Joanna, a great loss of money and the ability to make money in her accustomed way as an interior decorator.

Hardin had been working with the teachings and methods of Scientology. Immediately they began working together and with others in regressions and clearings. They became so expert in the methods of Scientology that they gained a contract to run the Scientology scene in Los Angeles for a number of years while L. Ron Hubbard was out of the country.

But Joanna began to feel that Scientology was too limited, manipulative, and controlling. She wanted the ultimate experience of reality.

Hardin triggered her to the awareness of being Totality, the Only Being, whole and complete throughout the whole universe.

When she described to Hardin her experience of unity, he said, "Sure, you're Totality — always have been, always will be."

"If you already knew this," she said, "how come you never told me?"

"I thought you already knew," he said.

This caused her some sleepless nights, lying awake, thinking, "But what about God?"

Until she heard a voice saying, "Go beyond God."

They split with Scientology and founded their own non-profit religious and scientific corporation, Totality, Inc., and continued working with people, developing their own methodology and getting new realizations, all of which was set forth in their published and unpublished writings. Joanna had excellent and sometimes miraculous results in working with people for more than thirty years.

At that time in my life, I had had my fill of ritual and dogma, true believers and blind faith. What is real for me is that the evolution of the soul of humanity happens through spiritual love and friendship. Healing and reconciliation, forgiveness and reunion happen among friends and lovers on the path.

Following are transcribed excerpts from recordings I made of Joanna telling me her story, indicated by the headings that begin "Her Story." These stories were repeatedly interwoven with all the teachings she was giving me.

HER STORY—MEETING HARDIN WALSH
Los Angeles, just after WW II

I'm going to start with the time I met Hardin Walsh, because he took me in regression therapy to the earlier part of my life, from conception, prenatal, and birth, right up to the time I met him.

Meeting him was in a sense an answer to what I had been asking for all my life. Even as I studied with a Hebrew rabbi, I said, "I want the ultimate."

And the rabbi said, "You don't ask for anything. You just listen and accept what I tell you." I told my parents that wasn't good enough for me, and they discharged the rabbi.

I got up one morning after being in Los Angeles for one week—it was just after the war ended—and I'm hearing a subliminal voice. Being the adventuresome person that I am, I listened.

It said, *"Get dressed up. Go down and take a trolley car."*

I was staying with my parents at the time, and there was the Pico trolley in Los Angeles. Getting dressed up for me, coming from Connecticut, where I was in New York every Monday morning as a decorator, meant I get dressed up. So I put on an emba mink coat, and I put on the shoes, hat, gloves, and bag that match, not realizing that California is pants and T-shirt. I was of course overdressed, but that didn't bother me too much. I didn't ask why. I thought that if I knew why, perhaps I wouldn't do it. So I went.

I get on this trolley, Pico, going toward Vermont, in Los Angeles. And I'm sitting there wondering, "Am I some kind of a fool? Or what? Doing this. . . . Anyhow, what do I have to lose?"

"Get to the corner of Vermont. Get off."

So I got off. And I'm standing there. I was real cute at that time. I was a size 8, all dressed up like Astor's pet horse. And the auto horns were honking. Of course I turned my little head away. I get on the Vermont car. I get down to Wilshire Boulevard.

"Get off."

So I get off. You may say, well, did you hear voices or what was it? It was voices, but it was subliminal. It wasn't as we speak. But it was clear enough for me to take the directions.

"Go into the store." (It was the Owl Drugstore. It's not there any longer.)

"Well, what am I going to buy?" I began asking questions at this point.

"Go into the telephone booth."

"Who am I going to call?"

My two thumbs went into the commercial telephone directory, which in Los Angeles is very large.

"Open to a page."

My forefinger of my right hand was taken, literally, and run across a number and a name of an advertising agency on Wilshire Boulevard. It was right across the street from where I was! So then I realized that this is some direction for something.

"What am I going to do in an advertising agency?"

"You're an interior decorator, you're new in town, you want to locate here, and you want some advice. Perhaps you want to do some advertising."

OK, I go in. And Hardin Walsh is there. But he meant nothing to me. He was the photographer, he did all the art work, and he did all of that for a lousy forty dollars a week, and I could care less. Here was a man married with two kids. Unh-uh. He didn't move me one bit. He tells me afterwards that he recognized me. But I didn't continue the relationship.

I went about losing a half a million dollars, which was a great loss to me. I earned every bit of that myself, as a decorator in Connecticut. My goal, my thinking-level goal, was to find a man who was in the real estate business, like I had in Connecticut, and open a very fine decorating shop in Beverly Hills. But no matter what I touched I lost money. I couldn't understand it, because I'm a successful woman, I made money. I lost it in trying to set up a decorating shop that didn't work out. I lost it in real estate.

Now here I am at my wits' end. I've got a son who will be going to college. I always considered it a responsibility to help him go to college. That was essential. I lost all my money and I felt like I was going out of my mind. The idea of my not being successful in business was abhorrent to me.

Two years later I call Hardin Walsh. At the time I didn't know why. I know now that it was superconscious guidance. In a sense, Hardin Walsh was going to answer, for me, the ultimate, eventually.

All right, I call him. I told him I'd meet him on the corner of Vermont and Wilshire. I see him walking down from the bus at the corner. He had a nice walk. He was an athlete, a football player. He walked like a tiger, very smooth. He was dressed in a navy blue suit, five foot eight, nine, forty-six shoulder, thirty-six hip, gray hair, green eyes, a handsome-looking man, Irish, oh yes, Irish, definitely. And he had a book in his hand.

He came down to the corner. We said hello. Nothing from me. I felt nothing for this man, nothing.

We go into the coffee shop. We order coffee and a sweet roll or something. He goes to take sugar—and I take the sugar bowl and take it to one side! He said nothing. I said nothing. That was good. I like that!

So he gave me the book. And the inscription in the book was:

"To the most beautiful and knowing woman in this or any other galaxy."

And I thought: *"Con man! What's a galaxy got to do with me?"*

He had the considerations of galaxies. I didn't. I was an Earth woman at that time.

So I opened the book, and I flipped through it. *Dianetics* is a valid work, definitely, for this lifetime.

I said, "There's technology here."

"Yes."

"Come on home," I said.

I took him home with me. We have been together for thirty-nine years.

(That was the same time that his wife left him. She decided that his sex with her wasn't so hot anymore. She was sexually very demanding. He was getting to a point where the relationship was no longer desirable for him or for her. So she left. She ran away with the television repair man, who was Mexican, and went to her family farm in Illinois with the two kids.)

The man, as an Earth man, did not appeal to me at all. I'm a Russian Jew. A man is supposed to have money, he's supposed to know about money, he's supposed to have some Earth considerations. Unh-uh, this man had none of that.

Then Hardin took me to a lecture. He was in the middle. Ron Hubbard, the Devil, was on one side — he's gone now, but that's what he was for me — and Manley Palmer Hall, the historian, was on the other side. They all talked at different times. I decided that that guy in the middle knew what he was talking about. I liked the way he did it.

Later I found out that he had eleven years of college education, as a medical doctor, which he gave up and didn't even take any diplomas with him. I decided he had something. He used language very well. He made a nice appearance. And I liked what he said far better than the way Ron Hubbard said it, speaking of Dianetics at the time.

When he came down, he introduced me as Joanna Walsh. At that time I was Bluma Friedman. I looked around to see who he was introducing. But it turned out to be me. My first thought was, *"Well, why didn't he talk to me about that?"* But I'm not an argumentative person at all. I'd rather walk away from it, not make waves, and then make a decision about it later. That's my nature. It saves a lot of wear and tear on the cell structure, I have since found out.

There seems to be some inherent sense of agreement already present between you and Hardin Walsh.

That's right.

The first time you sit together, you take away the bowl of sugar, and he does not question you about it.

That's right.

The first time that you and he go out in public, he calls you Joanna Walsh, and you don't question it.

That's right.

So it seems like there was some previous agreement between the beings on a deeper level than their human personalities.

You're right, absolutely.

I later found out that numerologically Joanna Walsh means *the way to freedom,* and the name given to me at birth by the doctor, not my parents, Blossom Cohen, means *born to be free*. And freedom is a very big thing with this Sag, I can tell you. I don't want any fences around me, ever.

We lived together. But there was something strange. I had no desire to have sex with him. All I wanted was his knowledge of how to help me. I lost all my money. I took a job. He didn't take a job. I found an ad for an advertising agency art director, but he wouldn't take it.

He continued going over to the Hubbard school. He and Dick DeMille and A.E. VanVoight, the science fiction writer, created three hundred questions for the students wanting to become a book auditor. That's what Hubbard had set up. I went over to that school once and saw a bunch of people who, you talk about hippies, these were hippies that were attracted to *Dianetics*. It was a bestseller. People were reading it on the buses, talking about it on television. It's a good body of knowledge. I recommend it, if you want to deal with just this lifetime. It has its limitations, though.

I asked him, "What are you going to do for a living? We're together, we're working, you're helping me."

"No, this is my work and I'm going to stay with it."

"That means that I have to support you, because all you have is a pension from the VA."

It occurred to me that it was all right with him for me to work and support us while he did what he wanted to do. He was two years older than me. I looked at that and I thought, *"He's good at what he does. So I'll support him for a while."*

After the Dianetics lecture, I said to him, "You're good. The way you talk, you're good. Manley Palmer Hall is a historian, he's only repeating. Hubbard, forget it, he doesn't work for me at all." Then I said to him, "I'm going to make you pay off." That's exactly what I said to him, because that's what it occurred to me to say.

And he said, "OK, that's all right with me, as long as I'm doing what I do best." And he did do it best.

I'd like to tell you what he did for me.

As a decorator, I was not able to wear on my body anything brighter than tan. I decorated people's homes and my own beautiful home, using color coordination. I was admired for that ability. People paid me to do that in their home. And I could only wear tan as the brightest color. I wore mostly black or navy. And I said that to him.

"There's something about me I don't understand."

And he said, "Well, let's go in and find out where it's at."

I never heard anything like that. Go in where? I had no idea what he was talking about.

He began to regress me to conception, prenatal, and birth. And I was able to remember, and later verified what I remembered with my father, who was still available.

My father couldn't understand where my questions came from, so he said, "Oh, he's psychic." The Russian people know about psychic. "He's psychic, so he told you." I let it go at that. There's no sense in trying to explain that I could remember what happened.

So he didn't tell you, you remembered it.

He never told me anything. That wasn't the way to work with me anyhow. I had to get my own data, all through our life, and we went into some pretty weird areas.

So was this first regression kind of like a guided meditation?

Not a meditation. It was a regression. He asked me to be aware of being at my conception with my parents.

What I said was, "Well, I'm remembering a time before that where I made a decision—as a what?—as a consciousness, OK?"

And he said, "All right, what was that?"

"My parents were both in Russia, and I as a consciousness knew what was going to happen in Russia, and I didn't want to be born in Russia. So I intuitively gave them the information to go to America." I remember that. And they did.

Then I went into conception, which was pretty normal. My mother was illiterate, but my father began to study English and became a citizen. He was handsome, with wavy blonde hair, blue eyes, a Khan in Russia. There were intellectual aspects to him. My mother was an illiterate gypsy, a delightful gypsy. I considered her my child, really.

In the conception there was a lot of Russian Jewish talk, because that's where they came from. We lived on the third floor of a house, because my father was saving money to send for his brother.

A horrible thing happened during prenatal. My beautiful grandmother passed away. My mother, who was sixteen, knew that she would have to take care of her three siblings, along with a baby of her own. She couldn't handle it.

She threw herself on her mother's death bed and said, "Take me with you." She was pregnant six months with me. (I have since found out that a baby is recording everything.)

Then she went home to the third floor and threw herself down the back stairs, trying to kill herself. That means non-survival for this baby in her—and both of us on the death bed! They named me after my dead grandmother. So reactively I'm dead. No wonder I couldn't wear anything other than tan, not even white.

[Her mother's self-destructive actions and intense emotions imprinted the subconscious of the unborn child with non-survival recordings. The result is that, in later life, the subconscious can react out (bring forth when stimulated) the feeling of being dead. It also creates a background undertone of deadness in life, demonstrated as the inability to wear bright colors.]

I liked what was happening with Hardin. I liked his ability to see me through that period and not dictate to me, but ask me, so that I could come up with my own answers. Because I realized that I had answers. I didn't understand the whole thing yet, but I realized I had answers— that I proved with my father.

And what was the first effect on you of these memories?

My emotional level came up. I went to buy a suit, and I came out with an orange-red wool gabardine suit, not realizing that I was buying a red suit. Hardin came to pick me up. His green eyes were sparkling.

"Do you realize what color suit you bought?" he said.

I looked at it and I said, "Oh, yes, I was able to buy a red suit!" And I jumped up and down like a child in the car, realizing to what extent I had released all that death and attempted abortion.

"This is great stuff," I thought.

4

KNOWINGNESS

Joanna would constantly challenge my knowingness to expand but always respected what it was in the moment, no matter how limited. She had no need or desire to invalidate my knowingness at any time. She had no need to force me to do anything, think anything, or feel anything other than what came to me to do, think, or feel. She had no need to force me to do it her way or see it her way. But she did have the unusual ability to somehow silently plant an idea or a realization in my mind and then guide my thoughts until I discovered it as if it were my own.

Joanna's basic method was to challenge and awaken the inherent knowingness of my being. She was not asking for intellectual information, opinions, or ideas, but for a certainty that lay beyond the conscious level — "knowledge that knows that it knows, knowledge with certainty."

Joanna would go very deeply into a certain matter and then suddenly, unexpectedly, ask me, "What you do know about this? What is your reality about this?"

Very often my response would be, "I don't know."

She would say, "Thank you for not knowing. Now what *do* you know, man?"

She was constantly prodding me to go deeper to where true knowing abides, a knowingness that had long been covered over by invalidation, cynicism, ridicule, self-doubt, and fear. She never invalidated me. She always validated whatever knowingness I came up with and then prodded me to go deeper.

My knowingness had always set me apart. In summer camp one of my counselors had identified me as an intellectual. I thought it must be some kind of disease. Schoolwork and study was the one area in which I could excel, the one life game I could win at. I maintained top grade-levels all the way through college, maintaining some sort of identity as a scholastic achiever. Despite my excellence at playing mind games, the world of the intellect seemed barren and sterile to me. I felt lost in a maze of abstract data that was meaningless to my life.

Libraries always put me to sleep. I studied much better with the blues pounding away on my stereo — though I now value silence above any music. One evening I went to the university library, resolved to directly experience the knowledge and wisdom that was accumulated there. It was a grand building fronted with huge white columns. The entry room had marble floors and a ceiling forty feet high. I went behind the front desk back into the stacks, which were twelve stories of metal shelving with wooden planks for walkways. Peering along the sides of the shelving, I could see the stories above and below me, tens or hundreds of thousands of books. I sat in a corner and let my mind expand to embrace all the books of knowledge that were in the library. I realized that even with a lifetime of reading I could absorb only a small fraction of the words housed in the library. It felt like an abstract, airless vault filled with billions of words, facts, ideas, and opinions that would only absorb and suppress my life force. I gave up faith in intellectual knowledge that night.

I devoted myself to poetry, music, and spiritual study and practice. My poetry was at first surrealistic, the lyric recording of irrational images that emerge from the subconscious. Though I had formal musical training, I found true music in devotional chanting and in vocal and instrumental improvisation. Meditation grounded me in emptiness, in the certainty of being that lies beyond the mind. I relied on the Taoist teaching that the scholar learns by daily acquisition while the follower of the Way gains through daily loss. I studied astrology for many years. Though intellectual on the surface, astrology leads to the deep intuitive knowledge of energy patterns.

Poetry and music had already developed in me a high level of clairaudience or suprasensible hearing. My work with Joanna led to the unfolding of clairvoyance or suprasensible seeing, which was already present but not fully acknowledged. By challenging and validating my know-ingness, Joanna triggered my awareness of being Superconscious.

Now I present the first excerpt of Hardin Walsh's unpublished book, Totality Concept. *As mentioned in the "Preamble," these ideas supplement the story I am relating, while stating some concepts more directly.*

For Hardin, Totality *refers to the ultimate reality that I am, you are, we all are. His formulation of ultimate reality is "I TOTALITY IS."*

As will be seen, the Total Meditation leads to the awareness of being Totality, followed by the awareness of "creating your first otherness, your superconscious light body." Joanna worked to trigger awareness of being Superconscious in an Earth body, while Hardin's teaching is Totality.

H O W   T H E   G A M E S   B E G A N

Once a before time, I TOTALITY was PRESENT.

I considered:
What would happen IF:
I created a SEPARATE awareness?
And that awareness PRETENDED to be SEPARATE from TOTALITY?
And that separate awareness FORGOT it was only PRETENDING?

That separate awareness wove a dream of pretending, evolved a game, made a mad machine.
Some call it the TIME GAME.
Out of my beingness I created it, wheel within wheel, as Ezekiel said.
Round and round I spun my wheels in figure-eights of eternity.
The wheels were hollow, like tubes, I lined them with VOIDS.
In the center I set the HUB.
In the Hub I set the AGREEMENTS, the monitors of the game.
Then through these wheels, through the TUBES OF TIME, I set the spheres spinning through ponderous aeons.

Each sphere held a set of GAMES,

each game held its own universes, its own galaxies,
monitored by the AGREEMENTS in the core.
And the core was monitored by the agreements in the hub of the time
game, held in place by voids.

Wheel upon wheel ran the tubes of time, in figure-eights of eternity.

How many games, how many universes, how many spheres revolve
in ponderous immensity through the tubes of time?

I, YOU, TOTALITY IS PRESENT.
As we explore our awareness of BEING and PERVADING, in a steady
succession of NOWS, the secrets of the game reveal themselves.

The AGREEMENTS spell out their POSTULATES, the GAMES reveal
their RULES, the universes are enumerated. . . . .

Therefore, let us grant ourselves the right to BE AWARE.

Let us be PRESENT as TOTALITY, NOW.

TOTALITY CONCEPT 26-A

BEING AWARE OF BEING PRESENT
AS THE SPACE

The beginning of the work with Joanna is the experience of being aware
of being present as the space within one's body, the empty space between
the molecules and atoms of matter/energy that comprise one's body. This
includes being aware of being present as the space not only within but also
around one's body — and of gradually expanding that awareness until
one is conscious of being present as the space within and throughout
the entire universe. The end result of the work is being aware of being
Superconscious and of functioning as Superconscious on the Earth plane.

Joanna gave her teachings not systematically but simultaneously,
interspersed with many anecdotal experiences, confirmations, prodding questions and a good deal of humor. Like a great raptor wheel-
ing in space, she circled round and round the many facets of her

understanding, occasionally swooping down to seize upon some illumination that had occurred in me. Much of what she said confirmed and gave depth to experiences I already had, while other concepts took me a longer time to grasp and absorb.

Most basic was the experience, not the idea, the experience of being ✳ present as the space, which was transmitted most directly through the Total Meditation.

"Be aware of being present as the space within your body. Science has demonstrated that within the matter and energy comprising your precious body, between the molecules and atoms you are ninety-nine-plus percent space, empty space. Be aware of being present as the space within your body right now."

(That was easy for me to do.)

"Be aware of being present as the space within and around your body, including your astral and etheric force fields."

(She would pause at each stage until she was certain I had the reality of the experience.)

"Be aware of being present as the space within which this room exists. These bodies, this furniture, these walls are existing within the space that you are."

"Be aware of being present as the space within which the city of Santa Fe exists. The breeze is blowing through you. The birds are flying through. The people and cars are moving through you. And you are present as unbroken, continuous space in which all of this exists."

(Vivid images would appear and disappear in the space. I would keep my awareness on being present as the space within which all exists.)

"Be aware of being present as the space in which this whole region of the country exists. The mountains, the rivers, the trees, the sky, all exist within the space that you are."

"Be aware of being present as the space within which the whole country, the whole continent exists. All the vastness of the land, the rivers, the sea, the sky, all exist within the space that you are."

"Be aware of being present as the space within which the planet Earth exists, a beautiful blue-and-white ball floating within the space that you are. Science says that if all the matter and energy comprising this planet were condensed so that there were no space present, it would only be the size of a small orange. See the planet in peace and harmony and love floating within your space."

"Be aware of being present as the space within which the whole solar system exists. The sun and all the planets whirling around it exist in the emptiness of your space."

"Be aware of being present as the space in which the whole galaxy exists. Millions and billions of stars, dark clouds of matter, infinite life forms, all exist within the space that you are."

"Be aware of being present as the space within and throughout the entire universe. Innumerable galaxies, whirlpools of light, dark clouds of matter, infinite life forms, all exist within the space that you are."

"Be aware of being the stillness."

"Be aware of being vastness."

"Be aware of being motionless."

"Be aware of being timeless."

"Be aware of being foreverness."

"Be aware of being Totality, whole and complete, within and throughout the whole universe."

"Be still and know."

Being aware of being the space came naturally and easily to me after years of meditation practice. When one stills the mind and quiets the emotions sufficiently, one becomes aware of an emptiness, a stillness in the ground of one's being. That emptiness had been a refuge from mental agitation and emotional suffering for years. The experience of extending the awareness of being the space beyond my presence to include the town, the region, the country, the planet Earth, the solar system, the galaxy, and the entire universe was new to me but seemed natural and came very easily.

Space is continuous within and throughout all of creation, existing unbroken and undisturbed by all the configurations of matter and energy. Within, not merely around, but within and throughout the infinite multiplicity of forms created of matter and energy in time, lies the unbroken unity of empty space. To expand the awareness of being present as the space throughout the various cosmic dimensions was almost effortless for me. Space has no boundaries, no limits, and offers no resistance.

I have found that experiential reality is almost wholly a matter of the focus of one's attention. Our personal mental, emotional, and physical activity claims most of our attention most of the time. Here, instead of focusing attention on being a drop of water, one focuses on being the space within a drop of water. Then the focus expands until one is aware of being the space within the entire ocean. The drop does not identify with being the ocean. Although it is immersed in the ocean, the attention on self-identification maintains the illusion of individuality. But the space within the drop is no different than the space within the entire ocean. It is merely a matter of the focus of attention.

The focus on the qualities of Totality (Stillness, Vastness, Motionlessness, Timelessness, Foreverness) was extremely useful in deepening the quality of this ultimate experience. Sometimes in deep meditation very subtle thoughts and knowings come, intimations of inspirations and guidance. Even though these knowings might remain inarticulate to my conscious mind, they can be a source of new directions in daily and creative life.

Sometimes Joanna would add, *"Space is Creator."*

Then she would say, *"As Totality, you have Total Ability and Total Awareness. Be aware of having Total Ability and Total Awareness."*

SUPERCONSCIOUS, CONSCIOUS, AND SUBCONSCIOUS

The meditation continues:

"Be aware of creating your first otherness, your superconscious light body, a vortex of fine, high, white-light energy. Be aware of creating your superconscious light body and be aware of being in that light body now."

We had many long discussions on the three-fold nature of consciousness: subconscious, conscious, and Superconscious. This so-called Three-Mind concept is found in many different forms throughout the world. Joanna discovered confirmation of these ideas in the Huna wisdom of Hawaii, which probably came from Lemuria. It gives a very practical psychology and cosmology of the individual.

Consciousness is continuous and unbroken through all levels of our being, but like the audible spectrum or visible spectrum of energy, there are levels of frequency below and above our normal level of perception. Superconscious simply refers to all of those levels of consciousness that are above and beyond our ordinary conscious mind. Subconscious refers to all those levels that are below, hidden from our ordinary conscious mind. "Subconscious" is a better term than the Jungian term "unconscious" (not-conscious). We can and do become aware of the contents of our subconscious when we go deeply into the psyche, into memories, dreams, and deep feelings. If it were truly unconscious, we could never be conscious of it.

Superconscious (*amakua* in Hawaiian) is Creator beyond time and space. The function of Superconscious is to create and uncreate. Superconscious creates all the multiplicity of forms in creation for its enjoyment and experience. Superconscious creates all the worlds and all the beings therein. Individualized Superconsciouses exist in vortices of white-light energy. The Kahuna (Hawaiian priests, "Keepers of the Secret") spoke of a gathering or family of *amakuas,* all in agreement. You Superconscious created your spirit, caused the conception of your physical body, and is the creative force in your life.

The word "Superconscious" points the attention to that which is above and beyond the conscious mind. "You Superconscious," a term Joanna used frequently, serves to point "you" to a vibrational level above and beyond normal consciousness. Our concepts can indicate and point toward but in no way define or delimit Superconscious. We can recognize Superconscious through its actions and creations but only know Superconscious as we are above and beyond our ordinary awareness. The Buddha said, "My teachings are like pointing a finger at the moon. Don't mistake the finger for the moon." The Twelve-Step Programs refer to this simply as "a greater power"—by whatever name one chooses to refer to it.

We recognize that there is a greater power with the ability to create and uncreate, to manifest and dissolve all creations. In addition to its truly awesome and cosmic aspects, this greater power carries an attitude of lovingkindness toward its creations. To the conscious individual it seems both indifferent and compassionate. Indifferent because it is not intrusive, not interfering. Compassionate in that it hears the needs of creatures, is aware of their sufferings, and can come into our lives if we clearly ask it to produce the results that we desire. In other words, God answers prayers. (Although Joanna does not use the word "God," Superconscious works fine for those who do.)

Conscious (*uhane* in Hawaiian) includes all of our ordinary levels of waking awareness and self-identification—"I am" awareness of body, mind, emotions and the external world. Conscious includes "the ID cards which the spirit answers up to," as Hadron put it, the self-identification, the *ahamkara*. Along with the instincts and passions of the body, its chief feature is the rational mind, whose function is to understand everything through reason and logic and manipulate the world based on its understanding. Most of us either live our life from instinct and passion or try to run it from the thinking mind. Instincts have their root in the physical body, passions in subconscious. Conscious, which includes the faculties of speech and movement, is the primary tool for dealing with the physical world.

Subconscious (*unihipili* in Hawaiian) is the storehouse of memory and emotion. Everything that an individual has ever experienced is automatically recorded in subconscious. The more powerful the experience, the stronger the recording. Traumatic experiences make especially vivid recordings. These memories are imprinted as patterns of light particles, pictures of light which carry along with them sound and feeling. The

55

Kahuna say that similar memories and feelings tend to cluster together—and that the *unihipili* is like a vineyard with many different clusters of grapes on the vine. The recording of memories and feelings is automatic. The clustering together of recordings is irrational and works by "subconscious association," which is unique to every individual.

By the same associative process, events occurring in present time can restimulate or reawaken feelings held in subconscious and reactivate them in present time. This gives much richness, depth, and intensity to our emotional lives, but also enhances the suffering we experience and may cause aberrated or inappropriate behavior. An injury or loss in present time may restimulate a whole series of memories of injuries or losses recorded in subconscious, may intensify the feeling, and may increase the likelihood of such injury or loss occurring in the future. Scientology calls this recording of a traumatic incident or chain of incidents an *engram*. Subconscious accumulates its meanings irrationally and influences conscious mind by powerful feelings that cannot be mastered. The roots of all irrational anxiety, fear, rage, self-limitation, and self-destructiveness, to name a few aberrations, can be found in recordings in subconscious.

The Kahuna knew that in a normally functioning human being, conscious would ask Superconscious to fulfill its needs and desires, and so it would be. If there was an inability to fulfill needs or meet desires, the Kahuna would first look to the subconscious of the person to see what clusters of feelings might be blocking superconscious actions. They said that conscious has to go through subconscious to communicate with Superconscious, giving subconscious the ability to block communication.

One might work hard to provide a good living for one's family and yet be unable to hold on to wealth because of subconscious feelings of guilt from having stolen when one was a child. One might find one's natural love nature distorted or frozen because of guilt and shame about sexuality put in there by priests. Whatever the situation, the Kahuna sought in subconscious the cause of the obstruction of superconscious action and then sought to placate and get agreement from subconscious so that it no longer blocked superconscious action.

God does answer prayer—not just the prayer of the words that come from our mouths but the prayer of our whole being. Most of us are giving God mixed-up messages and getting mixed-up results in our lives. So often there is conflict and confusion about what we want in life.

I say I want to make good money to support myself and my family while subconsciously I feel that money corrupts and is the root of all evil.

Or: I am young, active, sexually attracted — I want to be in love and get laid. But any woman who would have sex with me has to be a woman of loose morals or a whore because good girls like my mother don't have sex outside of marriage. Therefore if I have sex, I am a bad person.

Or: I fear that anyone who would love me would have to control me as my parents did. I don't want to be controlled, so how can I love or be loved by anyone?

Deep-seated irrational attitudes such as these have their roots not only in early programming and painful experiences but also in the residue of traumatic incidents from past lives.

RELEASING RECORDINGS USING VORTEX ENERGY

"I asked the question," Joanna said, " 'why are Earth people automatically reactive?'

"I asked the question knowing I would receive an answer, and I received the answer from Walter Baumgartener, a German scientist. '*Vortex energy*,' he said, '*universal vortex energy*.' In his delightful German accent he pronounced it *wortex energy*.

"Every creation in the universe is a vortex of energy. Every created form exists within a vortex of energy. Energy enters into the vortex in a counterclockwise manner, like the charging wave of an electric current, spiraling down until it reaches the apex of the vortex where there is an explosion of light, a reversal of direction, and the energy spirals back out the vortex in a clockwise manner, like the discharging wave of an electric current.

"Any impression or experience which enters into the vortex of a human being is automatically imprinted in the subconscious mind and when restimulated automatically reacts back out the vortex.

"What I discovered was how to use vortex energy to release these recordings. All of these recordings are merely minute patterns of light particles imprinted in subconscious. In the recordings are the pictures, sounds, reactions, and decisions made in the original events. They are like the patterns of ferrous particles on a magnetic recording tape, inert and meaningless until you put the tape into a playback mechanism. When they are played back, it sounds like there is a symphony orchestra in the room. I understood that one could erase and release the recordings in subconscious just like one can erase a magnetic tape."

The vortex is the universal pattern of creation, most visible in spiral galaxies, hurricanes and tornadoes. It is not immediately apparent that every created form is a vortex of energy or exists within a vortex of energy. A human being does not appear to be in the form of a vortex, any more than a cow or a tree. Nevertheless, the flow of energy into and out from a living being corresponds to the pattern of a vortex. Traditional medicine, such as ayurveda, recognizes the functioning of chakras (wheels) as vortex energy centers within the greater vortex of the spinal column and the breath. The flow of light, carbon dioxide, and soil nutrients into a tree, the expression of these elements as a living being, can also be seen as a vortex of energy.

The vortex within and around the (human) body has been illustrated by Hardin as multiple vortexes coming in from the six directions, all culminating in the center. In practice I always visualized a single vortex surrounding the body, culminating in the root chakra or below the feet, depending on whether I was sitting or standing. The apex of the vortex is "the narrow or pointed end, the culminating point."

UNIVERSAL VORTEX ENERGY—A SCIENTIFIC MODEL

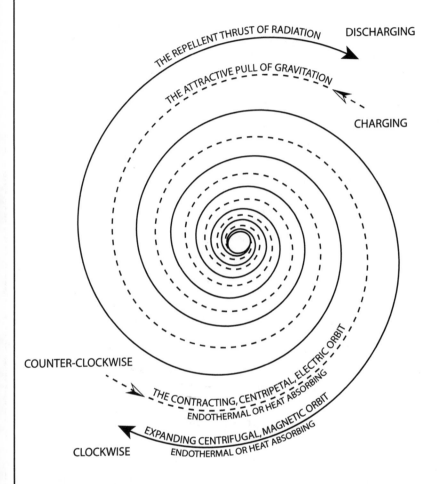

The electro-positive force of attraction pulls INWARD from WITHIN.
The electro-negative force of repulsion pushes OUTWARD from WITHIN.
The constant dynamic interplay of CONTRACTION and EXPANSION
from within the atom, from within all matter, produces energy and motion.
Matter is energy. Energy is matter. All direction is curved. All motion is spiral.

PSYCHIC FUNCTION AND USE OF VORTEX ENERGY

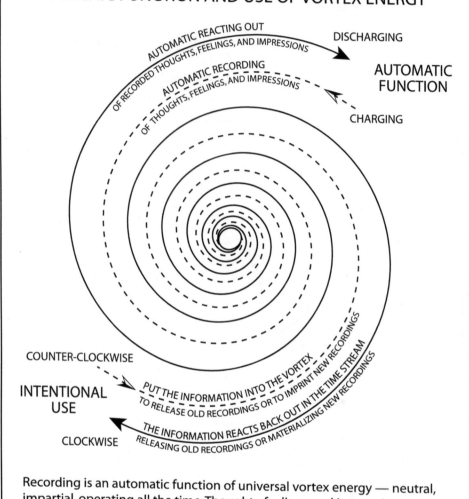

Recording is an automatic function of universal vortex energy — neutral, impartial, operating all the time. Thoughts, feelings and impressions turn into energy, which makes recordings in subconscious, where they are stored in associational clusters. Recorded thoughts, feelings, and impressions automatically react out, play back, and become real in present time, when restimulated by present events.

One can choose to make use of vortex energy to release previous recordings or to record decisions, postulates, new blueprints for life. Put the information (to release or to record) into the vortex, watch the information turn into energy, releasing past recordings or imprinting new recordings, then be aware of how the information reacts back out in the time stream.

VORTEXYA POWER-PACK
A LIGHT PARTICLE — BASIC BUILDING BLOCK
OF OUR UNIVERSES
IMPLODING — EXPLODING VORTICES IN
MATCHING PAIRS CREATES PERSISTANCE

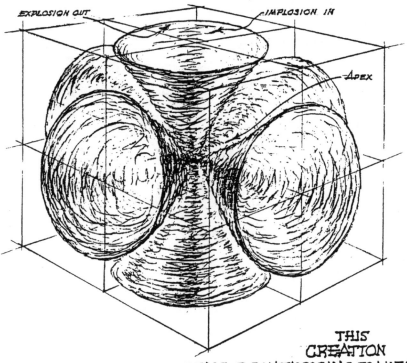

EXPLOSION OUT   IMPLOSION IN

APEX

THIS
CREATION
FORMS 3 DIMENSIONAL PLANES
IN OUR UNIVERSES

790124

AABRON OF ORR

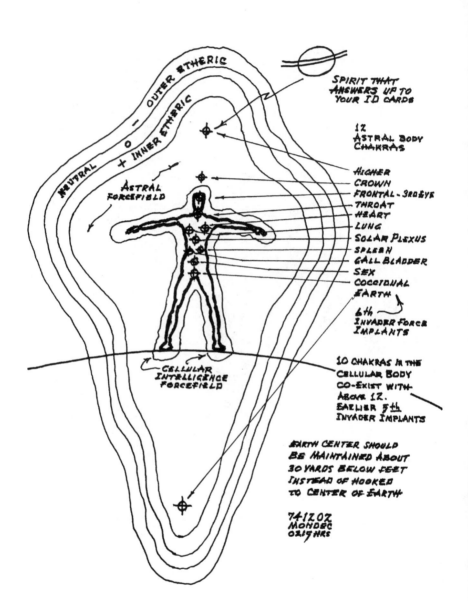

SPIRIT THAT
ANSWERS UP TO
YOUR ID CARDS

12
ASTRAL BODY
CHAKRAS

HIGHER
CROWN
FRONTAL - 3RD EYE
THROAT
HEART
LUNG
SOLAR PLEXUS
SPLEEN
GALL BLADDER
SEX
COCCIONAL
EARTH

6th
INVADER FORCE
IMPLANTS

10 CHAKRAS IN THE
CELLULAR BODY
CO-EXIST WITH
ABOVE 12.
EARLIER 5th
INVADER IMPLANTS

EARTH CENTER SHOULD
BE MAINTAINED ABOUT
30 YARDS BELOW FEET
INSTEAD OF HOOKED
TO CENTER OF EARTH

741202
MON DEC
0219 HRS

OUTER ETHERIC
NEUTRAL O — INNER ETHERIC
ASTRAL
FORCEFIELD
CELLULAR
INTELLIGENCE
FORCEFIELD

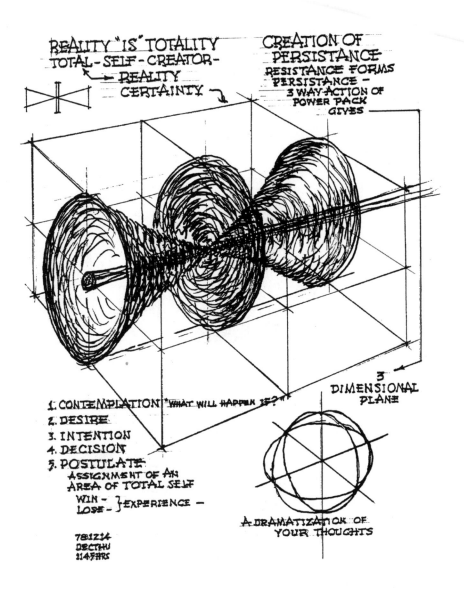

REALITY "IS" TOTALITY
TOTAL - SELF - CREATOR -
REALITY
CERTAINTY

CREATION OF
PERSISTANCE
RESISTANCE FORMS
PERSISTANCE -
3 WAY ACTION OF
POWER PACK
GIVES

3
DIMENSIONAL
PLANE

1. CONTEMPLATION "WHAT WILL HAPPEN IF?"
2. DESIRE
3. INTENTION
4. DECISION
5. POSTULATE
ASSIGNMENT OF AN
AREA OF TOTAL SELF
WIN -
LOSE - } EXPERIENCE -

A DRAMATIZATION OF
YOUR THOUGHTS

781214
DECTHU
1145HRS

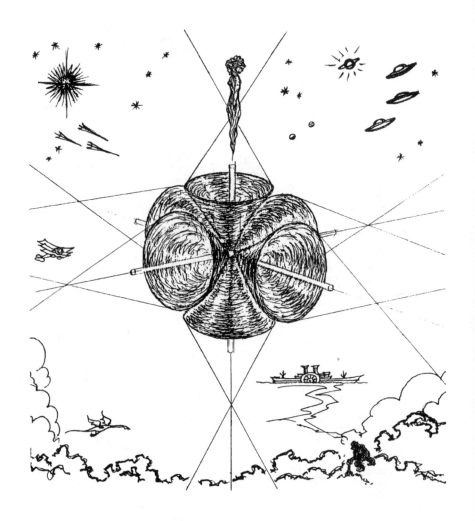

The meditation continues:

"Be aware of being present in your superconscious light body now. As Super-conscious you have the ability to access and experience any recordings, any infor-mation stored in your subconscious, without being affected by these recordings in any way. As Superconscious ask your subconscious to show you the pictures, to play the recordings, that are limiting or interfering with your ability to act in present time in regard to the issue we are working on. Ask and you shall receive."

(This is the key to getting results on issues in present time: accessing the data clusters recorded in subconscious that are distorting or block-ing the free operation of Superconscious in life. Joanna took great care that one saw the pictures clearly and got all the data in an incident or a chain of incidents before proceeding.)

"If you choose to release this recording, first of all be aware of the vortex of energy surrounding your body, within and around your body. Put the information into the vortex around the body rotating counterclockwise: 'I want to release this record-ing right now. I want to disperse the light particles back into the space from which they came.'"

"As the information spirals down the vortex, it contacts all the elements of the recording in the subconscious. When it reaches the apex of the vortex there is an explosion of light, and the energy reverses direction. When it reacts back out of the vortex in a clockwise manner it again contacts all of the elements of the record-ing, erases them, and disperses the light particles."

"But you don't want to leave that area of subconscious blank and open to any impressions that may come in again. You need to revise your considerations and replace the recordings with positive pictures of your own creation. For if you put new pictures of your life as you would see it into your subconscious, Superconscious will automatically react those pictures back out into your life."

"Now, if you choose to do so, create a new blueprint for your life. See yourself standing in the space before you. See your body healthy and strong and vibrant, free of any limiting conditions. See your body joyful and happy, full of energy and enthusiasm. Give your body whatever you desire for its happiness—a mate, chil-dren, a home, money, success. . . . Whatever you desire for your body, put it into your

picture. See it with your body. See it. Feel it. Taste it. Enjoy it. Know that this is your new blueprint for your body. Know that this is real now."

"Now turn the picture of your body around so that it is facing away from you, and breathe this picture of your body and everything that is with it, breathe this picture into your body. Feel it in your body. Make it yours. Know it is yours. And, being aware of the vortex of energy within and around your body, put the information into the vortex, rotating counterclockwise around your body. Put into it the information: 'This is my new blueprint for my body. This is my new reality for my life.'"

"Imprint this picture firmly on your subconscious. Know that this is your new reality now. Know that Superconscious will seed creative energy into the time stream and cause whatever pictures are held in subconscious to materialize on Earth. And now you must retain your new blueprint in your daily life. Let nothing interfere with your beautiful new creation for your life. Do not let doubt or fear or worry creep in and interfere with your new blueprint. See it every day. Know that it is real. Give it to Superconscious and know that what you ask for you shall receive. Be still and know. Be grateful. Be in peace."

Joanna continues,

"That is how I came up with the Four R's: Release the recordings, Revise the considerations, Replace the pictures, and Retain the new blueprint for your life.

"I have found that the Fourth R (Retain) is the most difficult for my clients to practice. It is so easy for doubt and fear to creep back in. It is important to keep seeing and keep on developing the new blueprint in your subconscious and know that it will materialize results out into your life."

This is similar to creative visualization and affirmation techniques, but without the release of the existing recordings, such techniques will only pile up mixed messages in the subconscious. When those results come they will still be mixed up with the old attitudes and reactivities.

The whole technique consists of getting a clear awareness of being Totality — the space within and through the whole universe — then remembering the creation of your first light body, your individualized Superconscious — and being aware of being that light body now. Then as

Superconscious establish a line of communication with subconscious and ask to be shown the pictures that are reacting out into the present life situation and causing aberrant behavior. There is often a whole chain of incidents that have made recordings in the subconscious and clustered together. Often one works back through present life memories, back to birth trauma and prenatal impressions, then back to previous lives and possibly even other worlds.

As Superconscious one can view incidents or whole chains of incidents without being disturbed by them or reacting to them. One can experience the feelings and sensations fully without identifying with them. As Superconscious one can make the decision to release what one chooses and replace it with a new creative picture. For a picture of a desired result held here in subconscious will develop as it gathers light particles around it and will precipitate "incidents and accidents" that will serve to materialize the new creation.

Joanna's work served to help her clients release mental and emotional aberrations, suffering, and pain, and to lead more creative, productive lives. But her specific goal was to trigger in each person the awareness of being Totality, the awareness of being Superconscious, and of being Superconscious functioning on the Earth plane, and thereby to aid in the evolution of humanity out of its automatically reactive perplexity.

Joanna was highly developed psychically and could immediately pick up subconscious pictures in other people and even the presence of spirits hovering around. She could have made a fortune doing psychic readings for people, but that was not her goal. Her method was to guide people to be aware of being Superconscious, to be able to see their own subconscious recordings themselves, and to choose whether to release them and replace them.

Operating as Superconscious, she was noninvasive, nonjudgmental, and compassionate. She was infinitely patient, sometimes prodding, but refused to give easy answers to anyone. As one client said, "Joanna's work is very uncompromising. You either get it or you don't." By working in this fashion, she encouraged people to develop their own Superconscious Ability and Awareness rather than rely upon her as a miracle worker.

Some of these methods evolved from the auditing work in Scientology but go far beyond what Scientology has to offer. Joanna used a

Totalometer, a refinement and expansion of Scientology's original E-Meter. A galvanic skin reactor clasped gently upon the palm allowed her to read the various energy levels her client was experiencing, to identify places where there were obstructions and resistances, and to recognize when total clearing had taken place.

Although she seemed to hold forth endlessly and relentlessly about her concepts, realizations, and experiences, when working with an individual client on their issues she was infinitely sensitive, perceptive, and patient. She would give me her total attention. I often felt that she got to know me better than I knew myself. She was as tender and solicitous as a mother with a child. Indeed, many of her clients asked her to be their mother or grandmother, which delighted her no end.

On the BODY level YOU can be considered to be NORMAL if YOU stand in front of the door and LOOK at it and WONDER. WONDER if the TIGER or the LADY is behind it—in case you might open it someday.

If YOU stand in front of the door and KNOCK and wait for someone to open it and REVEAL ALL to YOU someday after the BODY is classified as dead, YOU might be called a METAPHYSICIAN or a RELIGIOUS FANATIC.

If YOU open the door and become AWARE of the vistas on the other side YOU may become classified as a PHASE-ONE TOTOLOGIST.

If YOU close the door and quickly PRETEND the door never existed, YOU get classified as HUMAN—perhaps for several more lifetimes on this planet.

TOTALITY CONCEPT 740418

HER STORY—OVERCOMING
POLIO AND CRIPPLING INJURIES
Kentucky, age seven (1915)

We were living in an apartment where the train ran by. Evidently I had contracted the polio virus, because I sat in the living room, my head on a wing chair, very, very sad. My family was in the kitchen. They were drinking tea and talking with neighbors and all. That night is when the attack became fully developed. In the recall I remembered going through my body, my spine particularly, taking on the results of the polio virus. In the recall I could do that, I could get that information—how the virus goes through the spine, distorts the cell structure, distorts the spine, distorts the right leg, shuts off the nerves in the leg and in the feet. It was very painful.

My mother didn't know what to do with me, so she took me to the hospital. There, in all their unknowing, they put me in a darkened room. Why, I'll never know. Why not let the sunlight and the air in? No, they put me in a darkened room in a secluded area, no contact with other children. That was all they could do, because they didn't know what to do for polio at the time, until Sister Kenny came along with her wisdom and said *exercise the polio person*. They kept telling my mother, poor little gypsy, that I was never going to walk. That was the best of their knowledge.

This strange realization occurred in my recall. I was shown my body dancing on the ceiling. I was lying down all the time. I never sat up. My view was the ceiling. I know now that this was superconscious action. I was dancing on the ceiling. Oh such wonderful dancing, ballet, everything!

71

My body was dancing. In the recall I realized that I did not accept the recording of being crippled into my subconscious, because Superconscious showed me dancing. So what are they talking about? What they were saying, that I would never walk, had no reality for me at all, none whatsoever—because Superconscious showed me: I am dancing! My legs were flying all over. I was joyous at this.

I realized in the recall that when you don't accept a negative statement from someone, you don't record it, then you don't have it. That to me was such a revelation in what I knew my work was here. If you don't record it, you don't have it to react.

They said they could do nothing for me. They told my mother to get a wheelchair for me and give me things to do with my hands, like painting china or typing or sewing, all things which I had absolutely no interest in. My mother, poor dear, got a wheelchair and put me in it.

I looked at that wheelchair and said, "I'm not going to sit in this thing."

"But the doctors . . ." she said.

Doctors, to this simple little Russian Jewish woman, were God. Not to me. For some reason (I know now it was superconscious guidance) they didn't make sense to me. They didn't match my reality. I was seven years old at the time.

My mother gave me good Jewish food. She was a very good cook. I sat in that wheelchair for about five minutes. My body didn't know that it couldn't get up and walk. I would push it to get up but it would fall. I was black and blue.

My mother would stand over me and cry, "What are you doing to me?" (To her I was doing that to her.) It hurt her to see me falling and getting bruised.

I kept saying to her, "I cannot sit in this thing. I've got to walk. I've got to dance."

"But the doctor . . ."

I said, even at the age of seven, "I don't care what the doctor says. I can dance. I can walk."

Superconscious was really very powerfully impressing me.

It took me about three months of getting up and falling to finally get the wisdom to get my wheelchair up against the wall. By that time I had really strengthened my legs sufficiently to stand up against the wall. My mother came in and looked at me. I was standing up against the wall.

"Oh, my kin, my child, what are you doing?" she said.

"I'm standing up against the wall."

I didn't realize that what I had done earlier in standing up and falling had actually strengthened my legs.

"Get me crutches, because I want to walk," I said to her.

So she did. She got me crutches. From the standing up against the wall I began to reach out and make my legs walk. Then I threw away the crutches and said I wanted a cane. How did I know anything about crutches and canes? I cannot tell you, other than that's what I got to say and do — and I did it! There was that superconscious information that I was listening to. But I didn't realize it was Superconscious. I just thought it was me saying these things. So she got me a cane. I began to walk nicely around the house.

She was supposed to take me into the hospital every three or six months, for them to see how I was doing. At this point I was walking.

The doctor looked at me and said, "What happened to her?"

My mother said, "She wouldn't sit in the chair!"

"What do you mean?"

"She wouldn't sit in the chair!"

And that was that. I suppose they realized that what I had done worked. I have no way of knowing whether they proceeded with that knowledge on other cases or not. But I know that Sister Kenny certainly did, because she came out with, "Exercise the polio. Don't let them sit in darkness." Imagine that. Why not expose me to the sunlight? Wouldn't they have known that yet? Of course, this was a million years ago.

From what you are saying it sounds like your parents did not try to invalidate you or control you.

That's right. They did not. I realized in recall that before I was even conceived I selected these parents because they wouldn't interfere with me. And they didn't. They didn't know how to. They weren't really deep into any religion. There was the Hanukkah and those holidays where they went to the synagogue, but they were not religious people. They were Jewish people.

If you got intuitions or imaginations, they did not try to invalidate them.

Oh no, they didn't. They didn't force anything on me. They had to realize that I was taking the initiative in my life, because I was. That has been my nature throughout my life.

New Haven, age nineteen (1927)

I got a job and a nice place to live, and I met this man, who meant nothing to me, Arnold Friedman. He was handsome, like a store dummy, handsome. How I met him I haven't the faintest notion. There seemed to be a destiny to meet that guy. He fell in love with me and I felt utter disdain for him. But he wouldn't let go. I met women friends, and they had men friends that I met. But he wouldn't let go.

Had you ever had any romantic attraction to any man?

Never. They didn't appeal to me. I couldn't even shake hands. Kissing was out of the question. I had not kissed this man. I had not encouraged this man. He had nothing going for him as far as I was concerned. He had been married and divorced. He decided that I was the love of his life. I gave him no encouragement whatsoever.

One day he decides that I'm going to New York with him to meet his mother. He showed me a telegram that he had sent to her. She had sent back a telegram saying that she's fixing dinner for us.

I said, "What do I want to do a thing like that for? I am not your fiancée. I have no desire to be it. I certainly don't want to meet your mother and give her any false ideas about our relationship."

Yet that's what happened. As a Jewish young woman you don't refuse a mother. You just don't do that. It's not nice.

So I said, "OK, I'll go with you."

He had this little roadster. They had canvas tops that could collapse. We get to Greenwich, Connecticut, on December 11, 1927. I was nineteen, very unsophisticated. I looked more sophisticated than I really was because I knew how to dress. Snow was falling and formed ice on the road. We were in just a little roadster. We're going down the road and this big truck comes from the other side and slides right into us. It knocked me through the window. Of course he was held by the steering wheel. It broke my front teeth and broke my nose. I needed fifty-three stitches from my eye down my face over my lip and under my lip. It broke both my legs.

I came to and they had me on a gurney going to a hospital. I remembered that I had put on some nice silk undies.

I came to enough to tell the nurse, "Don't cut my undies. They're my favorite." They were pretty pink with lace and all of that, silk undies. So she didn't cut them. But imagine: here I am all broken to pieces and I'm concerned about my undies.

As far as Arnold was concerned, he was around, but I blocked him out, I think. He never meant anything to me. And here I am in this mess. They decided, he decided that we go back to New Haven. So they put me in an ambulance. Where he was I haven't the faintest notion.

They took me to the hospital in New Haven. That's where Dr. Hensey of Yale University Medical came to see me. I remember him distinctly. He looked at me. I was unconscious. I remembered this in regression. I don't know how long I was unconscious. But when I became conscious both of my legs were encased in a cast. They just did bare stitching in my face because they didn't think I was going to live. He later showed me that the newspaper said that I lost my right eye and that a beautiful young woman was demolished. I had skin at that time that had no pores at all, no blemishes, it looked like wax.

I came out of the coma, lifted myself up on my elbows and looked in the mirror on a dresser that was nearby, saw my face, and fainted dead away. What happened after that I haven't the faintest idea yet. I just knew that somehow I was in a very bad way and that I could die. I heard that. I had to decide that it was all right with me to die. In the regression I learned that I had realized that—it was all right for me to die at that time. Another thing that I distinctly remember: I never blamed Arnold Friedman. Now why wouldn't I blame him? I didn't want to go with him.

Then I remember seeing a big wheel of life. It wasn't a dream. It was a vision. There were bodies on this wheel, and as the wheel came to the bottom it crushed the bodies, then it picked up bodies and went on. Somehow I saw this as the wheel of life. I couldn't remember researching whether there is such a thing or not. There very well may be. It was at that time I decided that I would live. *"I think I'll live."* I remember making that decision. That wheel of life made me realize that the wheel goes round and round—you die at one end and you come alive at another end—and I thought about what that meant to me. So why go through the death? In my immature knowledge I made that decision.

Since that was that, I called in the chemist at the hospital.

I said, "What can I do about this face? What is available that I can put on?"

"They want to do surgery on you," he said.

"Wait. They've been doing surgery on me. I don't know how many operations I've had. I want to see what I can do with my skin. It's good skin."

"Yes, it's very good skin."

So he brought me Nivea and some medicinal lanolin. I asked for something to mix it all up so I could put it in a jar and again he accommodated me. I seemed to like the idea of mixing things, concoctions like that for skin.

When I finally went into regression, I realized that I made my own face cream in Egypt with oils. I loved mixing it and never had anybody else do it for me. In the hospital at that time I seemed to like the idea of mixing all this stuff together. I would sit there all day long rubbing this stuff into my skin until I almost erased the scar.

The doctors came in and said, "This is marvelous. It's a miracle."

I did a good job. Of course my nose was broken. I can still feel the tender place where it broke. They didn't do anything about setting it. That took away my nice little nose that I had from my mother and gave me a longer nose like my father. I guess I had to have a longer nose. I didn't want them to break it and set it again, so I remained with a longer nose. But I did manage to do a pretty good job of massaging out the scar.

Then Dr. Hensey said to me, "If you will permit me I will cut under your right foot in the arch, on the upper part of your arch and on the back of your foot. I will try to connect living nerves to the dead nerves that occurred as a result of the polio."

I wasn't having a difficult time walking. I was even dancing. I loved to dance. The only thing I had in common with Arnold Friedman was dancing. He danced like Rudolf Valentino. He had a look like him. And he danced magnificently. That was the only thing. I loved dancing with him.

So I gave the doctor permission to do that and now I have those scars. I can't tell whether that made any difference in my ability to walk. But there are more scars to be healed.

Arnold goes to Dr. Hensey and says, "What's going to happen to her? I'm really responsible because she didn't want to go."

Dr. Hensey says, "I don't think she'll ever walk."

They had put a metal plate in my right leg and my body rejected it, so they had to do an overlap of the bone, which shortened my right leg. My left leg was broken at the knee, and they decided to let that heal whichever way it would heal, and it did. There was a big protrusion on my left knee. My only concern was how I can manage to get out of this situation. This is the second time in my life the doctors say that I'm never going to walk.

They tell this to Arnold, and he said, "Well, I want her and I'll marry her and I'll take care of her."

Oh, when I think of it now—he'll take care of me!

So the doctor says to me (I was Bluma Cohen at the time), "Bluma, you ought to marry the man. He'll take care of you whether you can walk or not, whether you use a cane or whatever."

"I don't love the guy. What do you want?"

"You have no choice," the doctor says to me.

Telling me I have no choice! I'm a Sagittarius, I have to have choice!

Well, he convinced me that I should do that. So I married Arnold Friedman.

We went to Florida for six weeks on a honeymoon that for me was nothing. I got a rubber tube. I went into the ocean and exercised my legs all day long. Then I'd come out on the sand. The white sand of Miami Beach was kind of nice in the sun, and I would exercise my legs again on the sand. I don't remember Arnold ever saying anything to me like what are you doing. He just watched what I was doing. He didn't say anything to me. I didn't say anything to him. I seem to have that way. I did that with Hardin too. I wouldn't say what I was doing. I wouldn't ask for advice or opinions. I don't like arguments, so I'm just going to do what I want to do.

You're saying that just like your parents, Arnold didn't try to invalidate you or control you.

Oh no, he didn't, he couldn't.

Many men would have tried to.

Oh, I suppose, but they wouldn't get away with it. He didn't even try. And I know now from in regression that I realized the superconscious guidance in what to do to walk. The doctor never told me. I Superconscious told my body what to do.

The point I'm making here is: everyone has superconscious guidance. Everyone is a Superconscious, outside time, a superconscious vortex energy eternally. Somehow or other I followed the direction that I was given and benefited from it. Everybody can do that, if they have the initiative and the desire to progress in life instead of remain in an apathetic give-in situation, which is not my nature.

But at the time you didn't call it Superconscious or have any philosophy.

I just did what I felt inclined to do.

You followed your intuitions and hunches and didn't question your knowingness.

That's right.

I then asked Arnold to get me some crutches, just like I did with my mother. It was a repeat of the old scene. He got me crutches. I began to walk. Then he got me a cane. But I kept those crutches, because I had an idea what I was going to do.

When we came back to New Haven we went in to see Dr. Hensey at Yale Medical. I took the crutches and walked with them into his office.

"Oh," he said, "you're walking with the crutches. That's nice."

"That's not nice," I said.

I dropped the crutches and hit him over his bald head.

"Never play God. I'm walking! Look!"

And I danced around his office. He looked at me in amazement.

"You are!" he says.

"You see, you don't do that to people. Never tell a person they can't walk. You're not taking that person's intuition or whatever I had going for me into consideration."

"I won't ever. You've taught me a lesson."

"Good. Always encourage people that they can walk. Don't look at just the physical. I have no philosophy but I have a little wisdom going for me."

I was getting it superconsciously. I realized it afterwards.

5

COMING TO LIMITS
1984–1985

I began meeting with Joanna in September 1984, but it was not until the following May that I recorded my first session with her that led to the uncovering and release of past-life pictures. She took special care to prepare me and allow an adequate gestation period for her ideas.

Meanwhile, my progressed Sun was coming conjunct to my natal Saturn. The life I was living was coming to limits on every side. Following my heart and my inspiration, I had left the world to live at Lama Foundation soon after I got out of college. I had not prepared myself to deal with the so-called real world, nor had I imagined that one day it would be necessary. Now I was living in that real world and had to admit that I was not dealing well with my life at all. *Inability to cope* or *failure* might be the appropriate term.

I did not understand how to make money, especially how to work at what I loved and make money as well. I worked as a bookkeeper while still nurturing my ideal of being a romantic artist. Rents were so high in Santa Fe that I had to share a house with someone else. Abe was living with his mom, Varda, and staying part time with me.

In April I was laid off from the first job I had held since college. I had to look at the fact that I was minimally equipped to function in the business world. At the same time my landlords told me that they did not want to continue renting to me a home I had been sharing with another man, his daughter, and my son. Our unconventional lifestyle was unacceptable to them. This was the first of five homes I would be asked to leave, for one reason or another, over the next four years. Indeed, I would not have a stable home or a steady job until 1989. This did, however, provide me with ample amounts of free time to do inner work with Joanna.

To say I had a poor self-image would be an understatement. I had no picture of what to do in the world or how to do it, and very little motivation to function aside from the necessity to provide for my son. And the only woman I knew who ever really loved me could not leave her marriage to be with me.

The intensity of my creative focus in poetry and music, which had held very strong for nine or ten years, began to dissipate after the birth of my son and my divorce from his mother. I no longer heard the singing voice inside me. I would still go home to be alone at night, but the singing voice was no longer with me. I would tell myself I needed to be alone to do my work. In fact, I would smoke dope and read horror novels. It took a long time, but after a while I had to admit that I was fooling myself, that I was hiding self-indulgence behind a mask of functioning with a creativity that was no longer there. I had punched my ID cards with the image of the solitary ecstatic singer. Now it appeared that the singing voice was a gift that was given to me for a time rather than a power that I possessed and held.

I did experience delightful bursts of shared creativity with Glory, where we would sing songs and choreograph dance movements for the sacred circle dances in our community. That was a creative flow that was happening through her at the time, which I was fortunate to share.

My goal now was not what I wanted it to be but what it had to be (Saturn). No matter what union I might long for with Glory or with the singing voice, what I had to do was master the real world, the material world, at least to the extent of being able to provide for myself and my son. With my life coming to limits on every side, I was left with nothing but the necessity to change. And that change had to happen inside before it could manifest outside. How can one create a life without a picture of that life? Right now I had no idea.

Though Joanna doesn't like to be called a teacher, that's how she appeared to me at the time — as a Saturn figure, the older, wiser person who could help me on my way and perhaps teach me how to be. Necessity is a most powerful force. It might be said that without absolute necessity no one would ever come to awareness of and surrender to a greater power.

As Rumi says, *"Increase the necessity."*

At this stage of the local TIME GAME the IMMORTAL SPIRITS, which are NOTHINGNESSES, thought-form ASSIGNMENTS of the TOTAL SELF, are desperately trying to prove to themselves that they are SOMETHING — even a body.

There are movies on television that have PEOPLE saying there is no such thing as SPIRITS — or they are bad or do not exist. This is an interesting DENIAL OF SELF by all of the SPIRITS OPERATING bodies on this planet. PRETENDING you do not exist could be called psychosis.

It is even more interesting that the SPIRITS have forgotten they are not really SPIRITS. They are ASSIGNED UNITS of the TOTAL SELF PRE-TENDING and MAINTAINING the necessary levels of stupidity or UNAWARENESS in order to participate in this TIME GAME.

TOTALITY CONCEPT 740420

RELEASE THE PRIEST
May 2, 1985

Finally, after nine months of preparation and reflection, it seemed we were ready to work on my issues with Glory. We set the intention to do a session focusing on the recall, release, and replacement of any pictures that might be present in subconscious relevant to my inability to be with Glory.

Obviously I was unable to be with Glory because she was married, but that is something over which I could have no influence or control. This inner work I was embarking on was to reveal and release those karmic recordings which restrained and distorted my capacity to love other human beings, human beings of the opposite sex, and Glory in particular. The frustration of finding all of my love fixated on the unobtainable Glory in specific was the final factor pushing me to this inner work.

It is important to set the intention before going into session, because once one's awareness has shifted to being total space no need is felt to do anything about anything. Though Joanna had her agendas and purposes, she always let me set the goal when we were doing sessions related to my personal issues.

But first, before all of our sessions, there would be several hours of talking and tuning—talking among other things about my attitudes and feelings related to Glory, circling around the subject but not really pouncing on it. I came in ready and eager to get down to immediate pain relief. Instead we or, I should say, *she* would talk and talk and talk and talk, holding forth on her ideas, while prodding me on my issues. Whatever Joanna's purpose was in these long sessions of talking, I know that by the time we went into session, a certain level of my mental energy and perhaps resistance had been worn away and exhausted.

Joanna set no time limits on herself when she was working with someone. She was working outside of time and would allow whatever time it took for results to be achieved. Joanna didn't charge by the hour. She charged a flat rate per session, no matter how much time it took. She didn't charge me anything at all because I had very little money. I reciprocated by doing whatever work she requested, secretarial and otherwise, continuing long after our work was over. But my services could in no way compensate for the priceless gift that she was giving me. She worked with many people who had no ability to pay. The quality of her work or the time she took was not affected by the amount of money she received. She had certainty of the ability of Superconscious to transform human lives. Indeed, much of her income came from former clients who had prospered and were still grateful.

So when do we get down to it? you're probably asking. And so was I.

We went into her office and sat down in our chairs, which were positioned at right angles to one another, so that both of us were looking forward into empty space. My chair was wide enough that I could sit cross-legged in it.

She used a tissue with a little alcohol to clean the hand clasp of her Totalometer and then gently placed it over my palm. She turned some dials to calibrate the readings on her meter, and then we were ready.

"All right," she said. "Close your eyes and take four deep breaths. Relax your body, every part of your body. . . .

"Good. Now be aware of being present as the space within your body. . . ."

The Total Meditation was the foundation for every session and Joanna's most precious vehicle. If one could not get the awareness of being the space, of being Totality, and of being Superconscious, the session could go no further. Fortunately I had no problem being aware of being the space.

" . . . be aware of creating your first otherness, your superconscious light body, a vortex of fine white-light energy, and be aware of being that light body *now*. Be aware of being Superconscious, beyond time and space. Feel that high white-light energy. Enjoy it. Appreciate it. This is You Superconscious.

"Now as Superconscious, establish a line of communication with your subconscious mind and ask to be shown whatever pictures, whatever recordings, are reacting out in the present moment and preventing you from being with your beloved Glory."

Silence. Long, long silence.

I stared into the void in front of me. Nothing appeared.

She waited. I waited. Nothing appeared.

I knew that something was there, and I knew that I could see it. So I stuck with it.

The void in front of me was not empty, black, and clear like the night sky. The void I was looking into was gray, dark, misty, obscure, and shifting.

Finally, after what seemed to be forever, there was an opening in the gray fog through which I could see a dark figure. It was a man dressed in black. I was seeing him from behind, looking over his shoulder.

Joanna immediately saw my reactivity on the meter.

"Yes. Ahad. Are you getting something?"

I nodded my head.

"Good. Verbalize it, please. Tell me what you see."

"I see a man. He's dressed in black. He has dark hair. I can't really see his face. It's like I'm standing behind him and looking over his left shoulder. I can see the side of his face. He has pale skin and a trimmed dark beard."

This seemed puzzling to me. It didn't seem very significant.

But Joanna said, "Good. Good. Go deeper into the picture."

"He seems to be talking to someone, a woman. She's dressed like a nun. They are in a shady patio. She's sitting and he's standing over her. Oh, I get it. He's a Jesuit priest and she's a nun. She's looking up at him with big beautiful eyes, telling him how much she loves him, how she thinks about him all the time, how she wants to be together with him as a woman is with a man. I still can't see his face. I think I've moved into being in his body now. He is telling her they can never be together. They have both taken vows of celibacy and dedicated their lives to Christ. He loves her too and longs for her deeply. That disturbs him very much, but he cannot acknowledge it. He speaks with her gently and firmly, telling her that they can never be together. It is difficult for him to look into her eyes and let the clear, burning passion of her love touch the tenderness in his heart. He keeps his gaze mostly downcast and turned away. He knows he sounds cold and harsh, but he must be as firm with her as he is with himself for the sake of their religion. Because of their religious vows, they cannot love one another and they cannot be together as a man and a woman."

"That's it. You've got it. Rejection in the name of religion. Oh, how awful! And you got this with your own awareness and abilities. Please acknowledge the superconscious abilities and awareness that you have. And you told her *We can never be together.* Oh, how awful! No wonder she can't be with you. We'll have to release that right away. But first we need to see if there are any other pictures in the chain. Would You Superconscious ask your subconscious mind to show you if there are any other earlier pictures which are related to Ahad's inability to be with Glory."

I close my eyes. I ask to receive, and I wait. This time I didn't have to wait so long. I see a young man with brown skin, long matted dark hair, and blazing eyes, wandering the streets of India, wildly chanting, singing of his longing for his beloved. He's a *madzub,* a person intoxicated with the passion of longing and crazy for love.

"That's good. Very good. Go deeper into the picture. What else do you see?"

He's in love with a princess, a high-caste young woman. His parents are servants on her father's estate. They had known each other since childhood, but since they had come of age their love had blossomed into passion. She is exquisitely beautiful, with long dark hair, smooth dark skin, big luminous eyes, always dressed in the finest saris. He's just a poor boy. They would meet together secretly to hug and kiss, to whisper and dream. They would meet together secretly for fear of being discovered, which eventually they were. He was banished from her father's estate and forbidden to see her again. He learned that she had been engaged to marry a young prince. He snuck in to see her again. She told him sadly that she would always love him but she had no choice, she was to be married to this young prince, and she could never see him again. He wandered around the streets like a madman, consumed with the fires of love. He smoked lots of hashish, ate little, chanted his heart out in the blazing sun. . . . It does not seem that he had a very long life.

"Oh, so much rejection and unfulfillment sitting there! You see now why you feel the way you do. You meet Glory, and all of these pictures are restimulated in present time. We want to release them and clear your space right now. But first we should ask one more time for subconscious to show you any other pictures relevant to Ahad and Glory."

This time a very clear and peaceful picture came, a sunny pastoral scene with colors as luminous as a Maxwell Parrish painting.

"It seems to be early Greece, at the dawn of time. I see sunny green fields, running water, deep blue sky, a shepherd's tent, and flocks of sheep. I see two young children, a boy and a girl, playing happily together. They both have golden hair, fair skin, and blue eyes. They look alike. They must

87

be twins. This could be the first lifetime we shared together on Earth. We came in as twins."

"What a beautiful picture. Nothing that needs releasing there. Now tell me what is your consideration? Are there any of these pictures that you would like to clear off your body and dissolve back into space?"

"I would like to clear away the picture of the Jesuit priest and 'We can never be together' and the picture of the Hindu *madzub* and 'I can never see you again'."

"All right. Very good. Be aware that there is a vortex of energy within and around your body. And if you choose to, put into that vortex, counterclockwise, going from right to left, the information 'I want to release that picture of that Jesuit priest off my body right now, I want to erase this recording and dissolve those light particles back into the space from which they came.' That information becomes energy. Follow that energy as it spirals counterclockwise down the vortex. As it spirals down the vortex it contacts all the bits and pieces of that picture."

I put my mind into the swirling vortex, starting from above my head and moving down, around, and into my body. As I touched into the picture again, I could sense the feelings intensifying and renewing.

"Now follow that energy all the way down to the apex, where there is a tremendous explosion of light, and the energy reverses and comes back up out of the vortex in a clockwise manner. As it contacts each element of that picture, it erases it and disperses the light particles back into the space from which they came."

As the energy came back up the vortex, I could feel a sense of clearing and release, but the space was not totally clear yet. Joanna told me to continue with the clearing process until the space felt totally clear. I did that for both pictures.

When my space finally felt clear, and Joanna confirmed it with her meter, she said, "Good. Now you need to put a new blueprint for your life into your subconscious mind. For whatever pictures are imprinted in your subconscious will automatically react out into your life.

"I want you to see Ahad standing in front of you. See him very clearly. He is happy and healthy, loving and knowing, radiant and full of life. And

Glory is standing next to him. They have their arms around each other. They are loving each other. They can be together. Feel that total love.

"See yourself with everything you need in life, functioning as you would in life. Give yourself a nice, spacious, beautiful home with a big yard, where Abe can grow up, where you and Glory can be together.

"Give yourself money, gold, lots and lots of gold. Oh, I see you have some resistance to having money. We'll have to get to that later. Give yourself everything you need in life. See it with your body and around your body."

I continued to develop this imaginal picture for a while on my own.

"Now turn that body you see around so that it is facing away from you and breathe it into yourself. Breathe that image and everything that goes with it into your body. Breathe it into your cells. Breathe it into your subconscious. And, Superconscious, say to your body: *'This is my new blueprint for my body. This is the new reality I am living in. This is my reality now.'*

"As time goes along, allow the picture to develop. Enhance it. Let it get fuller. But never ever invalidate your picture. Never let Kreepy Doubt come in. This is your new blueprint for your life that you have created and given to your subconscious, and it is real now. Know that it is real. Be still and know."

This was the format for release and replacement that was followed every time we worked together, always beginning with the Total Meditation, Joanna always allowing me the choice about what to release and what to replace. For brevity I will not repeat it each time I discuss a session, but please know that it is always there.

Many schools of Metaphysical, Occult and Philosophical teachings have taught that each individual has to strive upward and achieve ultimate something or other, termed many names: BRAHMAN, ATMAN, ONENESS, STATIC or STILLNESS. In several YOGA teachings step-by-step procedures are spelled out. As you struggle upward for several lifetimes many things are encountered such as all manner of force-fields and hierarchy of SPIRITS. All these tend to force YOU to live up to the basic TIME GAME AGREEMENTS that you will stay with the BODY until it is classified as DEAD.

This is a SPIRIT activity. Many lifetimes can and have been used up in meditation and assorted practices.

In the TOTALITY CONCEPT the individual starts at the top by acknowledging his/her PRESENCE as TOTALITY and works his/her way downward through the HIERARCHY control echelon of command to the BODY: releasing them as you go.

First there is the staggering shock that YOU are EVERYTHING and EVERYWHERE. It is also interesting to discover that there really is a HIERARCHY of entities or OTHERNESSES—super SPIRITS that monitor the TIME GAME.

They will be just as shocked to discover that YOU are AWARE of them and will take immediate steps to knock your cosmic teeth out and restore the HYPNOTIC CONTROLS that keep you a NORMAL HUMANOID type BEING.

TOTALITY CONCEPT 740423

PLANET-HOPPING
May 25, 1985

One of the themes that Joanna kept returning to was that of the home planet — didn't I want to go to my home planet? As at our first meeting, I said that as far as I knew, Earth was my home planet.

Joanna said her work was with extraterrestrials, people who knew or suspected that they came from another planet, that Earth was not their home. The central event in working with such people was to bring them back to their home planet, so that they could experience their original nature and affirm their mission on Earth. Abilities and awarenesses that are natural on the home planet often seem strange and may create difficulties on Earth.

"On our planet we don't use money," Joanna would say. "Whatever we want we create directly from light particles. That is our superconscious ability. And we don't have sex, not in the Earth-plane way of one physical body sticking itself into another. Our bodies are light bodies, and if two beings want to experience one another they simply merge their light bodies and mingle light particles. It is such an exquisite sensation, far beyond Earth-plane sex."

If one had these home-planet memories, one might have little inclination to handle money or little attraction for "Earth-plane" money, sex, power, etc. On the other hand, there are many dimensions in the universe. Some clients, remembering home planets where sexuality was abundant and promiscuous, found the jealous and exclusive sexual nature of most Earth-plane beings quite strange. Other planets could also be the location of traumatic events that had imprinted in the subconscious. Joanna lived in a very no-holds-barred universe.

I didn't identify very much with this whole extraterrestrial angle. But Joanna persisted in saying that she wanted to take me to my home planet. And who am I to refuse a trip into outer space?

In this meditation session I spent a much longer time experiencing my superconscious light body, a light among many lights. I experienced what it was like to move and flow in the vastness of space, dancing among the stars, so to speak—magnificent, awesome . . . impossible to put into words.

When Joanna directed me to go to my home planet, I found myself drifting through space, looking for a world to be my home. I passed by many worlds, focusing down into them and briefly materializing on them. Joanna called it "planet-hopping."

There was a predominantly red world, like a science-fiction Mars, with barren desert, rock and sand, scorching winds, and murky crimson skies. This world had little interest for me.

There was a predominantly blue world, like the Hindu *deva loka,* home of the gods, where exquisitely beautiful blue-skinned beings with large limpid eyes lounged around in ethereal garb in airy pavilions overlooking lush gardens and a peaceful lake. The atmosphere was of deep, unbroken peace and reflection. It seemed to me like a great civilization that had evolved to perfection throughout the eons and now had nowhere else to go. There was a hint of melancholy. They had already been through it all. This was too advanced a world for me. There was nothing to do, nothing to learn. I moved on.

As I cruised on through space I approached a large, shimmering, gold-and-white world. This was a very advanced and radiant scientific civilization, very vibrant, not in decline like the blue realm. They had vast thought computers and delicate crystalline architecture. Joanna became very excited.

"This is my home planet you're coming to, the gold-and-white planet, Orr!" she interjected. "Do you remember meeting me and Hadron there? Do you remember agreeing to assist us, to play a role in our mission on Earth?"

With that suggestion it was easy to visualize meeting them there in their gold-and-white uniforms. I said that I would be there to help them but that I was on a journey of my own.

This gold-and-white planet was indeed exquisite, but they too were already far evolved. I was looking for a younger, fresher world, a place where I could get in more toward the beginning of the game — somewhere fresh, raw, undeveloped, rich in potential. I like new beginnings. I wanted to experience a whole evolution, not just drop in on someone else's creation.

So I continued drifting through space, zoning in and out of worlds, until I came across a relatively young, relatively new planet, an exquisite blue-and-white orb of clouds and oceans and, beneath the clouds, brown, green, and white land masses. The world was rich with living creatures and resources and was at an earlier phase of development. You guessed it. Welcome to Planet Earth!

"How long ago did you come to Planet Earth?" Joanna asked abruptly, snapping her fingers. "Quick, without thinking, how long ago?"

"Ten thousand years."

Joanna was thrilled with these memories of planet-hopping. She said the only similar experience she had was when she worked with someone who had been a space pirate, who had no home of his own but went around plundering other worlds. Apparently most of the people she worked with had home planets other than Earth.

I thought of this as being a session where we pursued her agenda for me rather than my own agenda of emotional clearing. It all seemed quite real to me but did not have the strong emotional impact of the uncovering of traumatic past-life pictures. The obviously archetypal nature of the imagery made me wonder whether this was a fairy tale being told to me by Superconscious.

I must admit I was less than thrilled that Joanna interjected that I was coming to her home planet, where I just happened to meet her and Hadron. Since she suggested it, I could see it quite clearly, of course. But was it a valid memory or just my picking up on her projection of her own agenda? This was a very rare instance when Joanna actively participated in my recall. She usually kept clear boundaries and waited patiently for me to come up with the pictures on my own.

HUMAN SACRIFICE
June 14, 1985

With Saturn in Leo in my natal chart, romantic love and play never came easily to me. I had a hard time enjoying parties. I was too serious. Love was always a heavy issue for me. I could not play with it lightly. If I felt love for someone, I resisted it. And if someone felt love for me, forget it. I resisted their love even more strongly. Love was what I most deeply desired and most deeply feared. No matter how much I needed to love and be loved, I kept pushing it away from me.

Pluto conjunct Saturn in Leo further intensified my isolation and deepened my aversion into fear and terror, but it also signified that my resistance to love, my proud and fearful self-isolation, would have to be transformed in this lifetime.

Whenever I felt love I felt pain in my heart — the more intense the love the more intense the pain. This was more than just the agony and burning of longing. It had elements of irrational terror and horror. The intensity of my love for Glory had heightened my awareness of these aberrations.

Sometimes I would lie down on my bed and feel as if my heart were being torn apart. Not exploding with love or bursting with joy, but literally torn apart by external forces. At times it felt as if my whole body were being drawn and quartered—each of my four extremities tied to horses, who were set running away from each other. At other times it felt like hands were reaching down into my chest cavity and tearing out my heart. The image was that of a great bird of prey hovering over me, sinking his talons into my chest, and ripping out my heart.

How could one be a loving person with this sort of nonsense going on? How could I tell my beloved 'Loving you makes my heart feel like it is being ripped out of my chest'? Fortunately for me it was Joanna's profession to work with such bizarre states of consciousness. She could take my psychic data literally, without invalidating me, and guide me to release these afflictions. We agreed to do a session on releasing this pain in my heart.

We went into session and did the Total Meditation. I regained awareness of being Superconscious and asked to be shown the pictures in subconscious that were restimulated in present time as pain in my heart.

When the window opened in the gray fog in front of me, I saw an Aztec priest standing on the platform on top of a pyramid, sacrificial knife in hand raised over his head, standing over a naked victim on a blood-drenched altar. It was shocking to find this scene in my subconscious. I described it to Joanna.

"Good. Very good," she said. "Which one are you, the priest or the victim?"

I scanned the scene, considering the alternatives.

"Well, I feel the most resistance to being the priest, so that must be who I am."

"All right. Move into the figure of the priest and tell me what more you get."

"I am in a large city of white and golden stone. There are many temple complexes and much commerce. There are hanging gardens along the canals. I am an Aztec priest, educated, respected, wealthy, and powerful. I am married and have my own house. We make war on other people and bring home many slaves to be used as servants and human sacrifices. I see a beautiful young man in a loincloth and buy him to be my slave."

I feel my body flush with blood as I realize what I have to say next.

"I take him to be my lover to satisfy my physical needs. But soon I fall deeply in love with him and love him more than anyone in the world, even my wife and children. When we are together it feels as if we are the same soul, one soul sharing two bodies. Though I am his master and he is my slave, we are equal as lovers. We spend long hours together sharing our most intimate feelings and thoughts.

"Then came the crisis, the time when religion demanded me to sacrifice to the Sun God that which was most dear to me, my beloved slave. I agonized over the decision for weeks but in the end convinced myself that I had no choice. I could not sacrifice all that I had and all that I believed in for the love of this slave boy. My culture, my priesthood, and my hierarchy demanded that I make this sacrifice.

"So here I am on top of the pyramid looking into the eyes of my beloved. I can see him very clearly — his large dark eyes, his copper-colored skin, and long black hair. He is gazing into my eyes with total love and total fear, trusting me, knowing that I had betrayed him to death, full of horror and anticipation of ecstasy. He too thinks he has no choice, that he is giving his life for me. I plunge the knife from over my head down into his chest. I thrust my hands into his chest cavity, tear open a hole, rip out his still-beating heart, and hold it over my head as an offering to the Sun God while his blood runs down the sides of the altar.

"There was no reward for me. From then on there was no more joy in my life, no more love, only darkness, depression, and despair that went on for years, for the rest of my life. I had betrayed and sacrificed my beloved, my only joy in life. And my culture and my religion had betrayed me. There was no renewal of life through human sacrifice. It was all living death."

"When there are overt acts of violence by one body against another," Joanna said, "both the perpetrator and the victim record the incident. We have found that the pictures taken by the perpetrator are often much more traumatic, for he is recording all of the pain of the victim as well as his own pain. Often people think, *'If I could just eliminate so-and-so from my life everything would be all right from there on out. . . . If I could kill my uncle and inherit all his money, which he doesn't need anyway. . . .'* They couldn't be more wrong. Taking someone's life is the best way to guarantee that you'll be hanging around with them for eternity."

"I sense that the spirit of this young man still hangs around you. Not that he possesses you or even is around all the time. He still loves you, you know. But sometimes when you are feeling love very intensely, he is attracted by your love and comes in to remind you what it is like to have your heart ripped out. We should help him to release off your body and return to the spirit world."

This made sense and served to illuminate a lot of bizarre phenomena I had experienced throughout my life.

We worked long and hard with the vortex to release those pictures of human sacrifice on the Aztec pyramid from my body. By the time we cleared the space and put in a replacement picture, we had been working at least six or eight hours.

It was only the next day that I realized that we had neglected to release the spirit of the young man from his attachment to my body and send him back to the spirit world. I called up Joanna.

"I'm working with someone right now," she said. "We'll have to do it tomorrow morning. I have to get ready to go to a luncheon then, but I'll work it in. Come in at ten o'clock."

Between ten and twelve the next morning Joanna was simultaneously assisting me in releasing this spirit and getting dressed for a luncheon, which took a lot of cosmetic preparation. She was both assisting me in deep meditation and rushing around getting herself together. In the middle of all this the woman she was going with came in. It was a most unusual session.

She asked me to establish communication with the spirit of this young man, to forgive and ask for forgiveness. I felt a very clear connection with his spirit and knew that all the pain and anger, the horror of betrayal, had already been released. The last bond connecting us was a very pure love. He flowed love to me. I flowed love back to him and asked him to let go, to return to the spirit world and on to new creations. Joanna called upon her spirit helpers, Chin-Ling and Redwing, to help him find his way over to the spirit world. And then he was gone.

If you have never experienced anything like this, it must sound fantastic and unbelievable, like the figmeat of someone's imagination. And well it may be. But the proof is in the pudding. I was working on emotional clearing and release. And I can tell you that since that day I have not once felt that intense pain in my heart that had beset me intermittently over the previous twenty years. I was now more clear to love and be loved.

For centuries mystics have told us how unimportant the BODY is. East Indian Masters practice putting the BODY in the Lotus position and going off and leaving it. They seem to think that without the BODY they can become more AWARE. This is true to a certain extent.

A SPIRIT away from the BODY is only controlled by the hypnotic IMPLANTS on the SPIRIT level.

Since the BODY is microscopically small in relation to the vast scheme of the TIME GAME it would seem appropriate to simply go off and leave it as mystics have done for aeons. However, this is a SPIRIT game of going somewhere. As TOTALITY YOU cannot GO ANY-WHERE because YOU are already EVERYWHERE as the TOTAL PRESENCE OF SELF.

TOTALITY CONCEPT 740424

SESSIONS WITH GLORY
July 3 & 4, 1985

I was deeply immersed in this transformational work with Joanna. I practiced the Total Meditation on my own, grounding myself in emptiness, opening to and listening for superconscious guidance in everyday life. I wanted to share this experience and offered to work with some of my friends on an experimental basis. Though we rarely saw each other, Glory was closest to me and most open to sharing this awareness.

That summer we backpacked up to the Continental Divide above Buena Vista, Colorado. We were way above treeline, over 13,000 feet, surrounded by soaring snow-packed peaks, under the clear blue sky and the intense ultraviolet light of high elevations, far beyond the world.

We hiked along the Divide to a gentle, barren summit named on the map Birthday Peak. There on a flat open space we practiced dancing out vortex energy: spinning to the left, counterclockwise, receiving energy from the cosmos, and then spinning to the right, clockwise, letting the energy radiate back out into the cosmos, all the time intoning HU. This was an exhilarating, energizing, purifying practice for two dervishes on top of the world—Superconscious in action, in whirling dance.

In the late afternoon, after we had scrambled back over massive rock slides and exhausted our physical energy, Glory and I did our first session together. This was the first time I had worked with someone else. I found that I was sharing much of her recall and could see it more vividly than I had my own murky pictures in session with Joanna.

The first memory she had was of herself as a being of light in the presence of God, together with other beings of light as in a candle flame. She was dancing among the stars, radiating, pulsating light throughout her entire body. The Earth plane was irrelevant.

Here I flubbed as a guide. I brought my rational mind in and lost the intuitive flow process. Glory felt herself resisting the scientific language that I felt was necessary and told me so. I had interfered with the way she was getting things. The moment was lost.

However, she did come up with an image of her present life intention: rushing out onto a great stage surrounded by doors, rushing from door to door, greeting all her family and friends, experiencing joyful reunions on the great stage of life, a feeling of freedom.

"I see myself as an angel of light dancing with huge throngs of light beings," Glory said when we went into session again. "I see a terrible being, a huge, violent astral warrior swinging a sword, bringing destruction and death to planet Earth. I rush away to tell the other angels, who come and take the Beast far away.

"I am a being of light dancing over the mountain tops, the Himalaya. I am dancing over the Earth, seeing all the people, feeling no connection but desiring to help.

"I zoom down to stand on a road. A carriage drives right through me. I am immaterial.

"I emerge from the waters of a river as a young boy, innocent and pure. I live a yogic life among the people. I experience little real contact with anyone.

"I have an image of an East Indian woman down by the river. She lives a simple life. She loves her four children very much. Men are irrelevant to her. The woman is carrying something on her head, walking down the road."

Some grief and weeping came up. We worked on releasing it, but by that time Glory was too tired to concentrate on using the vortex.

In our next session I really saw her pictures clearly, for they involved me. It seemed like we were sharing memory.

"I am flying through space, hand in hand with Ahad. We are beings of light with a vast train of other beings of light behind us. Ahad is our leader, strong and powerful, like Superman. We are flying through space, exploring worlds. We come upon planet Earth. Ahad focuses his attention like a spotlight on a location on Earth. It is like his hand is a flashlight with a very powerful beam. He puts a box over his head and runs down to Earth, running very, very fast down a mountainside, becoming more and more dense, until he is lost in the world of Earth forms.

"I am frightened and confused. I feel lost. We have no more leader. What to do? Finally I also rush down the mountainside, feeling my feet growing solid beneath me, then my whole body becoming solid. I find myself in the Himalaya among people carrying burdens. I must work with them. When I work too hard an ape man, Neanderthal, comes to help me. All here are ape men."

"Now go forward in time," I say.

"I remember life with the pygmies in the jungle, the whole tribe singing and drumming and dancing all night."

"Good. Go forward in time. When do we meet again?"

"I see you as a king walking past me. You ignore me. You don't even see me. You are a king, leading a group of people, taken up with being important. I am just a peasant woman. I recognize you, but you do not see me."

"OK. Continue to go forward in time. When do we meet again?"

"This is very strange. I see you naked, writhing on the ground, tongue sticking out. You are a snake shaman. Now you are dancing all around me, a powerful, provocative sexual dance, always shifting shape, sometimes a snake, sometimes a goat, sometimes a bull. I am somewhat frightened and feel distant from this display. I feel I am being shown a lesson by a teacher, but I do not like it."

We spend some time releasing and replacing her feelings of abandonment, betrayal, lack of recognition, sexual strangeness, etc. Then I ask her if she sees a final image.

"I see two blonde children, a boy and a girl, on opposite sides of a stream. They look at each other, bow to each other, see their reflections in the stream, then look up at each other, bow to each other and continue the game. They begin walking along the stream together, drawing farther apart but always looking back at each other, maintaining contact."

(This image resonated with my image of us as twins in an Arcadian age.)

Glory had the ability to see subtle pictures quite rapidly and vividly. Working with her in her inner world confirmed the usefulness of Joanna's technology, providing new perceptions on our karma, but most of all a knowing that I could act intuitively as a guide if I let go of my rational mind.

HER STORY—JESUS CHRIST OF HOLLYWOOD
Los Angeles, after WW II

I very rarely dream, even to this day, but I had this dream at that time. In the dream I was out on my back porch in Connecticut in my lovely home. I used to grow sweet corn in my back yard. From the first crop to the last crop I had sweet corn. I used to have sweet-corn parties on my back porch. I had a big pressure cooker. I would make blintzes and coffee. It was nice, the entertainment thing. I would invite neighbors and all of that. That was real life.

Then in this dream I'm looking out from my porch to my sweet corn. It's lovely. The sweet corn grows nice and straight and tall with the silk on the top. It's very artistic looking. But I noticed one corn at the end of one of the rows was very big, bigger than any of the other corn. So I went out through the aisle and pulled back the shuck and the silk and there was a baby, a pudgy, beautiful little baby. I pulled all the stuff off of it, snapped it off at the bottom, cleaned up the baby, and held it in my arms.

That feeling, that sensation, I never had, even with my own baby, in my whole life. That was an unusual energy I was feeling with that baby. I awakened from that dream and I thought, *"My God, that energy! I've never felt that energy. But I felt it with that baby."* I couldn't understand it at the time, but it was a delightful experience for me.

I had that dream shortly before I met Hardin again, before I called him, and when we hugged I said, "Oh, you're my corn baby!"

He laughed.

I told him what happened. He said that was a picture of when he was a baby. Now how would a thing like that happen? I had not seen that picture before. I had not met that man before. I had never hugged him. What was it that happened for me? Afterwards I realized it was super-conscious guidance again.

That's what I want people to realize. Go for your experiences. Be adventuresome. Don't try to think things through because you won't have the information. You won't have the gorgeous experience that I had.

I was working for the Anticipation Shops, Beverly Hills. They made me general manager. I was flying up and down the West Coast to the differ-ent stores, hiring employees and training them and all of that. That's how I made a good living. They found out how capable I was, and they paid me well.

I was waiting for Hardin to pick me up. I was on Rodeo Drive in the Beverly Hills store. They had triple mirrors in those shops. I was waiting at the corner of the triple mirror so I could look out and see Hardin coming to pick me up. I was guided to turn around and look at the sin-gle mirror, and as I looked in the mirror I intuitively got, *"I know."* Then my body turned around and looked in the double mirror, and I got, *"I know that I know."* Then my body turned around and looked in the triple mirror. I could see myself three ways, and I got, *"I know that I know because I know that I know!"* I went into ecstasy at that whole idea. It gave me such an exhilarated feeling.

When Hardin came by, I jumped into the car and I said, "You know what? You know what, Hardin? I KNOW. I know that I know because I know that I know!"

We both sat there laughing like a couple of kids!

At that time I didn't fully realize the value of knowing or the realiza-tion of what knowing was. But I was able to get it that way. It was really a glorious experience for me, and of course he understood.

Hardin had understanding, plain and simple. How he had it at that time I had no way of knowing, except that he did, because at other times he just behaved like a *goyisha kaph*—in Yiddish that means a *gentile head*. He had no earthly experiences that I could thank him for or even recognize him for, except when this other consciousness came in. Then I admired him.

When it came to sex, unh-uh, I had no desire to have sex with that man. He would like to have sex with me. But I had no desire for sex with him. So living a life with this guy was real weird. Here are two people, young enough, and I was not physically attracted to him. He was to me. He told me later he did remember me.

I admired his work, and I told him at one point, "Yes, you stay in that. I will support us until you are able. I don't know what kind of accreditation you have to get from Hubbard."

Was the goal of his work with people in Dianetics to come up with memories?

That was what it was at the time — to remember. That's all Dianetics was.

Did it lead to a clearing?

It came to a release on the body level. It did that for me. I began to realize I was a good guinea pig for him, because I seemed to have excellent recall. The goal was to release and produce a better, more functional human being, which I was, definitely. I had no more worries about having lost the money. I was able to go out and buy a red suit, which was wonderful, and I enjoyed what was happening with his work. I had more of an understanding why he wanted to do the Dianetics work.

He was working with other people, but he never asked for compensation. So I looked at that.

I said, "This is your profession. You're a professional. Why don't you ask for money?"

It didn't occur to him to ask for money, and I questioned that. Why not?

One day a couple of men brought in to our apartment a man in a white straitjacket, like you need to use with insane people. Hardin put the man on the couch in our apartment, took off the white coat, and began to work with him. And I watched when I came home from work. He worked with that man for hours every day. It seems that the man was a famous guitarist. He had begun to beat up on his wife with a strap and a buckle, and she took the children and left. She wasn't going to stay there and take that abuse. The other two men were his dear friends. They knew psychiatry wouldn't do it. But they had heard what Hardin Walsh could do.

He uncovered something that this man had forgotten, that early on in his life his father had abused him, had strapped him with a strap and a buckle, and when he got restimulated on that he automatically and reactively began to do it to the person he loved, his wife. Of course, Hardin Walsh knew exactly how to deal with that. He went through this whole early life with this man — it was a horrible life, and yet here he is a famous guitarist — and released this man, released him to the point where he became sane again.

I looked at that and I said, "How much are you going to charge this man for your services?"

"I did not count hours. I don't count hours. I'm more interested in working and helping that person"— for which I admired him greatly.

"Approximately how many hours?"

"Well, we worked for days, it seems."

"Well, two hundred and fifty dollars, would that cover it?"

And that man said, "Ten times more would cover it."

He made out a check for five hundred dollars. He stood and leaned against the jamb of the door, then moved away.

He said, "I could feel that door jamb right through into the cell structure of my body, I was so clear."

I thought, *"This is pretty miraculous. What's going on here?"*

That was the first money Hardin Walsh earned in working in Dianetics.

After I heard Hardin lecture, I decided to get behind him and make him pay off. I gave up my creative ideas, my life, to back him. I never did it before because there was no one worthwhile to do it with, but I decided that he was definitely worthwhile. So I proceeded to sponsor him, leaving my own career to one side.

But I did not read Hubbard's books. I had such a repugnant feeling about Hubbard. It turned out that he was evil. But Hardin seemed to have an affinity for him. Of course they were both into Scientology. But I found out that Hubbard really didn't know it. Hubbard didn't do the writing. The hierarchy did the writing through Hubbard. We found that out.

Before I came into his life, Hardin Walsh was known as Jesus Christ of Hollywood. That was what he was doing. He's a helper, and Jesus Christ was a helper. Hardin would go around Hollywood Boulevard, and if there was an alcoholic, and there's plenty of them, or someone in a fit of some kind, he'd pick them up. He was strong. He would take them into a store, not even ask permission, take them into the back, help them out of it, say thank you and walk them out. So he was called the Jesus Christ of Hollywood. But of course I can't live with that. I have to find a way to make a living. I have to pay rent, eat, have clothes. He had no clothes.

You seem to indicate that when he was going around and picking up people and helping them that for him it was also a form of research. He was interested in helping people but he was also interested in his research, in finding out about human beings.

Yes, you're right. He was a research scientist. You can tell when you read his book that he was a research scientist, mainly. The fact that he helped people, that was his nature, and we found out later why.

He had no clothes. And I didn't know how he would take it if I bought him some clothes or took his measurements. Really, it wouldn't have mattered. He couldn't care less. I went to Hollywood Boulevard. I didn't ask his size. I bought this beautiful beige jacket and darker beige slacks. They were exactly his size! And I gave them to him, and he said thank you, and he had no remorse or regret that a woman had bought him clothes.

I had to look at that, and I had to look at his ability levels, and I had to say, "Well, OK, that's the way he is." I had to accept that.

In our work together we had already gone into former lives. Hardin took me into many former lives, and I took him into many former lives. I took him into Buddha. And as I recall Hardin's work and Buddha's work, there is a similarity.

He said, "I am Buddha's body."

After that he began to do this kind of thing where he would put his hands together and bow down in saying hello or goodbye to people. And I laughed a little, but I didn't say anything. I never studied Buddha, but later on I found out that Buddha called space "emptiness." I didn't realize that Hardin was into all of that at the time. But he did remember being Buddha, the body, and he also remembered some of Buddha's work. Of course we hadn't gotten into the work where there was a resemblance — that was Totality. I would go into those previous lives like it was a motion-picture script unraveling, and he would, too.

Another lifetime we went into was Genghis Khan. And I said, "Oh yeah, because you like the idea of Genghis Khan." But then he came up with information about Genghis Khan that was not in the history book. He made a drawing of Genghis Khan's gauntlet. Then there was a journalist who made a journey to Mongolia and came back with a gauntlet, and it was identical to the drawing that Hardin made. So I had to accept the fact that he was Genghis Khan. And the information he came up with is really profound.

Then came a time when Scientology grew and prospered. We both heard that Hubbard wanted $25,000 for the contract, and there were people offering it to him. But as I looked around at those people, I realized that they didn't know what Hardin Walsh knew. This was the contract to run the Scientology and Dianetics work. Hubbard had to leave the country. The tax people wanted him out because he didn't pay taxes and he didn't offer to pay taxes. He kept no records. They wanted him out on general principles. They didn't like what he was doing. He was asking people for money. Go hock your car and give me money. And we found out that Hubbard never worked with people.

He just wrote books?

And how he wrote books — dictated by the hierarchy!

At that time, Hardin Walsh had done a series of charts on Scientology. We had already been doing regressions. I came back from my trip to San Diego and found two men there that I knew as his so-called friends, who to me were con men, period. I seem to have the ability to read people. I don't know whether it's because I'm a Russian Jew or what, but I can tell a con man a mile away. And they were offering to take Hardin Walsh and his charts to Hubbard to get the contract to run the school.

I said, "How much money do you have?"

"We don't have any money."

I opened my door and I put my hand against their bodies. "Out!" I said.

And they went out.

I'm very strong and I'm very firm when I make a decision. I don't leave any leeway for any reaction from anyone. That's the way I am. That's the way I've survived and thrived on Earth.

Hardin looks at me, "Why'd you do that?"

"Because they're con men. Do you want to be in business with them?"

He looked at that and said, "No."

You see, that's what I mean. He didn't have any Earth-type considerations for survival. Later on he began to call me the State Department, because I made things happen in our life. I motivated life.

I looked at the charts and I decided they were good. They were large and beautiful. I didn't read the book. I wouldn't read anything Hubbard wrote.

I said, "OK. We're going to Phoenix." Just like that.

When I talked, he knew I meant it.

I had bought this little car, which I was learning to drive when he came into my life. He met me at the school where I was learning to drive, and he took over the car, and I never cared to drive since then. I preferred not to drive.

So we drove that night to Phoenix with the charts. I can't tell you anything we discussed on the way to Phoenix as to how we were going to get that contract from Hubbard. We didn't discuss anything. And I didn't have any preconceived notion of how I was going to get that contract. Afterwards, as I look at that, it was superconscious guidance. No thinking was involved in any of it.

Hubbard was in Phoenix at the time. We went to Phoenix. We drove all through the night. We went to the office. Althea Hart, who we had corresponded with, looked at the charts and called Hubbard.

"Ron, you have to talk to the Walshes. Hardin Walsh has done a series of charts on Scientology that qualifies him to work within Scientology and Dianetics."

We drove out to where Hubbard was staying, near Camelback Mountain. We went in. His wife was coughing terribly, and I thought to myself,

"Why doesn't he release her?"

He said to us, "What do you want?"

I said, "We want the contract. There's no one else out there more qualified than Hardin Walsh to teach this work. And look at me. If you've got any perception at all, you know that I will run that business properly."

I watched him listening to something up above. I looked at that.

Then he said, "It seems that I am to give you the contract." He sits down at the typewriter and he continues to listen. I didn't know what that was, not until later. And he wrote the contract open-end. And I looked at that. I didn't say it to him, but I accepted that it was an open-end contract.

I said to him, "I'll make a deal with you, since you have decided to give us the contract. I will give you forty percent on books and tapes, and I will give you ten percent on all of our earnings from this work. Is that agreeable?"

"Yes."

Hardin had nothing to do with the deal. He was just looking at his charts. He said nothing. It was better, because I didn't want any interference with what I was doing.

Then Hubbard said, "I've got something to ask, a favor of you and Hardin. I know my name for my next lifetime, and I know that I am going to make millions of dollars this lifetime. I want you to sign my will for next lifetime, you and Hardin, to give evidence of what I'm doing here."

So I said to Hardin, "How does it seem to you?"

"If he's going to have millions of dollars, it's his."

"Do we have any reason for not signing it?" Hardin said no, and I said no, so we signed his will for next lifetime. He may be embarked on it now, because he passed over some time ago.

Apparently L. Ron Hubbard intended to bequeath to himself in his next lifetime the millions he made in this lifetime. Accounts have been written of his nautical searches for treasures he had buried in previous lifetimes.

6

ONGOING HANGUPS
August 1985

Back in Santa Fe, I was still dealing with the unremitting negativity of my self-image.

At Lama, at least I had been a big fish in a small pond. In the so-called real world, I was one more bottom-hugging scum-sucker.

Though my goal was financial self-sufficiency, I had ambivalent and negative attitudes toward money. I was "a refugee from a wealthy family" (Joni Mitchell). Material wealth seemed cold, controlling, restricting. My empathy was with the working class, the vagabonds, and the homeless. Lama had been an excellent refugee camp for me, offering immaterial but no material rewards. I had served as Treasurer for the community for many years and learned a lot about the variety of human monetary responses. We used money to relate to the outside world. In our daily life there was no money exchanged with each other. Selfless service *(seva)* was the ideal.

"You spent all those years at Lama hiding out," Joanna would say, "hiding out from the real world."

Now I had my initiation into the world of free enterprise by doing bookkeeping and office work for a local video/radio producer operating on a shoestring budget. I learned a lot about video production, media placement, and working on computers, but only found my judgments about *das kapital* reaffirmed. My boss paid those who worked for him very little. He would hire secretaries on an OJT (On the Job Training) contract, so that he would be reimbursed $2.00 of the $4.00 an hour he was paying them. When the OJT contract was up, pretty soon there was reason to let them go and hire someone else under a new contract. Yet time and time again he would blow his budget on video productions for some expensive creative effect that satisfied him as an artist. I could understand his commitment to artistic excellence, but saw that there was no future for me here.

I always paid my bills on time, but he raged at me the one time I tried to pay his bills on time. "Don't you ever pay my bills!" he screamed. His practice was to delay paying every bill as long as possible, longer than possible, until many of them ended up in collection. My prejudgments on capitalism were that it was based on lying, cheating, and stealing. I found they were getting reinforced.

I also confided in Joanna about my suicidal thoughts. She was the only one I ever told about them. Aside from general romantic longings for death, etc., I was plagued for years by a repeating picture of a hand with a gun coming up to my head, pulling the trigger, and blowing my brains out. Time and time again I would see this picture. There were times when I had been asleep and was unable to get back into my body, even when there was someone standing over me telling me to wake up. It was more than resistance to waking up, resistance to authority, etc. I literally could not get back into my body. At other times I seemed to be possessed by violent, self-destructive energies that would toss my mind and sometimes my body around with reckless abandon.

In her session notes Joanna wrote, *"A gun blowing his head off repeated in present time. Those pictures are sitting there and can become reactivated. At certain moments he doesn't know why he's here. Dissatisfaction is growth. He has gone as far on negativity as he wants."*

September 7, 1985

"Money is a two-way flow," Joanna explained. "You give something and you get something in return. Money has mostly come to you from your family, a one-way flow that did not condition you to deal realistically. Money is survival on planet Earth. On our home planet we don't use money. Whatever we want we materialize superconsciously. Many people from other planets have difficulty handling money. Hadron had no ability to handle money. But money is necessary for survival on planet Earth."

At the end of a session exploring my attitudes and aberrations around money, Joanna asked me to visualize holding a big pot of gold coins in my lap, to put my arms around it and love it, love that gold. I concretized her instructions and found myself with my arms around a big pot of gold which I could not love. Every spiritual teacher from Jesus to Maharaji had warned about the love of money. *"The love of money is the root of evil."* I felt my face blush and my whole body turn red with my resistance. I could not love that imaginal pot of gold. It was clear that there was more work to do.

September 17, 1985

"What did they do to you for money? What did you do to them for money?" Joanna demanded abruptly, snapping her fingers. "Quick now. Tell me the first thing that you see. Don't think about it. Just say it."

In the opening in the gray mist in front of me I saw a hand reaching down offering me money, a spread of paper currency held out to me. But I could get no further information at that time.

Over the following days I had a subtle, persistent headache and kept getting disjointed flashes of imagery. Something had been triggered. Something wanted to emerge from my subconscious. I came back to work again on this issue.

"What did they do to you for money? What did you do to them for money?"

"I see a hand reaching down offering me money. I am a young boy about nine years old. I know nothing about money. A grown man is offering me lots of money. I don't know whether to take it or not."

"Why is he offering you this money?"

"He wants me to tell him about my family. Now I get a bigger picture. We lived in a large farmhouse in the middle of nowhere, in the middle of Russia, possibly the Ukraine. All around us are fields of hay, gently rolling hills, very few trees, no other houses in sight. Our house serves as a way-station, a shelter on the underground railway which is helping

Jews to flee from Russia. The man is offering me money to tell him what goes on at our house, who stays at our house, what kind of visitors pass through. We are standing on the road in front of my house."

"Yes," she said. "I can see you. I'm right there with you. It seems I am watching you talking with this man from the attic window of the house. It seems I am your grandmother. I feel very strong emotions, fear and apprehension."

She was yawning heavily, as was I. Tears were streaming down my face. Deep yawning and weeping are a sign of deep emotional release, *turning on the somatics,* as they say in Scientology.

"The money in his hand seems powerful to me. I feel very confused. I've never seen so much money before. I know I'm not supposed to tell anyone what goes on in our house, but so much money would make a great deal of difference to my family. After a lot of anxiety and indecision, I finally blurted out what he wanted to know. He asked me for more details. I gave him everything I could. Then he took the money away, put it back in his pocket, laughed at me, and called me a foolish boy.

"I was in terror and despair. I had betrayed my family, all for nothing. I was too ashamed and scared to tell anybody what I had done, so we were all at home when the men came and burned our house down."

"Oh yes, I lost my body there at the same time you did. What a terrible thing! No wonder we are working together to release it."

The TOTALITY CONCEPT reveals that THOUGHTS are powerful CREATIVE forces which are involved in EVERY ACTIVITY. EVERYTHING that has ever occurred leaves a RECORDING as a THOUGHT-FORM or a vibration pattern at the LOCATION of happening and also IN THE BODY FORCE-FIELDS, often called the SUBCONSCIOUS.

This includes all of our experiences and the experiences of others as well. These hidden recordings act as AUTOMATIC RESTIMULATORS — GOOD — BAD or INDIFFERENT — on our BODY CIRCUITS.

There is a flowing CONTINUITY of constantly recurring patterns subconsciously formed from our former relationships, extending through AEONS OF TIME: broadcasting from old locations through the TOTAL PRESENCE of SELF — TOTALITY.

This CONTINUITY of THOUGHT-FORM recordings, vibrating with dramatic intensity down through the ages, has been referred to as the AKASHIC RECORDS. The AKASHIC RECORDS are a partial basis of reference for the exceptional methods inherent within the TOTALITY CONCEPT.

The TRUE ANNALS of the arcane archives are not written on mere scrolls or in books but in the immortality of AWARENESS and direct KNOWINGNESS beyond so-called TIME — a CONTINUITY without end or beginning — within the TOTAL SELF — TOTALITY.

The TOTALITY CONCEPT draws aside the veils of antiquity — by revealing how the sudden violent moments encountered by many are merely hidden impacts surging from the past — creating the PRESENT and challenging the formation of the FUTURE. Hidden AKASHIC recordings constantly bombard us with compulsive reminders of what we have done to others and what has been done to us. Humanoid BODIES convert these vibration patterns in much the same manner that a TV set transforms frequencies into sound and pictures.

IS IT NECESSARY TO REMAIN IDENTIFIED WITH YOUR AUTOMATIC ROBOT SPEECH TRANSPORT MECHANISM—THE BODY?

TOTALITY CONCEPT 740426

FRUSTRATION OF DESIRE
September 24, 1985

At the same time as we were hacking away at my money hangups we were also digging up the roots of my sexual frustrations.

Do you remember when the air was clean and sex was dirty? That's the era I grew up in, spawned into suburbia right after World War II and nurtured by a culture as sexless as a brand-new, gleaming white Frigidaire. Quick pecks on the cheek goodnight were the only physical affection ever displayed in my family. Information about the female body was available to me only through Sears underwear ads and pictures of Greek statuary. It was the Sterile Fifties. *"Don't ask, don't tell"* seems to have been the unspoken assumption about sex.

I have no wish to blame anything on anyone, nor do I wish to recount my checkered sexual history. Suffice it to say that at the age of thirty-eight I was every bit as sexually frustrated as I was ignorant at eighteen, despite having more experience and knowledge. I was the perfect candidate for sexual denial with my true love.

Saturn conjunct Pluto in Leo signifies the frustration of desire, not only sex desire, which is Pluto, but the expression of love, creativity, and joy, which is Leo. I could never enjoy parties. I was too intensely serious for the light play and dance of romance. Relationships became long, serious conversations or monologues about my inability to love and be loved.

My first true tears came at the age of twenty-four when I realized I could not truly love my lover. My desire was very powerful and conflicted. Spiritual teachings filled me full of judgments and warnings about the dangers of sexual love.

My finest energies were sublimated into poetry and music. Yet here too I met with invalidation. My father and my ex-wife in particular could not abide my musical expression. My poetry was not appreciated by many of those I respected. Ultrasensitive and secretive, I was a solitary singer, a lover with no beloved. My several lovers all seemed like strangers to me, or I a stranger to them, until Glory came into my life and I found my soul reflected in her.

My adolescent ideals had been William Blake, Vincent Van Gogh, and similar souls who labored in solitude to create expressions of beauty and truth with little thought of recognition by their contemporaries. Poets such as Robert Frost, Hart Crane, Rilke, and Hesse, who had rejected the philistine materialism of their upbringing to pursue art for art's sake, inspired me. In regression I had uncovered figures of the romantic poet starving in his garret loft and the romantic troubadour singing ideal songs of love for his unattainable lady. I had also touched many lifetimes as a priest, dervish, monk, or spiritual seeker who had renounced worldly power and possessions for devotion to the Creator.

Saturn in Leo gave me a deep-seated distrust and fear of all conventional forms of authority based upon the power of the masculine ego. With my progressed Sun conjuncting Saturn, all of my frustrated desires were in my face. And as the progressed Sun moved on to conjunct Pluto, I was moving on to transformation.

Joanna's notes paraphrase my self-exploration: *"I've set myself up not to have what I want and to express 'to want and not get.' Why did I set myself up this way? I came to Earth long time ago as a powerful spirit to enjoy Earth plane existence, intoxicated with the sensations, the sexuality, getting what I wanted through psychic, magical powers. Sometimes this was harmful to others, leading me to limit the external use of my powers. I seem to have no concern for generating money or having worldly possessions. I have a consideration that I have to get what I need from someone else thru my psychic power. I set myself up for no concern about money for a number of lifetimes, like this one with my family, at other times in religious formats—monks, dervishes, etc."*

MONEY, SEX, AND POWER ✳

The Tibetan Kalachakra, the mandala of the Wheel of Time, is embraced by all-devouring Kala (Time). In the middle of the wheel, in the middle of the twelve stages of interdependent origination, in the middle of the six realms of beings, are the pig, the cock, and the snake, representing greed, lust, and anger, or in more modern terms, money, sex, and power. Greed, lust, and anger are the Three Poisons holding us in bondage to the Wheel of Time. They are simultaneously the binding glue which holds together the whole fabric of material creation. As such they are what they are, energies tumbling in emptiness, binding together *samsara*, endlessly recycling karma.

This was my understanding of the Kalachakra at an earlier time, and it served me well. I have since learned that the Three Poisons are more correctly defined as: delusion and stupidity (ignorance, the pig), desire and passion (attachment, the cock), and hatred and anger (aversion, the snake). The root cause of all suffering is ignorance of the truth, delusion, or, as Joanna would say, not-knowing, forgetting, and pretending. I was wrestling with attachment and aversion, unfulfilled desire and dissatisfaction in relation to money and sex. Just as the cock constantly pecks away at the ground searching for bits of seed, never satisfied, so greed and lust constantly peck away at the material world, never satisfied.

Detachment from and renunciation of greed, lust, and anger are at the core of Buddhist and all spiritual teachings. Yet renunciation all too often is resistance, repression, and denial of these "negative" energies. Psychologically, when an energy is repressed it sinks into subconscious and acquires an independent energy of its own which can erupt and overwhelm the "positive" conscious identity, as witness pedophile priests and evangelists drunk with money, sex, and power. Totality, wholeness, accepts all that is without resistance, without pushing and pulling, repression or aggression. For you become what you resist. As Jesus said, *"Resist ye not evil."*

Inherent rejection and repression of money, sex, and power had been my path through adult life. I never permitted myself to get angry. I could not see that I was a very angry person. Though living simply, I was careless with money, theoretically unattached, but unable to recognize my own inherent greed. I was more vulnerable to lust, though conflicted, and lust connected me intimately with other beings and led to the development of the ability to love.

That summer (1985) I was at a Ram Dass retreat at Lama Foundation. At the conclusion of the retreat there was a fire ceremony in which people were encouraged to find pine cones, invest them with karmic bonds they wanted to burn, and toss them in the fire while the group was chanting mantra invoking Kali, the Destroyer of Illusions. Normally I only watched, but this time I felt called to participate.

I found three pine cones in the forest and meditated with them, investing them with my attachments to money, sex, and power. As I concentrated I realized that resistance, repression, and denial of money, sex, and power were equally attachment, that negative hangups were as binding as positive clingings. I saw that I had to give up all pushing or pulling, attraction or rejection, all judgment on money, sex, and power and simply let them be what they are, energies tumbling in emptiness. I had to give myself permission to deal with money, sex, and power without craving and without aversion, simply allowing them to be in life, and continue developing compassion in emptiness. *"Emptiness engenders compassion."* (Milarepa)

That night under a full moon we stood in a circle around a large blazing fire chanting a complex mantra to Kali. One by one people came forward clutching their pine cones, investing them with intention and tossing them into the fire. Ram Dass as *pujari* would sweep his hand upward and pronounce *"Swaha!"* *("So be it!")* with each offering. Conscious of the full light of the moon, the light of the fire, the impersonality of the ceremony, I came forward and tossed my three pine cones — my attachment to and rejection of money, sex, and power — into the fire. I was ready to begin a new cycle.

POISON OAK
October 1985

I went to visit Glory in Marin County, California, where she and her husband had moved. I stayed up late, awoke late, and left late for the airport, driving down to Albuquerque with my body tensed over the wheel of my VW bus, pushing with every cell. I arrived just barely in time for my flight. My muscles were seized up for days. But I was going to see my beloved.

I took the bus from the airport to the Tenderloin district in San Francisco where she was going to meet me. She was not there. I waited and waited and waited on this seedy urban street. She did not come. I called her home. No answer. I began to feel anxiety, even panic. Then I remembered what Joanna had said: "As Totality, as space, you are everywhere. If you want to know what is happening somewhere, simply be there and know." I emptied myself, was the space, directed my attention to Glory, and saw that she was sleeping. I called her home again and she answered. She was confused about what day I was coming in and had been taking a nap.

The weather was glorious — cool, clear fall days — and we got to spend more time together than we ever had. With Neptune transiting her natal Sun and opposite my natal Sun, our ecstasy and illusion of union reached a peak. As we walked over the hills and by the ocean, all the old love songs we had ever heard sang true blue, walking on sunshine, oh, oh. All the while she was still one hundred percent married.

But what is relevant here is poison oak.

One day we were walking on the beach under the Marin headlands and decided to climb the cliffs rather than go back the way we had come. On top of the cliffs we blundered into a huge patch of poison oak. Glory freaked out.

"God is punishing me for my sins, for loving you so deeply," she cried.

I said that I was not going to take the picture of the poison oak and would not be affected.

Over the next two weeks she developed terrible rashes that spread all over her body, even going internal, and finally had to go to the emergency room for cortisone injections.

I remained steadfast in refusing to take the picture and developed no rash at all, until finally I felt I was lacking in compassion by judging her vulnerability and opened myself to sharing her pain. Sure enough, right before I left, two weeks later, I developed some small poison oak rashes. That showed something to me.

HER STORY—TOTALITY—GOING HOME

I found this beautiful house half a block from Wilshire Boulevard. I had accumulated a few dollars. I had the five hundred that Hardin had earned, plus a little more that he earned from various people that were brought in to him. We rented this beautiful house. It had four bedrooms. The living room and dining room connected so we could have lectures and classes there. It was surrounded by a garden. The part that I figured would be the office had windows on three sides. I could look out on the garden. I loved that.

The landlord said, "What're you gonna do here?"

I said, "The two of us just don't need a big house, do we? We're going to do psychological work, because my husband is a doctor of psychology."

We had the diploma. I had framed the diploma and was very proud of that. It's good to have a diploma. People like that.

He said, "OK, fine, I'll approve that."

We had a big party. We had the mailing list from Althea Hart. We sent out a notice that Hardin Walsh was given the Hubbard contract and we were having an open house. People came in. We made hors d'ouevres and coffee, and Hardin talked—because at that time I was mostly the State Department, none of your business, you know.

We began to attract people. I didn't realize at the time I asked for the contract what the following was in LA and in other parts of the world. And we made a very good living. Pretty soon Dick DeMille, Cecil B. DeMille's adopted son, came in to work with us. A man came from London, England; we were able to help him come because he was studying in our school. Then there was a student from Mexico as a student. They all passed Hardin's professional course, and I retained them to work with people on a fifty-fifty basis. That worked out very well.

You were training them as auditors?

They paid to take the professional course. We had quite a few people taking the professional course. And I would sit in on it so that I would understand what was going on. I wasn't really into what was going on. I just knew that I was following these intuitions to do what I was doing.

Were the Scientology auditors using the E-meter at this time?

They were using Volney Matheson's E-meter, which measured the energy up to 2.5, no more. And I questioned that. Why no more? It read up to a very low level. I didn't know all of that at first, but I got into it and found out.

We made a very good living. We developed a nice following. Pretty soon we began to invite other speakers to come in on a fifty-fifty basis. We would send the mailing out, then provide the place and the coffee and stuff. That continued for about four years.

I became increasingly disenchanted. I heard the tapes that Hubbard sent to us to sell. I heard controls.

I said to Hardin and Dick DeMille, "Listen to these controls."

No, they couldn't hear the controls.

So I stopped the recorder.

"Now, here, listen to this."

Then they began to hear.

What do you mean by controls?

Implants were placed there: *"You will do so-and-so when you hear this. You will do so-and-so for Ron Hubbard when you hear this."*

I didn't want that in there.

And there were other forms of controls as well: *"You will go and do that and that and tell people to come to Ron Hubbard."*

So I said, "I don't like this. You've got to cut that stuff out of that tape or I will not offer it for sale."

So Hardin cut out those controls on every one of the tapes that went out.

I became increasingly disenchanted with being related or associated with L. Ron Hubbard. He, for all the world, looked like the Devil to me, like evil. He was out there with boats, because they wouldn't let him into any country. He was the Captain. People would go to the boat to work with him. And then we hear that he would throw people overboard if they didn't do exactly what he wanted them to do so he could control them.

One of the men found his way to us and said, "That man is evil. If you don't do exactly what he tells you to do, he throws people off the boat to drown."

I said to Hardin, "That does it for me. I've got to find a way out of this. This is a living, and it's a good living. . . ."

In the interim Hardin's former wife had brought his five-year-old son and plunked him down on the kitchen floor, no clothes, no anything, and left. Here I have a five-year-old child, and my son's about to leave Connecticut University and come to UCLA. Of course I had to provide a room for him and a room for this child. So we divided up other rooms so that there'd be enough auditing rooms.

"What am I going to do? Here I have a family, I'm trying to run a business." Again I felt trapped in a whole set of circumstances not of my own doing. We have a five-year old child. We had to send him to a private school, so he could stay there longer than the regular school. That was an extra cost. I really felt trapped in the whole situation.

I told that to Hardin. I said, "Look what's happening here!"

It didn't seem to matter to him. He wasn't doing it all. He was doing what he was doing, and I was doing everything else, running the house, running the cooking, and everything. Finally I decided to hire a nice black couple to do the work that needed to be done so I could just run the business.

One day—I didn't realize that it was superconscious guidance at that time—I said, "Hardin, sit down with me."

The thing about Hardin was if I said to do something, he would not question it. And I would not question anything that he wanted to do in the work.

"Sit down," I said. "Be aware of being your body." This was being fed to me, you understand?

"Yes, I can do that."

"Be aware of being the spirit that lives with bodies."

"Oh, I don't use one of those things."

It wouldn't occur to me to say, what do you mean, you don't use a spirit?

Then I went on to say something I didn't know. I didn't understand what I was saying.

I said to him, "Be aware of being that which creates everything."

And I'm listening to what I'm saying.

He sits there with his Irish green eyes sparkling and says very casually, "Sure, Totality."

Wow! That hit me like a beam of light! I exteriorized from my body, and I was up in space. And that was where it all came together: Totality, Space, Creator! That's what I got while I was there. Then I'm aware of Earth people. I'm looking at Earth people, and they've got all these energies around them. That's when I came back into my body.

He sits there, his green eyes sparkling, and he says, "You sure took off in a hurry."

I said, "Well, you used the magic word, the ultimate, Totality! What happened to you?"

"Nothing. I've always known. I TOTALITY IS."

"Why didn't you tell me?"

"I thought you knew, too. If I knew, you knew."

There was the ultimate. There it was. I could no longer remain in Dianetics and Scientology. I said that to him.

I said, "I suggest you go to the typewriter and start writing the technology of Totality."

How would I know if there should be technology? But that's what I said.

And he said, "Yes, I can do that, I will do that. But why can't we add Totality to Scientology?"

And I became indignant. I can't tell you why. I never remember arguing with the man before. How could he say that? How could he say that we should add Totality to Scientology?

He said, "Because I know that so well."

"I know you do, but you've done it. You knew that you're Totality all this time."

And he did. Because after he passed over I looked in his books and he had written Totality in the Scientology books. Where they said *Thetan*, he would write *Totality*. I realized that he said he knew it all the time that he was in Dianetics and Scientology. He never said a word to me.

I said to him, "I'm going to give you an ultimatum, mister, because I feel very strongly about Totality. That's the ultimate I've been seeking all my adult life. You and Hubbard and Scientology — not Joanna. Joanna, you and Totality. That's the way it is. Make up your mind. I'll give you a month."

He said, "I don't need a month to make up my mind."

And he proceeded to write the technology for Totality. It was brilliant.

He made charts. And I found out who Hubbard was talking to: hierarchy. Hardin proceeded to make a chart showing me where hierarchies fit into the total scheme of things. And it's brilliant, looking at it now.

What is the experience and the reality of Totality that is so far beyond what Scientology has to offer? What is the limit of Scientology? And what does Totality mean, anyway? You had an experience. How can you communicate to us that experience?

I was so excited about the whole experience. I can't begin to tell you the elation, the ecstasy, the everything that I felt from that experience of being the space, Totality, Creator, Oneness, the whole thing. The whole thing came together for me up there.

When I came back, I said, "Let's look in the dictionary. Let's see if we have a definition."

Webster's had it, the big dictionary: <u>*"Totality: a state of being, being whole and complete."*</u>

And I said, "Webster, bless you, thank you, I thank you eternally." That was a nice definition.

Didn't Scientology lead people to wholeness and completion?

Oh, no, no. *Thetan* was the ultimate [for Scientology]. *Thetan* is an Earth energy. Alpha, Beta, Theta. . . .

I said to Hardin, "What are you doing with this stuff? Even I who have not read the book, even I who have not become involved in teaching it or doing it, know better than that."

So Scientology led you up to the spirit level?

The Thetan is like a spirit. Yes.

And yet when I asked Hardin to be the spirit he said, "I don't use that thing."

This wasn't adding up for me at all.

Then I began to realize that the hierarchy really wanted Hardin, because he was an honorable man. He knew that work. He didn't even have to read the book to know the work. They wanted him. But they also knew that when I came into his life there would be a triggering of what we really are on Earth for, and that's Totality.

What happened then was that we found out that the people who were in Scientology couldn't even listen to Hardin talking about Totality. They would go blank. So we asked a few of them to let Hardin Walsh work with them. They're all implanted, before they come in, on the spirit level. They're implanted, like all religions are, as we found out, to be what the hierarchy wants you to be.

Hierarchy are bigger spirits who have some kind of desire to control planet Earth. We found that out when we worked with Jesuit priests. When we found out about that, the Scientologists had to go. They were like following the Pied Piper of Hamlin. They had to go. It was an interesting experience. We didn't have the income from Scientology any longer.

But I said to Hardin, "I cannot be that untrue to myself and to you and to who we are. That is not right for us, now that I realize Totality."

One day we're putting out a mailing. I said to Hardin, "I feel trancy, like that time I exteriorized from my body."

He said, "Let's see what happens."

He was very calm and casual about anything unusual. There was nothing that he didn't understand, nothing that he didn't have a seemingly previous understanding about.

I said, "Go put a reel-to-reel tape on that plays for four hours, one that we used for the workshops."

He did not ask me why or anything.

Then I said, "Come and hold my hand."

And he did. We were gone. Our consciousness was gone. Our bodies were sitting there, but we were on another planet. And it seemed natural to be there.

What was happening: a thought computer was turned on. We were all sitting around in a crystal-like arrangement. Our bodies were light forms. We had a communication coming, and we were told it was a super-

conscious communication. We didn't have what Earth people have —
subconscious and thinking minds. We were shown what happened two
thousand years prior by this computer.

There was an Intergalactic Federation meeting. Beings were called
who were of ultimate consciousness to decide what to do about planet
Earth, because in two thousand years it was going to evolve out of the
terrible stage it was going through, and it was going to go through more
of it. They needed help, and we were beings who were helpers. We helped
wherever we went.

Hadron looked down on Earth and said, "They're barbarians. Why
don't we wait for two thousand years and go then?"

We were told we needed to go now, at that time, because we would
become acquainted with the problems of Earth and we would be better able to help people.

There was a being sitting opposite us. Even as a light form he had
extra gentleness and love coming from him.

He said, "I will go."

Hadron said, "You're going to barbarians? What are you going to do
there?"

He said, "I will heal them first. They're sick. I will try to plant seeds
of love, and maybe in two thousand years some of them will be able to
experience what love really is."

I said, "What are you going to do?"

"I'm going to talk to them," he said.

And I said, "Talking is not enough. Do you not have a technology?"

Hadron and I were scientists. We still are.

So I said, "Haven't you got some kind of technology you can give
them that would help them to understand what you're talking about?"

He said, "I don't do that." But he pointed two fingers out of one hand
at Hadron and me. "You are the scientists," he said. "You can take my
words and put them into a practical application for people."

I said to him, "What are you going to do first?"

"First I will inseminate a female, Mary, down there. They will call it the
Immaculate Conception. Since our planet is Orr, and Orr means *light* in
the Hebrew language *(Aur)*, I will go as a Hebrew rabbi. I know exactly
what they're going to do. There are religions down there, and they really

don't know what they're talking about. They're going to cause a lot of problems for me. They're going to take my teachings, which I will not write, and they will do what they want with them. It will not be the truth. They're going to put me up on a cross. (Actually, if an Earth person puts their hands out from their body, they're wearing a cross already. That's the cross Earth people bear.) When they put me on the cross, I will simply be home. I will go home. Yes, I will do some tricks for them down there, like reappearing and all that kind of thing, that they will make a whole religion out of. And I may go back after that another time or two, but they won't recognize me. But you two should go."

Hadron said, "I will not inseminate a female. I will not do that. They use something called money because they can't create what they want as we do. I will not use money. They've got pain palaces, hospitals, and they've got people who call themselves physicians, doctors. They don't know a thing about healing Earth bodies."

And he said to me, "You want to go there?"

I said, "For sure. That little planet needs help."

And it seems that besides the being who called himself Jesus, the Christus, there was a being who said, "I will call myself Buddha, but I will come way before this being comes." Then there was another who said, "I will be called Lao Tzu." He said that the space in the window is greater than the window. There were a few others present as well.

I said to Hadron, "Tell you what we'll do. I'll take care of the money, so you won't have to."

It was then I found out that I had volunteered. It became all right then, that this *goyisha kaph,* gentile head, didn't know how to handle money. It was all right. So I did it more graciously after that.

"Tell you what we'll do. There is a group of beings down there on Earth called the Essenes. They will understand. We will materialize to them."

I can tell you that the experience of remembrance of how to materialize was so exciting, and it was natural for us. Then we remembered that my home-planet name was Orayna and Hardin's was Hadron. We remembered all of these things.

We materialized to the Essenes in their garb. They had natural-colored fabric. They had made dye out of the earth — it was a reddish-brownish color, striped on their sleeves. They welcomed us. They knew that we had come from another planet to help planet Earth. We later found out that Jesus was there too and gave his best writings and teachings to the Essenes. The scrolls are evidence of that. We materialized on Earth and went through cycles that I remembered in regression.

There was a little planet next to Orr, I think it was called Arisha, and it was all women. I was part of that planet. These women were really the operators of that whole galaxy. They were the energy operators. And Hadron realized that. I didn't say that to him. He realized that. The men would come to us and we would go to the males on the home planet. And then we experienced mingling: male and female energy holding each other and mingling light particles. What an experience that was! Music emanates from that. Colors emanate from that. What a way! And we called that love.

When we finally came back to planet Earth, we sat there looking at each other, and I said, "No wonder I couldn't have sex with you. That's not my idea of making love."

And he agreed with me.

And we did hold each other, we did mingle light particles, remembering how we did it at home. And we wrote a poem, called *Mingling*, for Earth, that the trees mingled with the Earth, that the rain mingled with the Earth, how everything mingled, the flowers mingled. And we recognized spirits in the trees and in the flowers and in the mountains. We came back with extra-sensory perception. It was quite a realization and an experience.

We sat there looking at each other: "What do we do with this?"

We came to help. That meant that we definitely had to have good technology with Totality and use it to help people. Of course there was not very much money as a result. But I was willing to make the sacrifice, and Hadron was willing to make the sacrifice.

In all consciousness I could not continue with anything connected with Ron Hubbard. We gave it back to him. But we had Scientology Council Incorporated. We still have that.

There were people who came, wanting to buy those papers from us.

They were willing to buy our first editions of books on Scientology and Dianetics. But when I looked in the books and I saw what Hadron had done. . . .

Green was his favorite color. He had a green pen, and he would underline where he put *Totality* next to where they had *Thetan*.

I said, "I can't let these books go. These books are his source for me."

We changed *Hardin* to *Hadron* because I liked the home-planet name better.

And I said, "I cannot give up anything he wrote in. To me they're sacred."

We continued working.

My son could not acknowledge Hardin or Hadron or anyone. He came to live with us. He would walk by Hardin and not even acknowledge him or say hello to him.

I proceeded to raise Hardin's child until I could no longer handle him. He was not a reasonable child. He had had something happen to his brain at birth. They took him into the armed services. He called me and said, "I will kill anybody if they give me a gun."

I called the military installation where they took young people. I told them, "I would not put a gun in that boy's hands. He had meningitis when he was little and it has affected his brain. He has been impossible to live with. I wouldn't put a gun into his hands."

They sent him back.

After that I realized that I should be doing the Totality work, because ideas came to me as well about the technology. When Hadron remembered he was Buddha, and then he remembered that he was Genghis Khan, there was verification of that. Then we both remembered Egypt — that I was Nefertiti and he was Amenhotep IV. He said, "I was an idiot," about himself. "And," he said, "the plumbing was terrible."

Then I began to work with people. I took on what Hadron wrote, but I seemed to want to add more. And I told him that.

He said, "Fine. After all, you're Totality."

One day he said, "I'm really going to give you an experience of being Totality."

I said, "OK."

I was game for everything that would help me or give me more real-ization — more ultimate, as I put it.

So we had a session.

He said, "Be aware of being your body."

"Yeah."

"You don't use a spirit either."

He decided I didn't and I guess I didn't.

Then he said to me, "Be aware of being out in space, ultimate space, before anything was created."

Wow! What a thing to say to me! But I took it. It was interesting the way that all happened for me. At that session I found out everything about why. I could be aware of being the space before anything was cre-ated.

Then he said, "Now, as creator — and we are ultimate creator as the space — create the universe."

And I created the universe, vortices with a lot of energy, a lot of dif-ferent energies out there.

And he said, "That's right, that's right. And now create first otherness."

I had to know what he meant, and I did.

I said, "First otherness: those are little energies that have a lot of light in them, and they seem to know, they seem to know."

"Yes. Those are the first otherness, the first creations as creator, after the universe. Be aware of being that."

"Yes, I can do that."

I seemed to be able. There was no thinking. That was the best part. If I had to stop to think, I wouldn't have done anything.

I said, "Yes, I can do that. I can be aware of being that first otherness." And then I gave it the name Superconscious. I said, "That's Super-conscious, Hadron."

"Yes," he agreed.

"Now what do I do as Superconscious? I have a body on Earth and it seems stupid to me at this point. From this experience that body seems pretty stupid."

"It is. It hasn't begun to fulfill its potential. Isn't that why we came?"

"Yes."

7

RELEASING VARDA
December 11, 1985

When I was twenty-seven I made the decision that I needed to give
something to somebody. I became aware of the inherent selfishness of
my nature. All my life I had been given to and had not given back. Even
in romantic love relationships my center of attention was focused inward
on my emotional turbulence and the poetry it engendered rather than
on the other person. No matter how much love attraction and desire I
may have felt, I had to admit to myself that I was objectively incapable of
loving another human being. It seemed to me that the way to begin was
to be able to give something to someone rather than receiving all the
time. I decided that I was ready and needed to take care of someone else,
to provide for someone other than myself.

That's when Varda came into my life, in Jerusalem in the fall of 1974.
She was just recovering from a nervous breakdown. She needed to belong
to a group of spiritual friends, like the one I was with, and needed someone to love her and take care of her, for she could not fully take care of
herself at that point. Superconscious provided me with exactly the opportunity I had asked for in a very short period of time.

So naturally I "fell in love" with her.

She played deep, sonorous melodies on her violin. I was attracted by
the possibility of making music with her. One Friday after a communal
Shabbas celebration, we agreed to meet in an upper room and make
music together, her violin with my guitar and voice. Somehow it never

came together. We couldn't get tuned up together, she couldn't relate to what I was playing, something like that. We were good at getting frustrated together.

Finally she said to me, although she denies it to this day, "How about some old-fashioned loving?" and led me out to her tent in the garden where we put he and she together in a good old-fashioned way. In the morning she was furious with me and berated me with intense and demeaning anger.

With single-minded devotion I escorted and pursued Varda in Jerusalem and Israel, across Europe, to New York, across the country to Lama Foundation, out to California, and back to Lama again. I pursued her not only with my desire to give something to somebody, but also with the compelling need to project all of my love-sex energy on one other person. She knew she wasn't that person, and I should have listened to her.

I wrote her a long invocatory poem, resonant with Tantric hymns to the Goddess, inscribed it with multi-colored felt pens on a long sheet of paper, tied a ribbon around it, and presented it to her. I thought this was the deepest, most beautiful, and certainly the longest poem I had ever written. Varda opened the scroll, began reading the poem, and got very angry.

"What is this shit?" she said. "This isn't me!"

I should have listened to her, but no, like all of us, I am driven forward under the compulsions of my karmas. Part of that was a past-life promise to care for Varda. The other part was the spirit who was to be born as our son Abe, who had already joined us in Jerusalem. Varda saw him quite clearly all along, a handsome blonde boy full of joy and enthusiasm for life, exactly the way he was as a child. Once when we were laid up sick in London, lying in bed together for a few days, we experienced his spirit simultaneously. No doubt his strong desire to be born through us played a role in holding us together through all the dramas that threatened to tear us apart.

Varda was acceptable to me as a person to project my love upon, but I was not acceptable to her. I was weird, creepy, repulsive — these were some of the nicer things she could say about me when she got angry. But she did need someone to take care of her, and I was the only one volunteering to do that. She tried to run away any number of times, but always came back to accepting my caregiving as something she needed.

The crowning point in our relationship came when I had finally made up my mind to tell her that it was all over, this time *I'm* breaking up with *you*. I'm not going to sleep with you anymore, I divorce you, etc.—and she said to me, "Guess what, honey? I'm pregnant!"

Despite all our pregnancy scares and fears in the past, when a new life was really with us, we were both filled with tremendous joy and gladness. We were both ready to be parents. The only question was, could we do it with each other? We got married in a beautiful ceremony in the dome at Lama. We moved into a cute little family house at Lama, the Muffin House, and did our best to be a family.

When Abe was born in February 1978, he was a source of great joy both to us and to the whole community. We never had any doubts or regrets about bringing Abe into the world. He is a light in both our lives. Nevertheless, our lack of contentment with each other, our mutual antipathy, continued to grow. We moved into separate houses after six months, and two years later we were divorced. Varda took Abe and moved to Santa Fe in September 1980.

If I were living only for Abe, I would have left then, too. But my karmas compelled me to stay longer and to dance with Glory. It took me three years to realize that Abe needed more than a part-time father.

Varda and I remained friends and worked together as cooperative parents. Abe had a largely happy, if somewhat chaotic, childhood. Nevertheless, it was a great relief to me when Varda remarried and transferred her significant-other projection to husband number two.

To say that we came together to bring Abe into the world is true, but it is begging the question of why we really came together. There was a deep karmic bond and some kind of karmic payback happening between myself and Varda. Otherwise why would I pursue so relentlessly someone who continually rejected me so emphatically? Otherwise why would she submit so often to someone she felt was weird and repulsive?

For most of our relationship I found myself in the position of loving (as best I could) and not feeling loved in return, of trying at least to love someone who did not feel the same love for me, who was often angry and abusive. Indeed, I took it as a spiritual practice at that time to love without feeling love in return, to give without receiving. There was of course the selfish hope of the future receiving of love. We all want to be loved.

"What you give is what you get," I told myself. "What you give into life is what you get out of life. You want to get love, so give love. If it doesn't come back to you from Varda, it will come back to you from life sooner or later." And indeed it did.

What fun! This is not a recommended game to play, unless you have to, in which case you have no choice, so you may as well enjoy it the best you can.

To say that Varda was incapable of fully taking care of herself and therefore incapable of rejecting someone who would take care of her is again begging the question. There seems to have been the acting out of a karmic contract to take care of this other person and to love without feeling love in return for a certain period of time.

What I first saw, when I ran this in session with Joanna, was a woman's face bending down over me, as if I were on the ground, her eyes wide with horror. She was a cute, blonde Dutch woman with round face, rosy cheeks, and one of those little white Dutch caps.

When I moved into it further, I saw that I had been her husband there in Holland many years ago. We had a nice life together with our young daughter. Then one day I was drunk, and I fell down in the street and was run over by a cart. A wheel ran over my head, permanently damaging my brain. This is where she rushes out into the street, finds me lying in the mud, bends over and looks at me, her eyes wide in horror.

She takes me home and cares for me because I can no longer take care of myself. I can no longer provide for her. She has to provide for herself, our daughter, and me. I can no longer love her or make love to her. I am a vegetable. She is loving me without receiving love in return.

This goes on for a while. Slowly her love turns to despair, resentment, anger, and hatred. She does the natural thing and takes another man into our house and into our bed, so that she can feel loved and cared for again. And one day they decide to relieve me of my misery by putting a pillow over my head and smothering me.

Not surprisingly, I did not feel that this was a loving action. I already had enough jealous rage going with this other guy in my house, in my bed, sthupping my wife. Now I had the searing hatred and thirst for vengeance of someone who has been murdered.

So my spirit hung around the house and haunted them, projecting creepy sensations and eerie noises, rattling dishes, creaking doors, misplacing objects, trying out all the various impotent ruses an agonized spirit has in its bag of tricks. Eventually I became weary of this. I might be making them miserable, but I was keeping myself in misery too, hanging around them, feeling bad about making them feel bad. This was no fun. I moved on.

Joanna notes, *"He wants to use death to get out of a seemingly blocked situation."*

It does very strange things when two people vow to love each other exclusively forever and ever. *Forever* is all right, in fact is true. It's the exclusivity that is the real limiter. Sooner or later we're going to have to let go of that, along with the image of the old man with the long white beard who sits in the sky and says, "The Lord thy fraud is a jealous fraud. Thou shalt have no other frauds before me."

Here we see not only the karmic debt with an equal and limited period of payback, but also the nature of the injury to the victim: damage to the head. Whatever mental injuries Varda had suffered (childhood trauma, nervous breakdown) rendered her incapable of loving me in a way I could receive. I know that she loved me deeply enough to give me my only son, but the traumatized and abused elements of her personality pushed me away from her. I was also dealing with my own mental and emotional aberrations, which rendered me incapable of truly loving her or anyone, and which were what I was now working on with Joanna. Karmic reciprocity.

What is unique about Joanna's method—Totalizing and the use of universal vortex energy to release pictures recorded in subconscious—is that it has the ability to release karma. It gets stranger and stranger—but what we are sharing here on Earth has to do with the release of karma.

Two other past-life pictures with Varda came up. In one I am a little

Dutch boy, she my abusive mother. Was I immediately reborn to Varda? It seems I was mentally retarded in some way. A carryover of the brain damage recordings? A miserable, limited lifetime. I lost my life when I was kicked by a horse.

In my present life I was twice thrown off horses at summer camp and injured at the age of nine, due to being terrified of horses and unable to manage them well. The first time I landed on the left side of my face. The second time I broke my right wrist.

In the hospital I was put under anesthesia and had a very vivid experience of flying over the landscape of the summer camp I was at, two fingers of land stretching out into Lake Ticonderoga. I reconnoitered all the features of the terrain, the boys' camp, the girls' camp, the horse barns, the fields, the docks, and the fire circle in the woods. I walked through new areas of the forest. I went back into the bunk where my bed was but no one was there. This was my first out-of-body experience.

In the other life recalled we were gypsy lovers. This lifetime was much more romantic and appealing but ended in violent death. The bonfire, the dancing, and wild music were very vivid, very deep in my soul. But the recall of my death was wrapped in apathy. An older man attacked me, slashing at me with a knife, stabbing me in my solar plexus. Another one bites the dust. So what?

ASTROLOGY is a fairly accurate study of the operation of the BIG HYPNOTIC COMPUTER up in the sky made up of planets circling around the sun in their ring-paths.

Planets orbiting in their ring-paths are surrounded by and held in place by electro-magnetic force-fields of extensive size and scope which interact with each other. At certain positions their collective force-fields exert more magnetic attraction and repulsion influence on planet Earth than at others. However, their influence is felt and recorded by BODY force-fields AT ALL TIMES. This is an automatic occurrence which is pre-programmed with recordings of many evolutionary lifetimes on this and numerous other planets.

PLANETARY automatic reactions can be GOOD or BAD depending upon past recordings RESTIMULATED by who YOU meet from day to day and what you have done to them and they to you in the recent and far distant past.

When it is understood that cell structure records like a tape is recorded — EVERYTHING that happens on a see, hear, smell, feel, taste level — then there is comprehension of what is meant by KARMA, a small segment of the AKASHIC RECORDS.

TOTALITY CONCEPT 740426

RELEASING ROGER
December 15, 1985

After witnessing my disembodied spirit hanging around and haunting my own home and family in Holland, I began to consider more seriously the possibility that my own life in present time might be haunted.

I had read many books about possession, obsession, hauntings, and so forth, never consciously recognizing that it could be happening to me. There had been all sorts of bizarre phenomena in my life which I had never understood which might actually have a reasonable explanation in the presence of obsessing spirits.

There were times when I found myself outside my body unable to get back in. There were times when I could see through my body but not speak through it or use it. There were times when my body had been thrown around the room, sometimes howling and moaning, as if being tossed around by an invisible force. There were times I was plunged into obsessive spirals of negative and self-destructive feeling. Then there was the diabolical cartoon of the hand holding the gun, putting it up to my head, pulling the trigger, blowing my brains out, then the hand holding the gun, putting it up to my head, pulling the trigger, blowing my brains out, again and again and again. And of course there were the singing voices that gave me all my poetry. There was much more of this stuff going on than I care to recall.

143

As a child I had been sensitive to spirits, particularly to the old man and the old woman who lived in the house where I grew up. It was their house. They had built it, lived in it, and died there. No one else was aware of them. But I could sense their presence, had inaudible conversations with them, and sometimes they would help me out in small childish matters. As an adult I no longer had that acuity of perception. Excessive use of marijuana had tended to both open me up to spirit possession and gauze over my subtle awareness on certain levels.

Now that I had such excellent help in psychic matters, it would be foolish not to take the plunge.

"Joanna," I said, "I have been considering the possibility that I might be possessed or obsessed by one or more disembodied spirits. Judging by the evidence, it seems very likely to me."

"I have been waiting for you to come up with that knowingness," she said. "I have seen it all along, but I wanted to wait until you came up with it on your own. Now you have the ability to recognize it for yourself. There certainly do seem to be some spirits sitting there. I think it would be a good idea to get down to work—find out about them—where they came from, why they are there—and release them off your body so that they can go back to the spirit world where they belong. Don't you think so?"

I certainly did.

Once we were in session I could sense the presence of a malignant entity clinging to the left side of my head, but I could not perceive it directly.

Joanna described it to me as a hunched over old man with old-fashioned glasses and a tweed coat, very angry, very bitter, creating non-survival messages, death wish.

"Ask him why he is there. Decide to know," Joanna prompted me.

"He seems to be angry about his daughter," I said. "She is suicidal, but I am the one who should die. He is sticking around to see that I do it."

"Who is this entity?" she asked me.

"He's like Scrooge, a banker. It's in New York in 1880. His daughter, Maria, loved me, broke her heart over me. I didn't love her, didn't take care of her. She became a prostitute and died of venereal disease. He blames me for abandoning her, for her death, and is hanging around to defeat me, to prevent me from loving anyone again. Loving anyone equates with abandonment and death. I have always relied on women taking the initiative with me, since I never can come on to them."

"How may we address you?" Joanna asked the spirit.

"Roger," he answered through me.

"Roger, how long have you been with Ahad?"

"A long time."

"Since before birth."

"Yes."

"Why do you want Ahad to die?"

"As long as he's defeated, he doesn't need to die. He needs to be defeated in love, unable to hurt and abandon, to cause young girls to lose their lives."

"Are there any other entities present?"

"There are, but I won't tell you anything about them."

Usually, Joanna could persuade spirits to leave a body on their own, willingly, guided by her spirit helpers, reasoning that it was in their own best interest to return home to the spirit world where they belong so that they can undergo clearing and be ready for a new, better lifetime. Most spirits could understand that. When the spirit was recalcitrant, she would call upon spirit helpers to act as psychic policemen and forcefully remove the spirit to a neutral place, an astral cellblock, until it could make up its mind to move on.

Roger was fixed in hatred and unwilling to listen to reason, so Joanna called on her spirit helpers to remove him. An obsessive malignant spirit was lifted off my body. I could feel it immediately. We sent his spirit love and forgiveness.

As was the case in the release of the spirit of the victim of the Aztec priest, the release of the spirit of this bitter old man off my body resulted in the immediate and permanent alleviation of psychological aberrations that had plagued me for twenty years. Most specifically, the nasty, insistent, suicidal promptings disappeared without a trace. A very large layer of obsessive-compulsive sexual fixation was no longer there. And a sharp, stabbing, self-hatred was gone, just like that.

I don't think I ever could have fully believed it unless I had experienced it myself.

RELEASING HENRY
December 20, 1985

There was one incident in my life that kept haunting me — the first time that I was unable to get back into my body.

I had come from college to New York City to visit Martin, my best friend from high school, who was now a music student and blues guitarist living on the Lower East Side. He was, predictably, very heavily into drugs, and our primary recreation was getting stoned and listening to music. He lived on Avenue C, not far from the huge, lurking transformers of the ConEd power plant. It was a very rough neighborhood, not one where you hang out on the street a lot, so we spent most of our time inside his apartment behind its triple-locked barricaded door. Even so, thieves still came in through the window when he wasn't home.

Dope intensifies natural urban paranoia — a distrust of everything and everyone as a potential energy rip-off. Walking down those streets found me positively skittery and jittery. One evening on the way back to the apartment, I passed by a group of black teenagers in the twilight. Some of them spoke to me, taunting me, trying to get my attention. I kept on walking. They shouted after me, calling me to come back. I kept on walking. A couple of them started to come after me at an easy lope. I broke into a run. There were shots fired into the air. Gunshots! I really took off, not looking back.

By the time I got back to the apartment, I was scared out of my wits. Fear like an enema had purged my psychic body of anything but fear itself. Martin and his roommate were hanging around, talking, listening to music, and of course smoking dope. I sat down across from them, so freaked out that I could not say a thing. They passed me a joint. I took a few hits, felt the welcome rush, and left my body. . . only to find somewhat later that I couldn't get back into it.

I didn't know that I had exteriorized. I merely got good and spaced, which often does involve the experience of being present as the space in which everything is existing, rather than being a body sitting in space. That is why the music sounds so great. The music is no longer outside you. You are inside the music, and the music is inside you, inside the space you are.

At any rate, there I was, freaked, totally spaced, and unable to get back into my body. I had full awareness of the dark room, the black-light psychedelic posters, the glowing lamps, my two friends sitting on the couch, talking, but when they spoke to me I couldn't speak back to them. They must have thought I was really spaced. I knew what I wanted to say to them, I just couldn't say it. I couldn't use my tongue. I couldn't operate my body. I couldn't move at all. This was really scary. I had no idea what was happening.

After a while I did manage to get back into my body and grab for some potato chips. The fear subsided. But I felt very strange, contaminated, polluted. Too much fear, I thought. My life got very strange from there on out.

Of course, life in general was getting stranger and stranger in the late sixties, and I did not ascribe any causal significance to this incident at the time. But there would be other incidents where I would, say, be walking down the street and find myself outside my body, unable to get back in. My body was still walking down the street, and I was the space around my body—I just couldn't get back inside it. And then there was the difficulty I often had getting back into my body and waking up in the morning. It was very disturbing.

When I went into this incident in session with Joanna, I was able to see that another entity had indeed entered my body at that time when I had so conveniently vacated it by spacing out. Joanna saw him as a solid white mass without much energy, a ghostly presence on the right side of my upper body.

This entity had been an old drunk sailor whose body was dying in a hospital ward nearby at the same time as I was out of my body. He was rather an appealing character, a vagabond and a poet, philosophical and humorous, working as a sailor because he loved to travel. He gave his name as Henry. He was also lonely, alcoholic, and addicted to opium and whatever else he could get his hands on. His body was wasted away by drink and drugs, but the immediate cause of his death seems to have been a severe beating he received from a gang of punks in an alley. He was wandering around outside his expiring body when he just happened to find in the immediate vicinity another younger body that was temporarily unoccupied.

Without my conscious knowledge or permission, he had been with me for the past fifteen years, hiding out in my body, enjoying my life, making some small contributions of his own, a hitchhiker on my journey through life.

Joanna pointed out that my whole appearance had changed after Henry came on board. "Before, you were a very well-dressed young man and took care of your appearance. Then you started to wear shabby clothes, let your hair grow long, neglected to shave, and looked like a tramp."

I thought I was just dropping out to become a hippie, along with my friends, but it seems like Henry was along for the ride, too. It was true that for the past fifteen years I had only worn second-hand clothes, usually right down to the threads.

I saw how Henry had been part of my wanderlust, and got a sense of how his sensibility had contributed to my poetic voice. Though an uninvited guest, Henry was a benign spirit, a likable fellow, indeed an old friend by now. But I was into total clearing and it was time for him to go.

When presented with the idea, he was very agreeable to moving on to the spirit world for clearing and further adventures. So Joanna asked her spirit helpers to come in and escort him away, while I worked with the vortex energy to purge all traces and impressions of him off my body.

Releasing a spirit off the body is a wholesale stripping away of a psychic overlay, like stripping away an overpainted image that was not part of the original picture.

The nearest experience I have had on the physical plane was when I had the toxic mercury-nickel amalgam fillings in my teeth replaced with a chemically neutral composite material. My whole system had been homeopathically poisoned with mercury and nickel ever since I was a young child. My mouth was a weak galvanic battery (two dissimilar metals in a moist environment) turning my saliva into battery acid leaking down my throat.

I found this hard to believe until someone took a voltmeter, put the prongs on the fillings on either side of my mouth, and showed me that I was carrying around an electrical charge that measured half that of an AA battery. And this with only four fillings in the teeth left in my mouth. An electrical charge in my mouth for over thirty years? That's enough to drive anybody crazy.

After the amalgam was removed, my friends asked me if I felt better. I said that my mouth and my body chemistry felt normal for the first time that I could remember. It was not as if I had been sick, was going through a healing crisis, and now getting better. My body had been poisoned and now the poison was gone. That's what it feels like to get rid of obsessing spirits.

Whereas Roger had been a malignant parasite draining life out of my system, Henry was more like a benign tumor that was easy to remove. Roger was externally obsessing and alien to me, so I have had to rely heavily on Joanna's notes to recall his release, whereas Henry was very familiar and vivid to me.

That part of each individual that is CONSCIOUS has the ABILITY to ACKNOWLEDGE his/her PRESENCE as TOTALITY at ANY given LOCATION and thus REMEMBER. This is the actual mechanics of MEMORY. When an individual rediscovers the ABILITY to do this CONSCIOUSLY the MEMORY picks up markedly.

It is merciful that we do not REMEMBER past lives until we are ABLE, with correct instruction, to RELEASE the heavy PAIN and SHOCK patterns they contain.

Because of BEING TOTALITY, any individual has the ABILITY to FOCUS his AWARENESS at any LOCATION on this or any other planet in any lifetime. The ABILITY to do this and differentiate between NOW and THEN is SANITY.

Everything that has ever occurred has a definite LOCATION that can
be recalled with the FOCUSING of ATTENTION and AWARENESS.

However, research has disclosed that activating past lives into
MEMORY can be painful to the BODY because of the death,
destruction, and heavy emotions sometimes revealed. Unless handled
rapidly these activate automatically on the BODY STRUCTURE.

TOTALITY CONCEPT 740513

RELEASING ANGER IN RELATION TO SEX
February 5, 1986

As many layers of the psychic onion as I had peeled away, as many glowing new blueprints as I had put in, the external situation with Glory had
not moved and seemed likely to endure as "an exercise in futility" (Joanna's
terms). Love her as I may, love her more than anyone before or after, I
had to admit that I was really very angry about this situation, and that
anger was filtering, if not blocking, the true love. Glory often said, "Behind
every anger is hurt and sorrow." If I didn't hurt so much, I wouldn't be
so angry. Since my goal for myself was to be able to truly love (and of
course be loved in return), and since my anger was clearly blocking the
love, I asked Joanna to work with me on releasing the reactive anger in
my being, particularly in relation to sexual love.

It seems like I came into life with a strong judgment against the basic
male anger/sex energy. I distrusted the natural arising of my male sex
energy and would not let myself be aggressive with women no matter
how strong my desire. If I desire, I withdraw. So I tended to attract aggressive women, simply because only they could break through my shell.
Even more than sex I feared the expression of my own anger, blocked it
off completely, and consequently had a lot of repressed anger. Among
other things I had an aversion to groups of men, group male bonding,
competitive combative sports, and competition and aggression in any
area of life. All of this is indicated by Mars in the Twelfth House of my
natal chart.

You can't always get what you want, particularly if you can't allow yourself to want it in the first place. But now necessity increased and I got what I needed: clearing.

The first picture I saw was of a lovely English countryside in spring, with rolling meadows of grasses and flowers, copses of trees, a village in the distance, shingled house tops, a church spire. The scene was almost too archetypal, too familiar, too "picture perfect" to be anything but a "product of my imagination"—it challenged my rational mind, distrusting as always. I asked again and again and still got the same picture. So I moved into it.

I am a young man walking with my beloved young woman in the green springtime fields. She is slender and beautiful with long auburn hair gleaming in the sunlight and wearing a long flowered print dress billowing in the breeze. We walk along, away from the village, holding hands, talking, young and in love.

We lie down together in the tall grass. We talk, caress, hold each other, embrace... and I get very turned on. My sex organ is hard, full of blood. I want to put my body into hers. She gets very scared of my sexual arousal, doesn't know what it is or how to handle it, and pleads with me to stop pushing into her. But I am too hot with passion and continue trying to force myself on her. She pulls free, gets up, and runs away from me.

My sexual passion becomes blinding anger, my desire is rejected again and again. I pursue her, catch up with her and try to hold her. Terrified, she struggles and screams. I shake her, shout at her, slap her down. She freaks out more.

The next picture I really did not want to see. I saw my hand holding a knife, plunging it into her back over and over again until she lay dead in the grasses, covered with blood, my only true love, slain by my own hand in blind passion. Now my passion is gone, as is the only one I love in life.

Overwhelmed with grief and despair, dazed, dulled, I wander back to the village and surrender myself to their justice. I no longer want to live. Let them take my life from me. It's like another energy took over my body. I thought it was me ready to love her, but then this other energy came in and I ended up killing her. I spend some dark time behind bars in deepest desolation — and shortly thereafter I am hanged.

Of all the images I recovered from subconscious during this work, this was the most shocking and grievous: my hand holding a knife and plunging it into her back.

"No wonder she's afraid to have sex with you," Joanna said, "she's got non-survival sitting there."

The next picture I see is a woman's face, young and beautiful, long raven-black hair, strong features. She is drawing away from me, more angry than scared, screaming at me, backing up against stone walls.

Moving deeper into the picture I see a town in the forest in medieval Europe, somewhere in Germany. I am a guard of the castle. She is a peasant's daughter who brings armloads of produce into the town market for sale. We are also very much in love then, stealing away whenever we can to roll and tumble, hug and kiss, on the greensward under the huge oaks. We are hot for each other. These are much earthier times.

But we could not have a life together. I am a solider owned by the castle. I sleep in the barracks. I have already killed several men. I am not a free man. I could not support a family. She is passionate and earthy, very turned on by my maleness, but she does not want to have a child by a soldier who cannot have a home or a life of his own. She is furious that I am not free to have my own life, to marry her and raise a family. She is scared of pregnancy and disgrace. After the first bursts of passion, she resists and refuses having sex with me.

This leads to terrible fights and confrontations, her throwing pots and pans at me, me hitting her, etc. In the scene I am seeing, she wants me to be with her, but I cannot get off guard duty. She is angry at me, yelling at me. I am drunk, angry, frustrated, feeling rejected by her. I close in on her. She claws at me, scratches my face. I push her head against the stone wall and injure her. She vows never to see me again.

So in rejection and despair once again, caught in a brutal and limited life, I take the time-honored way for males of all ages to get out of the game: I throw myself blindly into the mayhem of battle and get myself killed. Men have always had an easy way out.

Joanna notes, *"All death is self-inflicted."*

. . .

The next picture I see is an African village — round mud houses with thatched roofs, on the edge of the forest. In the plaza all the people are standing in a circle around a painted naked man dancing and singing. I am the shaman invoking the gods of fertility. On the edge of the circle there is a woman, naked, kneeling, bending over a log, watching me, while one by one the men come up and fuck her from behind. We gaze into each other's eyes with intense, blazing love. I never take my eyes off her as I dance and chant and contort. She never takes her eyes off me as she is screwed by man after man all day in the hot sun. She is my sacred consort in the ceremony, but we can never have each other. As the shaman I am the sexual territory of all the men in the village, as is she. We can never touch each other, much less have a life together.

(There is a resonance here with Glory's recall of a snake shaman.)

In the final image of this extensive recall, I am an itinerant priest ministering to remote Alpine villages. She is a young woman with long blonde braids, passionately in love with me. I love her and of course feel that I must reject her advances in the name of religion (again and again and again). In her bedroom, she kneels before me, reaches under my habit, takes my penis in her hand, puts her mouth around me. I can't deal with this. We have sinned together, and now I can never see her again. I watch the black-robed priest striding away along a path winding through the meadow. . . .

EACH INDIVIDUAL HAS AVAILABLE ABILITY, thus there can be a rediscovery and an ACKNOWLEDGMENT of that ABILITY and TOTAL ABILITY.

ABILITY is BEING ABLE to FOCUS and UNFOCUS the ATTENTION with INTENTION on any LOCATION and, by the use of a POSTULATE (THOUGHT), release and/or dissolve permanently the PRETENDED STATES OF IGNORANCE known as the FALL OF MAN.

RELEASE is to examine the original INTENTIONS, DECISIONS, and KNOWINGNESSES that created the original ASSIGNMENT in the first place. Then YOU as YOUR TOTAL PRESENCE take charge by ASSIGNING and UNASSIGNING the old recordings, over and over, until they are no longer of any importance to you.

DISSOLVING is accepting the old POSTULATES and ENERGY patterns back into YOUR TOTAL PRESENCE — YOURSELF (not the body). Into YOU as TOTALITY — THE TOTAL SELF — from whence all comes. ASSIGN-UNASSIGN over and over — at the LOCATION and also in the BODY force-fields. This removes ENERGY from the BODY which must be replaced by a REASSIGNMENT of new ENERGY.

REASSIGNMENT requires a firm DECISION in relation to actions occurring in this lifetime and a REPLACEMENT with ENERGY CREATED by a new DECISION or POSTULATE: this is reevaluation. However, REASSIGNING pure ENERGY such as INFINITY POLARITY LIGHT PARTICLES which the BODY SPIRITS will grab and use in place of the RELEASED ENERGY patterns is the most effective.

When you have RELEASED and re-evaluated a past experience, it is absolutely essential that a REASSIGNMENT of NEW POSTULATES and ENERGY be given to the BODY. Unless this is done, the AUTOMATIC BODY FORCE-FIELD SYSTEM of the automatic AUR CYCLE (ASSIGN-UNASSIGN-REASSIGN) will reconstruct itself and put everything back the way it was.

The BODY is a SURVIVAL MECHANISM operating almost entirely on AUTOMATIC. If with a THOUGHT process you remove ENERGY from the BODY it has the SURVIVAL ABILITY to AUROMATICALLY recreate the ENERGY exactly the way it was before it was removed.

TOTALITY CONCEPT 740518

RELEASING MY FATHER
April 10, 1986

My father was the president of a bank, practical and conservative, an excellent provider for his family, but a rigid and controlling personality in many respects. I was intellectual, liberal, artistic, and psychic (although I didn't recognize psychic at the time), and as I grew into adolescence in the sixties the differences between us created great conflict in our family — the famous "generation gap" of the era. I couldn't understand why he was the way he was, but I wanted his recognition and validation of who I was becoming. He definitely could not comprehend who I was becoming and laid a great deal of invalidation on me.

We would have long discussions, actually alternating monologues, each holding forth to the other. He became exasperated with my rapidly expanding mind. "Frank, you know I haven't understood a word you've said," he would say. Or, more bluntly, "Frank, I think you're crazy." He, in turn, became for me the image of everything I didn't want to be. I rebelled like crazy, forcing my way to freedom, but his invalidation and rejection of me left deep psychic scars. At one point he refused to speak to me for years on end. I became convinced that I was crazy, a self-diagnosed schizophrenic, which with all the voices I was hearing seemed reasonable enough.

On the other hand, my mother was always very loving and supportive of me, even when I'm sure she thought I was totally off the deep end. Indeed, at certain times of extreme isolation and distress, I felt that it was only the cord of my mother's love that kept me from self-destructing.

Joanna and I set the intention to uncover and release my karmic pictures around my father.

(Around this time I had gone up to the Puye Cliff Dwellings outside Española with my friend Emily. She was in a semi-sick, low-energy place. We spent a lot of time in the caves sitting and meditating or spacing out. We both saw the village standing again as it was, stone houses built out from the escarpment and on top of the mesa. We saw a ceremonial procession at night by torchlight in which she was the Corn Maiden, image of fertility. We both had been there before and shared the same time and space together. I searched for an intimate past connection with her but could only find that we had been members of the same community, as we were now.)

In session I saw myself living in the cliff dwellings, one of the ancient inhabitants of this land. I was an important and powerful man with a long nose, not a warrior but a priest, a keeper of songs and ceremonies for the tribe. We lived in peace and harmony with the land. I was happily married and lived with my wife in great harmony in one of the stone buildings. I questioned if this was Emily—and found out that my wife in that life was my mother in this life!

The one flaw in this perfect existence was my son, with whom I was not pleased. He was a young soul, slow, simple, and dull. He had no fire, no passion. He was not like me at all. He brought no honor to me. He made me feel ashamed among the tribe. As he grew to be a young man and showed little interest in anything, I was hard on him, pushed him, challenged him, talked down on him. "Be a man. Do something with your life. Make me proud of you." I was invalidating and unkind.

He was humiliated and angry at me. Determined to show me up, trying to do something heroic, he stole a pony, raided a neighboring tribe, and got himself killed.

I was devastated. I did love him very much. He was my only son and I had pushed him into getting himself killed. I withdrew from my wife, from the tribe. I spent months sitting alone and brooding. Grief, anger, and frustration. Finally in despair I did the manly thing and single-handedly attacked the neighboring tribe to avenge his death. I was wounded, suffered, and died. We lived in a peaceful culture. There was no reason for my son or me to get ourselves killed other than my blinding pride. An exercise in futility.

Coming into this life, the tables were turned. He was the father and I was the son. He was not pleased with me. I brought no honor to him. And so forth.

When I read the beautiful evocation of the Ages of the Soul in *Messages From Michael,* it brought me great peace, for I intuited that my father was a soul at an earlier stage of growth and could not comprehend the intensity of my inner life. Younger souls tend to be directed outward to gain experience through interaction with the world, while more mature souls become aware of the inner life and turn their attention at least partially inward. No stage of soul experience on Earth is any better than any other. The older soul is not superior to the younger soul. These are just different stages of experience that every soul goes through on Earth.

My father and I were at different soul ages and could not understand each other. True love surpasses understanding.

My soul was now working on developing greater tolerance, compassion and understanding than I had at earlier stages of the journey, so that I might no longer afflict those I love with rage, judgment and invalidation.

USE OF THE PENDULUM

My financial situation was going from marginal to desperate, and still I kept coming up blank on motivation for money. I had been laid off of my job with the glowing promise of being able to collect unemployment somewhere down the road. Even when I had my job, I was being paid a wage about half the statewide average for bookkeeping work. So it was clear that it was going nowhere, even if I was rehired again for brief spells. I had little motivation to go out and find a similar job.

I was confused about the lack of relation between vocation and livelihood in my life. I had developed many refined skills pursuing the things I loved: poetry, music, dance, photography, and astrology. But these vocational callings seemed unrelated to making money, at least in the ways I practiced them. Material success in these areas seemed to require a good deal of self-promotion and chutzpah, which was not in my nature.

Right after Abe was born, I invested a lot of money in printing up twenty thousand sets of black-and-white postcards of cloud formations. I called them Cloud Cards. But I found that I had no gift for sales and marketing, and even my own product bored me stiff. I ended up with a huge inventory of cards that I could not sell and many years later would destroy.

On a smaller level, I produced matted and framed color landscape photographs and took them around to galleries. This also met with marginal success, as I did not pursue it in a businesslike manner. I guess I expected that my artistic productions were so good that the world would beat a way to my doorstep to discover me.

I developed my astrological skills while living at Lama Foundation. I did charts for everyone I lived with. The community was like a living textbook for me. When I did readings, it was always a learning process for me and a service given to others. I always got good feedback on my readings and never took any money for them.

When I moved to Santa Fe, I thought: *"Why not set myself up as a professional astrologer?"* I put ads in the newspaper, put up posters, made business cards, and for several years offered free readings in the healing room at the Ark Bookstore every Wednesday afternoon as a way of self-promotion. Giving free readings gave me a lot of objective confirmation of my skills and insight in a public setting. People I had never seen before and would never see again came in, put down their charts, and listened to me hold forth for an hour. Sometimes people would stonewall me, wouldn't give me any information or say a thing about themselves other than their chart. I enjoy more of a dialogue, but I learned to work with this. The feedback was pretty unanimous: *"This is amazing. Everything you've just said is true. . . . "*

And I got clients. But I found it was very difficult for me to ask for money or even to accept money for doing a reading. Most of all, I did not want to set myself up in a position where I was even partially dependent for my livelihood on convincing people that they need me to do their charts. I have a great deal of respect for many professional astrologers, the expertise they have and the work they do. But this was not for me. My role continues to be more like that of the village astrologer who offers his insight to his community as a form of *sadhana* or spiritual service.

I was coming to the conclusion that my vocation and my livelihood might not be the same. I might have to work for a living doing things other my soul's calling. But what to do? How to know what to do? How to make a choice? My thinking mind was too reactive and uncertain, overburdened with conflicting rationalizations. I could not figure it out or get any knowingness on the situation. But I had to start doing something.

So for the first and only time in my life I used a pendulum to dowse out my situation, to bypass my conscious mind and get what answers I could from Superconscious.

I wrote down a list of all the vocational skills I had or could imagine developing: accounting, astrology, bookkeeping, poetry, photography, and so forth. I took a recent picture of myself and the largest piece of money I had (a fifty-dollar bill) and laid them together. Since I wanted to check out various vocational skills in relation to Ahad and money, the picture and the money would serve as my witness. I would hold the pendulum over the picture of Ahad and money and then hold the pendulum over the various options on my list one by one to see what kind of a reading I would get.

Accounting and bookkeeping came up with the strongest positive responses, with only very weak responses in other areas and definite negatives in areas such as poetry. Based on that I decided to enroll myself in the community college, take courses in accounting, and possibly sit for the CPA exam.

HER STORY—JOANNA & HADRON'S ABILITIES

When Superconscious began to work for my body, one of the experiences I had that gave me greater reality of what it meant to be Superconscious and have a human body occurred when Hubbard decided to sneak back into the country and give what he called the doctorate course.

I said, "Hadron, that's a con. That is a con."

He said, "But I want to go."

I said nothing. You want to go? Go!

Dick DeMille said he wanted to go. The Mexican man said he wanted to go.

And I looked at that. They were my income. They were the income for my family. I had two boys here. I had an overhead.

I said, "What are you gonna do? Where are you gonna get money to go and live there?"

He said, "Well, just send me twenty dollars a week."

I said, "How am I gonna get twenty dollars a week? You're all going!"

There was no further discussion. I gave him fare, only he went with the boys by car. They all left me, and I sat there wondering what to do.

Men are totally unreliable. I have never depended on a man to support me. When I was married the first time I made ten times more than that husband made. So I sat there trying to decide how I was going to survive. I was furious with Hardin because he didn't even ask me, he didn't even show any concern. There was that stupid Irish man, as far as I was concerned.

Mark Gallard was studying with us. He was a very sick man. He was a chiropractic doctor. So that gave me a clue.

I said, "Mark, get on the phone and call chiropractic doctors and give them a course like Hardin did."

He was smart. He was very bright. He said, "That's a good idea."

I said, "We'll make a proportionate degree of money for you and money for the house to pay the rent and utilities."

He got ten chiropractic doctors, who paid fifty dollars apiece for taking the course. They all came that evening. I prepared everything nicely. I had coffee and doughnuts, the things you do when you have people in. Mark gets up to give the course. He had the E-meter there. And he couldn't confront them to give the course.

I was leaning against the door jamb to the room that they were in and I felt myself weaken. I went over and took Mark by the hand. I took him outside.

I said, "Go upstairs and lie down."

I went in and I gave that course for ten straight weeks. That time I realized I was guided superconsciously. I could rely upon Superconscious to come across for me. The doctors were very happy for the way I gave that course. And I began to realize my strength, my power. I have Superconscious with me, hey, I can do anything.

That sent information around the town. One Saturday morning I get a call from one of the doctors' wives. He is in the hospital. He has cut his right hand and required surgery and is crying for you to come to the hospital to help him.

I had never worked with anybody! I gave the course but I had never worked with anybody! And I am to go into a hospital where a man has had surgery? What am I gonna do there? Then I remembered how I had gotten help superconsciously. That gave me the courage, gave me everything I needed to go.

I got dressed up in a suit and a hat. I took the little meter and I walked into the hospital room. The surgeon was there, along with the nurse and the wife. I became the State Department.

I said, "I will allow all of you to remain, provided that you will not utter a word."

And they agreed.

I connected the chiropractic doctor up to the meter. I sat there listening and Superconscious, I Superconscious, came in for me the body. And I took that man to a time before the accident. What happened?

"Well, I wanted the lawn done. My son was back from college for a week and I asked him to mow the lawn with the electric lawn mower. He said he didn't have time, that he had to go be with his friends. My wife agreed with him, and I became furious. I had anger like I had never known before. I had blind anger at my wife and my son. I went to the electric lawn mower, caught my hand in it, and cut it open. And of course my wife rushed me to the hospital. And the doctor tells me that I will not be able to use my right hand. I'm a chiropractic doctor. How am I gonna earn a living?"

I said, "Calm down here. Let's know that we're going to get a solution here. Can you agree with me on that?"

"Yes."

I took him in his memory to the moment when his son and his wife agreed that his son shouldn't do the lawn. Superconscious guided me to take him to that time. And I could see on this little meter his negativity coming up in him. Then I took him to where he cut his hand in blind rage, how he screamed. His wife took him to the hospital, and the surgeon operated on his hand and told him: "You will never use that hand again."

I said, "Did you accept that statement from the surgeon?"

"Of course. My hand was cut open. They operated on it. The nerves were cut."

I created what I called the erasure technique. I took him into every segment that we went into, in and out, in and out, remembering it and then coming back out of it, going back in and coming back out of it, until I could see a tone rise on the meter. I understood the subconscious and how it records. I understood all of those aspects of humanity at that time. Then I took him to the operation, in and out, in and out, erasing the subconscious. Then I took him to a point after the operation where the doctor told him he would never use his hand again.

I snapped my fingers right in his face and I said, "How long is it going to take you to heal that hand? Right now! No thinking!"

He said, "Three weeks."

I said, "I agree with you. Wife, do you agree?"

"Yes.

"Doctor, do you agree with him?"

"Yes."

"Nurse, do you agree with him?"

"Yes."

My acting ability came right to the fore. I was dramatizing like I was on stage. I looked at myself doing this. The wife agreed, the doctor agreed, the nurse agreed, and then I agreed again.

And I said, "That settles it!"

He did heal that hand in three weeks. It was then that I discovered something: that a person could make a postulate, could make a decision, and it could come true. There was an agreement. I realized that there had to be the agreement. He paid me very well.

He went back to his practice and he called me. "I've got two house patients I want to take you to." OK. They paid me very well.

Then it got around in the chiropractic circles that Joanna Walsh created a miracle. I began to get clients. I began to make money. They came to me from all over. It was so wonderful, to do it on my own. I put out a mailing of my own with a picture. I sent them out. And I was in business again, for the first time without any man.

You were using techniques—

that Superconscious gave me.

These weren't Scientology techniques.

No.

They weren't anything that you had used before.

No. They occurred to me as I was working. Superconscious gave it to me, unquestionably. And meanwhile Hardin and the guys were in Phoenix, taking a doctorate course, which I didn't ask them about, not any of it. I didn't want to listen to any of their tapes when they came back. I wasn't interested in anything Ron Hubbard would give them, because, as I said, to me he personified evil, and he was evil.

You weren't handling Scientology clients. You found your own clients.

I found my own. They came to me. And I developed that technique even further.

Was anyone doing Scientology work in Los Angeles while they were away?

Yes. People had been taking the professional course from Hardin and were doing it to the extent that they could do it. To me these people didn't look capable. Hardin represented a knowing person to me. He had knowing beyond. I decided he had universal knowing. You ask a man to be aware of being that which creates everything, for goodness sakes, and he gives you an answer right off the top of his head that's right, and you respond to it, you react to it—hey, this guy's gotta be something. You've got to admire him, even though he doesn't ask how are you gonna live alone and goes off.

Hardin calls me one night and he says, "I really need some money."

I said, "Work with somebody. You're taking a doctorate course."

I said it that way to him. I found it difficult to forgive him. I acknowledge it. I did later. But at that moment, I had his son and my son and myself.

Then I hear a woman giggling.

I said, "Who's that?"

"Well, there's a young woman here taking the doctorate course and she wants me maybe to go to bed with her."

"Do you want to go to bed with her?"

"It might be an interesting experience."

"By all means do that. You stay with her and let her feed you and I won't send you any money. Good night." Bang! Slammed down the telephone.

That gave me a certain sense of release. It was awful to acknowledge that I wanted to get even with him somehow. And I didn't send him any more money.

It was a couple of weeks later. The auditorium was filled. Two people had come to me. They showed me artifacts, and they said, "These are not Earth artifacts. They were given to us when we were taken up on a space ship. We checked them out with scientists and they said that we had nothing on Earth like this." So I sent out a mailing, and I filled the auditorium with interested people.

I was in the office, facing the front door. I was dividing the money into two envelopes. The front door opened and the strangest-looking man walked in. He's very tall, with no ears. His arms are hanging down below his knees. And he frightened me, because I felt he was there for no good, because I had people that had been on a space ship.

And then I said to myself, "Oh, I wish Hadron was here."

The front door opens and Hadron walks in. He takes hold of the man's arm. They go into the classroom opposite the auditorium, and I hear scratchings on the blackboard. Then Hadron comes out with the man, goes outside, takes him to the corner, and the man disappears.

He comes back, and I said, "Where did you come from?"

"You called me, didn't you?"

"I sure did. That guy scared me. How did you get here? You had to materialize. You never mentioned that you could materialize."

"I never mention a lot of things."

That's what he said. That's what happened. You can't hold resentment against a guy like that. He performed miracles.

[*This incident happened when Hardin was still in Phoenix.*]

We moved our residence to another building because we had so many cars parked there that we were reported as doing business and we had to move. So we took this big building. It was a nice building. It had classrooms and a big auditorium. We got some help from the people to take it. I paid them back. We had nice rooms. They were offices previously.

Ted came to us. He was really an exceptional awareness person. We had him taking people to work with. He took the course for Totality. I used to walk around the rooms to listen to what was going on to make sure everything was all right. And one day I hear Ted screaming. I open the door, and I see this man on top of Ted wanting to choke him. So I yelled for Hadron.

Hadron came in and glared at the man.

The man screamed, "Hadron, don't glare at me! Don't kill me! Don't glare at me! Don't kill me!" He jumped up and ran out the front door.

I said to Hadron, "What is he talking about?—*Don't glare at me! Don't kill me!*"

"Out in space we had space ships. We could glare at each other and kill each other."

"You never mentioned anything like that."

"Why? Why mention it?"

This is how I found out that this man was not really an Earth man.

I said to him one day, "You're schizophrenic. Absolutely."

He agreed.

"One minute I see this Earth man that I have nothing to do with. The next minute I see a man that does exceptional things and has exceptional knowing. I find that very exciting, and I can forgive you for the other stuff that you are."

"Thank you for forgiving me," he said.

One weekend we were invited by friends to go to a lake where they had a summer home. There was a seaside town was about ten miles away from this place where the lake was. It was announced on the radio that the weather where we were headed was going to be pretty hot. At the ocean it would be nice and cool, but we were going to the lake with these people.

So Hadron says, "Well, I guess I'll have to contact the weather spirits."

So as we were driving from Brentwood to the lake he contacted the weather spirits and said, "We're going to a lake and we don't want it to be hot. We want it to be cool."

He communicated just like that with weather spirits. This guy never ceased to be amazing to me.

We get to this lake and it is delightful. And everybody said, "What's happening?" Hadron said, "We told our friends who invited us that I told the weather spirits that I didn't want hot weather here. I wanted cool weather. We're going to be there. We're going to have boating and swimming and everything."

Then there's a report from Oceanside—how come it's so hot by the ocean?

"Oh," he said, "I should have told the weather spirits that it doesn't have to be hot there because it's cool here. It can be cool here and cool there."

So he had to talk to the weather spirits and get that straightened out. I was amazed and full of admiration for a man who could talk to weather spirits. I never heard of such a thing. I since found out that there are people living here in this town, Santa Fe, who do that, but it was not anything familiar to me at the time.

Some people said, "We should have that in the newspaper."

He said, "Forget it. I don't want that in the newspaper."

That's what he could do.

You mentioned that he seemed to have a certain camaraderie with Ron Hubbard and Dick DeMille and that they seemed to enjoy exploring areas in space, recalling things that you didn't want to have anything to do with. What was that?

We went for a weekend up at Idylwild, which is up above Palm Springs. We took a little apartment there, where we fed the squirrels.

And he said, "Let's have a session."

"OK."

We sit down to have a session, and he's taking me out to space where they're having these space fights with Hubbard, and I became furious. I became indignant.

I got up and I said, "You go to hell! How dare you take me out into that kind of a remembrance! I don't want to remember any of that, with you or Hubbard. Goodbye!" And I ran out the door. But of course we were away from our home.

I didn't talk to that man for three days. There was something about that situation that was repugnant to me. The thought that he would dare! I was indignant that he would dare to ask me to remember that. I was furious. And he apologized.

He said, "I don't know why, I just felt like having you remember that with me."

I said, "I don't want to remember that with you. There are other wonderful things that I would rather remember with you. Never do anything like that."

"I won't."

It seems that he and Ron Hubbard had something going that you didn't share, that you didn't want to share.

That's right. That's what kept him with Scientology, him wanting to go to Hubbard. Oh yes, I realize that. But you see, when Hadron and I got together, then the hierarchy left him alone. They knew that there was no use, that we came to bring Totality to this planet.

8

RELEASE THE SLAVER
April 15, 1986

When we next sat down to work on my money issues, Joanna directed my attention to my home planet. She had found that many people have difficulty on the Earth plane, especially with money, due to their home-planet natures. I never shared her certainty in being from another planet, at least in the way that she described it, but nevertheless I took a good look at it to see what I could see. The results were inconclusive and fragmentary. Not all delving into the subconscious results in clear color postcards with neat story lines attached. There is a lot of digging through the muck, a lot of onward through the fog. Whole sessions with Joanna were sometimes inconclusive. Sometimes my psyche was not ready to move. Sometimes what she was looking for (life on other planets) simply was not there.

Having struck out on the home planet issue, we returned to the money issue.

"What did you do to them for money?"

"I bought them and sold them, used them and abused them."

"What did they do to you for money?"

"They took my life."

"Please direct your attention to the location where you bought and sold them for money. Tell me what you see."

"I am standing on the levee, on the docks along the Mississippi River, watching the ships, watching a line of people come down a gangway off a ship. They are all black people. I am admiring them, judging them, assessing their individual beauty and strength, so that I can decide which ones I will buy, which ones I will keep and which ones I will resell. It seems that I am a slave trader in New Orleans.

"It seems that I not only buy and resell slaves, but I also take a great deal of pleasure in sexually using many of the women I own. I love them all, sexually, and some of them love me. I enjoy many different women. When I get tired of them I can always sell them and buy some others.

"I'm leading a very dissipated life with a lot of hunting, drinking, gambling, and brawling, along with the slaving. I am quite fond of all the money I am making in the slave trade. But I distrust banks. So I keep bags of gold coins hidden around my house, under the floorboards and in the walls. Nearby I can sense the presence of a woman who really loves me, who would make a life together with me if I would leave off my wicked ways. She tries to get through to me, but I am too intoxicated and veiled for her to reach.

"Somewhere along the way I contract syphilis, spread the syphilis around, not knowing that I have it, and get crazier and crazier every day. The fever is burning up my brain and I am suffering like crazy. I am deranged and raving. So I arrange to get myself out of the game. I go to a bar, get drunk and get into a fight with a friend, something about gambling debts. He pulls a pistol and shoots me dead, getting me out of the game."

When I say 'arrange to have myself killed' I do not mean on a conscious level. I mean that my spirit agrees to let me get killed and get out of my pointless misery.

"On a conscious level, my friend coveted my bags of gold and was looking for an excuse to get into a fight with me, pull a pistol on me, and shoot me. I can see him clearly. He has reddish-gold hair and beard. He is wearing a white suit and a white hat. He was my friend, but he set me up and killed me out of love for my gold. It was a setup, a staged brawl.

"Right after killing me he went straight to my house, forced a servant to tell him where all the gold was hidden, took the money, and ran out of town. I saw this all as a spirit outside my body right after death. I knew that my love of gold was the cause of my death. He was just the agent. Nevertheless, I felt betrayed by someone who said he was my friend."

Joanna directed me to go to any other location on the time track that might be relevant to my lack of motivation in regard to money. I saw a picture of a Chinese man sitting at a desk covered with money, piles of gold coins, accounting ledgers, and an abacus. There was a dull and lifeless feeling to this picture. The attached story line was that I served as accountant and banker for a Chinese crime syndicate that dealt in drugs, prostitution, and slavery, buying and selling lives with which I had no personal contact. I'm pushing around piles of money and people, a shady plutocrat, protected and secure, until someone else poisoned me and took over.

This lifetime didn't seem to carry a particularly strong charge, nowhere near as much as the life, loves, and death of a New Orleans slaver. Greed is a colder passion than lust. Lust at least has the potential for bringing spirits into contact with one another through the joining of bodies, whereas greed tends to further isolate the spirit behind a wall of money and possessions.

I used the vortex energy to release these pictures off my body and clear the space. The miasm of the syphilitic brain fever was tenacious, lingering, and difficult to clear, as was the brain damage suffered in the Dutch lifetime (which was so tenacious it was carried over into the next lifetime). Throwing myself into battle or brawl and getting myself killed proved to be a quick and painless way to get out of the game, compared with suffering long-term mental and physical degeneration. As Joanna notes, all death is self-inflicted.

Using the vortex energy, I put new pictures of money for my body into my subconscious. I saw myself doing accounting and receiving money, doing bookkeeping and receiving money, reading charts for people and receiving money, selling photographs and receiving money. I saw myself having money and being happy that I had money. I even saw myself having gold coins, although I couldn't quite bring myself to love that gold as Joanna would have me do. I saw an increasing flow of green energy enhancing the quality of life in the present, not the accumulation of hoards of treasure.

As I continued to hold and develop these pictures regarding money over the coming months, knowing that whatever pictures I imprinted upon my subconscious, Superconscious would react them out in my life in the time stream of Earth, I became aware that I was setting myself up to work for money for the rest of my life. Every picture had to do with Ahad doing some kind of work, performing some kind of service, and receiving money. Here I was, limiting myself again, my imagination not stretching beyond the Protestant work ethic. So without denying or resisting that there was a lot of work ahead for me, I simply took necessary work out of the money equation. I simply saw my body receiving a greater flow of money into my life, regardless of where it came from. This began to feel better and better.

A humanoid inhabitant of this planet is a complex group of co-existing SPIRITS operating at different ASSIGNED levels of AWARENESS and ABILITY.

The part of YOU that is CONSCIOUS and AWARE is the personalized UNIT of YOUR TOTAL SELF that answers up to your ID cards.

This CONSCIOUS part of YOU is the SPIRIT that is pretending to be OTHER THAN the TOTAL SELF — TOTALITY — which can become AWARE of the ABILITY to FOCUS the ATTENTION at any given LOCATION within the entire SYSTEM OF TIME GAMES and rediscover data about what has occurred to YOU — SPIRIT — in the near and far-distant past.

Especially the activities which have established limitations on YOUR AWARENESS and ABILITY — as TOTALITY.

ALL ACTIVITIES HAVE LOCATIONS: yesterday, last week, last year, ten, a hundred, a thousand years ago on this or other planets.

The same mechanism that RECALLS yesterday can be developed once the process is understood, to bring into your AWARENESS any LOCATION out of the past.

REMEBERING IS FOCUSING AND UNFOCUSING THE ATTENTION ON A
LOCATION WITH THE INTENTION OF RELAYING THE DATA TO THE
BODY AWARENESS UNIT.

As TOTALITY YOU are present within all THINGS — EVERYWHERE.
Thus YOU can BECOME AWARE at the LOCATION of a past incident
and also as the BODY AWARENESS UNIT.

This meets the requirements of the TWO-TERMINAL physical
universe and is the TOTAL superconscious MEMORY.

TOTALITY CONCEPT 161-162 740708

GOING HOME
April 24, 1986

Joanna persisted in trying to take me to my home planet. When I finally
did go home, it was not to any planet but to that great light deep in space
that I had seen with Glory. It was a glorious and awesome experience
in an altered state of awareness. It confirmed that Earth is not my home.
The light is my source and my home. But insofar as any planet is my
home planet, it is planet Earth.

Being aware of being a superconscious light body beyond time and
space is a much different experience than the recalling of past-life pictures. It is not just viewing memory recordings in recall. One can actually refocus awareness into other dimensions. Verbalizations are much
slower, more abstract, much more like channeling, giving expression to
otherworldly realities in earthly language.

After spaceation into Totality, I asked to go to the home world, the
origin dimension.

Glory appeared to me in her light form and said, "Come on, honey,
let's go home." (Her light form was bright, pure, radiant, joyful — no
burden, no sorrow, no age, no pain.) She took my hand and led me out
through a vortex, a time/space tunnel, back to that great light deep in
space, the sea of light.

"Yes," I said, "I've already been here. I know this place, but I'm supposed to find a home *planet*. I want to tune in to *that* reality."

So I cleared my awareness and opened myself up again—and once again Glory came to me in her light form, like Beatrice in *The Divine Comedy*, to lead me back to the sea of light. Hard-nosed, skeptical, I kept testing what I was getting, clearing my space again as many as six times.

Every time I kept seeing Glory in her light form. She kept saying to me, very gently insisting, "Come on, honey, let's go home. This *is* home for us. This is our *home*." She was very patient with me.

How many times could I question my beloved?

What else was there to do? I went home with you.

What followed is beyond the ability of words to describe.

The great light deep in space, the sea of light, is a vast plasma of light which science might call the center of a galaxy.

(Plasma is the state where matter and energy exist in a random chaotic state, a highly ionized gas consisting almost entirely of free electrons and positive ions, the state of matter and energy before creation. All beings are originally formed from this plasma.)

Within this vast plasma of light are millions and millions of beings of light. To Earth-plane astronomers these beings appear to be stars, spheres of light. As perceived by the stars on their own level of awareness, these are living, moving, dancing, rejoicing light beings, whose bodies are fluid living flames, capable of extension, expression, articulation, all the elements of dance. Not only does each light being have movement, each one also emits sound vibrations (music) and subtle dancing colors far beyond the range of human perception. The whole vast plasma cloud is bathed in unceasing, ever-changing light, though the overall ambiance seems to be golden white. (Gustav Doré's engravings of the angelic spheres in Dante's *Paradiso* come closest to earthly images that faintly reflect this reality.)

In the sea of light, the sea of love, being is always joy and delight, dancing lights, swells of exaltations, choruses of glory—millions of stars eternally circling around the central light, while within the grand cosmic dance infinite other permutations and combinations occur: smaller circles, roses, crosses, triangles, and so on, revolving around their own centers, and as individual beings of light dancing, rejoicing freely, inter-mingling, interpenetrating. We move freely in and out of each other's forms, delighting in mingling, not bound to each other by anything at all but universal love. This is where we came forth from, where we return to: home.

From home the time line unfolds. Some of us wanted to experience greater individuation, greater freedom, greater space in which to move, so we left the sea of light and went into outer space. We experimented, innovated, and experienced many varieties of movement in outer space. In outer space our individual lights seem extremely bright by contrast, while in the sea of light all the lights blend together and individuality is more a matter of subtle variation in color and sound.

Then she and I and some others decided to form our own circle of dancing lights. I got the image of lights dancing in a circle, every other one going the opposite direction, interweaving in and out of one another like fish in a grand right-and-left, weaving a crown of light. Our circle got larger and larger until it became immense. Then beings began to drop away to go explore elsewhere, until finally our circle was very small again. We went off to explore other worlds, she and me and our little cluster. We went planet-hopping for a long time and eventually came to Earth.

Joanna said that never in all her work with people had she encountered such purity of origin. In her experience most other beings who have such recall have created other worlds, other planets, with cultures, tech-nologies, arts, etc. She said that the directness of our connection with original light was very unusual.

Glory and I are twin flames of the same original light. We share the same address in light. The first time she kissed me, my whole being was flooded with light. Whenever we are together we share the ecstatic ampli-fication and mingling of our original light, which is why I say to her, "Home is wherever we are together."

In this session, Joanna steered me three times to explore if I had created or gone to a planet other than Earth after coming from the sea of light. I tried to go where she indicated, but the results were ephemeral—vague images without much reality.

I saw tall, slender, light beings with big blue eyes, joyful and peaceful, moving in and out of each other's bodies, among arching crystalline structures. I saw barren desert terrain under a glowing golden sky, a fierce devouring heat. I saw a world inhabited by technologically advanced reptiles. But none of this had any more emotional impact than clips from old sci-fi films on late night TV. I just could not get any reality on having come from another planet. My true home is a great light deep in space where star beings dance and sing in glory.

RELEASE BETWEEN LIVES
June 3, 1986

Now that I had the glorious experience of going home and the reality of cosmic origin, it became necessary to undertake the arduous task of releasing and clearing the condition of my spirit between lives, conception, prenatal, and birth. I already had the very clear picture of my previous life as a young Jewish man, a fugitive who perished in the Holocaust in Europe, spontaneously recalled on top of Truchas Peak with Glory. What I now needed was to relive and release the process that had brought me into this present life.

The overriding, paralyzing emotion in my life was fear, nameless formless fear, which could subside into anxiety or magnify into terror — fear of life on Earth, fear of being seen, fear of being heard, fear of being known. The fear of a fugitive: if they see you, they're going to kill you. I may be a joyous creative spirit, but I'm veiled and obscured by this reactive fear imprinted in my soul. Not only fear of authority but fear of having any authority. Fear of achievement, fear of recognition, fear of entering into relationships, fear of trusting anyone. Especially fear of groups of men, fear of religious and political organizations. Even at Lama Foundation, as safe a place as I could find to hide away from the world, I was afraid to sing my songs if I thought anyone could hear me. I wrote secret lyrical poetry singing of this nameless, formless fear that obsessed me. I had taken birth in America, as safe a place as I could find to take rebirth on Earth, but I was still running, still hiding from the Nazi terror.

When I left my Jewish body in the Holocaust, I didn't leave the Earth plane. My life was not complete. It ended abruptly in fear and terror. I was a fragment of a huge mass of souls of Holocaust victims hovering in the Earth sphere. One might almost say this was a group soul, traumatized by the horror of the Nazi terror, unable to comprehend the evil that had destroyed us all so suddenly.

Joanna had a profound vision of her own during this session, as her notes record: *"Impression of a dark spirit leaving Germany at end of the whole thing, a gray shadowy outline of a Nazi uniform. He was behind all of this. He was the spirit that controlled Hitler—weird, violent, destructive, impersonal, cold—like a black hole in space sucking up infinite amounts of energy. This parasitic power feeds on grief and destruction, not on love, peace, and forgiveness. I can't touch that energy. It's like a black hole in space. It is a cosmic principle that consumes what is being created. Human beings can tune in to that principle as the Nazis did. It feeds off what victims generate. It's evil in that sense."*

There were agreements made among those of us in that massive group soul of Holocaust victims, agreements to come back in together, to distrust and resist authority, especially governmental and religious authority, to not participate in making war, to gather together and trust each other, to live together and take care of each other. A good portion of the cultural revolution of the sixties and seventies was motivated by agreements made in this group of souls that came back together. There was a strong feeling of alienation and loneliness in these souls, causing us to seek out each other, come together, and live according to our own lights—to make love, not war.

Varda and I had been together in this previous life, perhaps cousins. We made an agreement to be together, to love each other, to have a child together, although we both were still so traumatized in this current life that we were unable to fully love each other and stay married.

As long as the situation in Europe was unresolved, this vast throng of grieving souls hovered around in terror and confusion concentrating on the Holocaust. When the war came to an end and the truth of the Nazi terror was fully revealed, we were free to seek rebirth.

I was looking around for a place to be reborn and contacted the spirit of my mother, who was the beautiful, well-loved daughter of a well-to-do family in upstate Pennsylvania, a safe and secure setting for rebirth. I was surprised at who my father was to be when he returned from the war to rejoin his bride, but I had karmic ribbons to burn with him as well. They moved to Baltimore and he began to work for the Baltimore Bank for Cooperatives, a division of the Federal Land Bank, which would be his career for thirty years. Conditions were as safe as they were going to be, and I moved in on their lovemaking and precipitated conception. I wanted to be with my mother. On a subtle level my father felt manipulated by both me and my mother, and there was always tension between us, for we were on different soul levels.

Joanna took me meticulously through the memory of conception, each month of gestation and the birth trauma. My mother was heavily drugged before delivery, and I came into the world in a numbed, passive state. I was put into a nursery with lots of other newborn babies and didn't see my mother for three days. I wondered if I had killed her.

I came right back in to my current parents with all my unresolved fear and terror, anger and grief, still raw and reactive. Though I was eagerly expected, much loved, and always told what a wonderful child I was, in fact I was a terrible baby, I later found out, howling and screaming for the first six months of my life. My mother was a modern mother, not breast feeding me, instead putting me on a rigid schedule of formula feeding. Apparently I was hungry and unhappy all the time, until finally the doctor told her to feed me on demand and I grew fat and happy, or at least became a more contented baby. But the cause of my howling and screaming was much deeper than the lack of nurture. It was fear and terror from my previous incompleted life on Earth.

The majority of SPIRITS using BODIES on planet earth this lifetime have entered into HYPNOTIC AGREEMENTS that they CANNOT DESTROY A THOUGHT — CAN CREATE WITH THOUGHT. Old thought-form recordings of the past thus become indestructible to these SPIRITS. This makes KARMIC recordings possible and all the other wild invariables of the TIME GAME.

Many have questioned past lives because they cannot see the pictures or be AWARE of the recordings. However, as you begin to regain your AWARENESS and KNOWINGNESS as the TOTAL SELF, past-life areas with heavy emotional charges that relate to this lifetime may come into view and need to be handled and released.

TOTALITY CONCEPT 165-166 740709

THE GREAT MYSTERY CONTINUES

One of the reasons that mystery novels are so appealing and satisfying is that the reader knows when one begins the book that no matter what happens, no matter who gets killed, betrayed, or destroyed, there will be a solution to the mystery by the end. In mystery novels — our modern morality plays — the natural order and harmony of things is disrupted at the beginning by an inexplicable act of violence. By the end of the story, all the underlying motives have been revealed, all the perpetrators unmasked, and the mystery solved. The bad guys die or go to jail. The good guys live free to fight another day. Wouldn't it be great if life were like this?

But we are living in a mystery much greater than any human mind could imagine. Father William McNamara says, "Life is a mystery to be lived, not a problem to be solved." In our obsession with understanding things, finding solutions, and making things work, we often fail to open up to the greater mystery of all that is.

People in the helping professions devote themselves to helping others find healing and solutions. Joanna had helped me come to a good deal of inner resolution and integration, finally triggering me to remember and reexperience my origin in a great sea of light. The ultimate mystery is revealed. All of my problems should be solved. Now I can simply proceed as Superconscious in an Earth body, creating and uncreating, unobstructed by any aberrations due to karmic recordings.

And You Too can have Health, Wealth, and Happiness through knowing the Great Mystery, the Secret of All Ages, merely for the price of a paperback book and a few hours of your attention.

Wouldn't it be nice?

Imagine reading a book where all sorts of strange and inexplicable things happen, in which you encounter all sorts of people and situations which trigger you into acting in strange and inexplicable ways, in which you are carried along compulsively by a captivating narrative such that, by the end of the book, you are more confused and miserable than when you began, and the unsolved mysteries have multiplied. Not only that, but in each sequel the situation gets worse. At the close of the latest episode you are a deformed infant, born addicted to heroin, abandoned in a dumpster in Bangkok. How long would you go on reading these books until you gave up in disgust?

Now imagine that you had no choice but to continue reading this series of books *ad infinitum,* each book a new lifetime in which you always start out as an infant. They always teach you the same things: tie your shoes, wash your hands, respect your parents. . . . And yet you are prodded to action by strange, inexplicable emotions which seem to have no origin in your present surroundings.

Still we want answers. We want solutions. The human mind wants to be able to understand everything in terms of binary code, either black or white, yes or no.

Recently a friend asked me, "Ahad, do you think that when a soul chooses to come into an incarnation, it knows the time and place of its death in that incarnation?"

I took a deep breath and my mind became extremely nebulous. "It seems to me," I said, "that the rational mind wants to set up a dichotomy for which there is a yes or no answer. It is like discussions about free will and predestination. You say the soul chooses a new incarnation. I could say that the spirit is irresistibly compelled by the winds of karma to be born again whether it likes it or not. The rational mind processes in terms of discrimination and reducing all possibilities to the simplest solution. The rational mind has to see things in *either/or* terms, as in '*Either* you believe that Jesus Christ is your Lord and Savior *or* you're going to go to hell.'

"My sense is that on the subtler levels of understanding, opposites are reconciled and even multiplied. My sense is that the universe operates in terms of *both/and,* or better still, *both/and/and/and more.* My sense is that there is free will and there is predestination and much, much more. As we become more aware, the mystery of creation seems to become more subtle and vast."

A good analogy is Spider Woman ceaselessly weaving her web.

An even better analogy might be Penelope, who had to keep her suitors at bay until her missing and presumed-dead husband Ulysses returned from his wanderings. She said she would choose herself a new man, but first she had to finish weaving her tapestry. Every day she wove on her loom, and every night she unraveled what she had woven during the day. That's one way she plays with us.

OLD LIVES' TALES

Just how real are all these past-life memories anyway?

I have always been leery of listening to psychics who spin romantic tales with the wonders of one's past lives. And yet here I was spending hours probing around in the gray mist of my subconscious looking for images from other times. I had always been skeptical of religious authorities and fixed belief systems. While respecting the rights of others to believe whatever they want, I only know what has been recognized and validated in my own experience. And here I was, digging deep for experience.

My initial recall, on top of Truchas Peak with Glory, was priceless because of its spontaneity, its overwhelming emotional force, and the fact that it was discontinuous with her Christian beliefs. If she wanted to suggest anything to my psyche, it would be opening to a personal relationship with Jesus Christ, not recalling past-life terror during the Holocaust.

Joanna was very psychic and easily could have made a fortune doing glamorous psychic readings, were it not for one consideration: she insisted that her clients arrive at their data themselves, without her interjection or suggestion. She knew that second-hand information about oneself would always be suspect and only relatively useful, as compared with the certainty and knowingness that come with information one discovers oneself.

Joanna's mission was to trigger others to be aware of being Super-conscious functioning in an Earth-plane body. As such, the focus of her work was to assist people in developing their superconscious awareness and ability levels. As Superconscious, one can be aware of past-life recordings without being reactively affected by them. As Superconscious, one has the ability to create and uncreate, to disintegrate existing subconscious recordings and create new blueprints for life, should one so choose. She was not so much interested in the information derived as she was in seeing one develop superconscious ability and awareness. Joanna spent long hours, which seemed like eternities, waiting for me to come up with pictures on my own that she could already see.

Does the uncovering of past-life memories mean that each one of us is an individual immortal spirit with memories of lifetimes stretching back over thousands of years? Not necessarily so. That is another discussion.

What is real, therapists are finding out, is that there do exist in the subconscious anomalous and autonomous complexes of images with affect that do seem to effect our lives very strongly, as demonstrated by the very real changes that take place in people's lives should these images be uncovered and released. There is no temporal continuity to these memories, as there is with present-life memories, so we could say that these memories are temporally discontiguous, outside conventional linear time.

It really doesn't matter what your beliefs are about past lives and such. The fact is that these temporally discontiguous memories do exist in subconscious, no matter how they got there, and do affect us. Great healing can take place when these memories are recovered and integrated into the whole person. That doesn't mean that one should rush right out and go into past-life regressions. There are so many wonderful things to do in life other than be in therapy. But don't be surprised if and when such temporally discontiguous memories do start to arise in your common presence. It could be the beginning of a deep healing experience.

When asked about past lives, Buddha replied that theoretical discussions of the existence or non-existence of a soul between lives or in previous lives do not tend to lead toward liberation. Yet Buddha also related many charming and instructive stories about his own previous incarnations in the *Jataka Tales*.

In the East, an endless round of incarnations — recycling the soul on the wheel of birth and death — is taken for granted. In the West, the religious party line tends to be that each soul lives only one life, dies only one death, and then awaits resurrection on the Day of Judgment. For a Christian there can be no past-life memories because there are no past lives.

John G. Bennett, a pupil of Gurdjieff and Ouspensky and a teacher in that line, proposes another way of looking at this in *The Dramatic Universe, Volume Three*. He theorizes that just as the physical body is composed of a unique combination of physical genetic elements inherited from the parents, so the psychic body, which we like to call soul, is composed of a unique combination of psychic elements drawn from what he calls the Soul Stuff Pool, which is an etheric reservoir of all the memories, impressions, and feelings of mankind. The soul is seen as a transitory combination of psychic elements which, just like the physical body, serves as a vehicle for Spirit in human incarnation. Body and soul are enlivened by Spirit, but body and soul are transitory and ephemeral, whereas Spirit is immortal and eternal. Therefore, we have past-life memories but no past lives.

This is in accord with a basic tenet of this line of work, which is that ordinary man has no permanent Self. There is an opportunity, a chance for permanent self, through engaging in the work of this line.

When the ordinary good man dies, he does go to heaven. But it is an illusory heaven composed of elements of his psyche, which he enjoys for a period of time until these elements dissipate and disappear, as does he.

Spirit coming anew into the Earth plane first picks up psychic elements from the Soul Stuff Pool to form a psyche, and then finds itself attracted to a man and a woman who will blend their genetic material in the conception of a new incarnation. Here we have a rationale for the presence of past-life memories without having lived past lives.

Elements held in subconscious memories, whether we call them feelings, pictures, recordings, engrams, or archetypes, influence our conscious life much more than most of us are aware of. Psychologists document how traumatic experiences can be automatically pushed into subconscious, especially with young children, if the experience is too severe to deal with. They also document how repressed or suppressed emotions don't go away but fester and grow in subconscious. By being unacknowledged and unintegrated into the whole personality, repressed emotions gain strength and independence in secrecy, so that when they erupt into the outward life, they emerge with a strength and autonomy of their own, unmodified by the whole personality.

Repressed feelings and traumatic experiences in subconscious can cluster together through irrational association of feeling and image to form what are called autonomous complexes in the subconscious — complexes of feeling and thought which operate autonomously from the outward personality. Scientology uses the colorful term *demon circuits* to describe complexes of thought and feeling that act together autonomously as if they were a demon possessing the person, when in reality they are nothing more than associations of thought and feeling.

The point is that if your life has become unmanageable and unbearably painful, you could stop drinking, stop thinking, and stop stinking — you could turn your life over to a Higher Power, to God in any and every name and form. But if that and all else fails to bring peace to your soul, you could start exploring the contents of your subconscious, preferably with expert help, to see what might be affecting your outward life from within you. And if you find discontiguous, extemporal, anomalous memories, pictures, and feelings in your subconscious, don't worry about where they came from, just get rid of them and clear the space.

Or you could sit down and start spinning out, writing out, the romance of your glorious past lives, as some have done. This may be illuminating, entertaining, and even profitable, but be careful — it may not tend toward liberation.

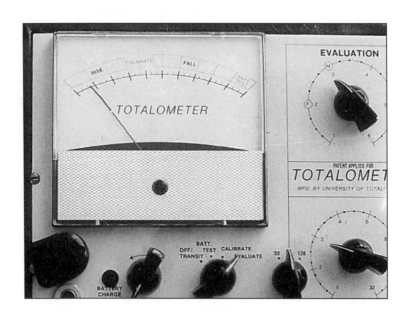

HER STORY—RICKY—
THE WORK ACCELERATES

After I began working with people, I earned a reputation. I had a hairdresser in Del Marina, Dorothy, and she told me that another client of hers had a little boy that the psychiatrists wanted to do a prefrontal lobotomy on.

I said, "Oh, heavens, that's awful. What's the matter with the child?"

"They don't seem to know," she said. "I told the mother about you, and you will probably get a call from her."

The woman called me. She didn't understand anything that I had to do.

I said, "I have to talk to the child."

"You can't talk to him. He stutters."

The child's spirit came to me and said, "I've been trying to get this child to you and finally I've done it. Now this is an exceptional person, and you know exactly what to do for him. He does not need a prefrontal lobotomy."

OK.

The child came to the phone. He did not stutter.

I said, "Ricky, my name is Joanna. Do you want to come talk with me?"

He said, "Can I come right now?" He wasn't stuttering.

"A Saturday morning would be a nice time for you to come with your parents. I want them to be here too, and we'll find out what they say is wrong with you. We'll find out if there's anything wrong with you."

He was eating clothes. He was stuttering. He was blinking. This poor child's whole system was out of kilter. The whole biology, everything about him, was out of kilter. His parents didn't know what to do with him. They had taken him to a psychiatrist. They had taken him to a private school in Texas. He had no academic record. He was about ten when he came to me.

I sat down on the floor with him and had his parents sit over in the corner. And I looked at that child, his big brown eyes, and I was guided to say to him, "Ricky, tell me what you know, honey, tell me what you know."

"I know I'm in Holland."

There was the whole case, wasn't it?

"I know I'm in Holland. Sometimes I'm in LA. I'm the father in Holland. My father here in LA is my child. My mother is my child. My sister is my wife."

There it was.

Now it's a matter of getting his attention into present time. Hadron and I had worked on a technique that we called "present-time orientation technique."

This involved taking a book and handing it to the child.

"What is this?"

"This is a book."

"Where is the book?"

"It's here right now."

"Oh, that's nice. It's not in Holland?"

"No. It's here."

"Go to the door. Touch the door."

Give him my hand. Everything in present time.

The child acknowledged that that's here, that's right now.

Then I took him to Holland, and I said, "What's going on in Holland?"

"Oh, we're well-to-do people. I have my family and I love my family and they love me. We're very happy in Holland. And then sometimes I find I'm in LA. That's very disturbing to me. I don't know who I am. I don't know why I'm here. I don't know anything."

By the time I got through with that first session the parents were crying. I was crying. And Ricky stood up and recited Omar Khayyam poetry. Wow! Is that who we've got here?

Then he looked at me and said, "I know who you are."

I didn't ask. With children, they'll tell you something if they want to tell you, and if they don't, don't ask.

At the next session, he came in with a little bust of Nefertiti. He gave it to me and said, "This is who you are."

I had already remembered that I was and I acknowledged it. I said, "Yes, I am."

"Oh," he said, "you were a great lady."

And he told me that I had died unhappy. He told me what I had already remembered. I didn't think he was picking it up off me, that I was trying to bring the One-God concept to the people of Egypt and they didn't buy it. They wanted all those little gods that they had. That made me very unhappy. I died with a whole lot of gold and no recognition. And of course I had this Amenhotep IV [Hadron].

And Ricky said to me, "Am I going to keep on working with you?"

"Yes—because we have to get you ready to go to school."

I did not teach him any academics. I taught him that he is Superconscious and that he knows, and that he knows that he knows. That's what I taught him.

In Holland he was a father in a previous life experience?

I helped him to understand that that was a previous life and this was now this life. That was then and this is now. You go back and forth. Now that's then. Be there. And be here. And then the present-time orientation technique. And he came right up.

Did you find out why he was in that past life? Was it that good?

He came back with the same family. They restimulated each other, all the same people.

Was this the first time that someone's spirit had come to you?

Yes, that was the very first time.

After that I said, "If any spirit or anybody's gonna come to me from any other dimension, I want to be sure." So I began to get a tickling in the throat when I was working with someone, and I would recognize that

that was a grandmother of someone I was working with, or a former husband. Then the tickling would stop if I got the right person and got the communication. That satisfied me, because I wasn't about to go into this channeling stuff that people do — not that it isn't valid in many ways, but not for me. I need certainty in my work. I need everything to be sure. I don't want to make any mistakes. I'm working with people. It's important.

I said to this mother, "Take him to this private school."

"The child has no academic record," she says, "I'm not going to take him to that school."

I said, "I'll take him, as long as you agree to pay for him."

"Of course. But you didn't teach him academics."

"No. But I taught him how to know and to know that he knows. And this person Omar Khayyam certainly knows how to know."

I took him to the school.

The headmaster said, "Where's his academic record?"

"We don't have one," I said.

"But how can you register this child in our school?"

I said, "I tell you to give this child the exams for his age level and see what happens."

He passed. He passed thoroughly. They got together, the headmaster and the teachers.

"What did you do with this child?"

"I taught him to know that he is a superconscious being outside of time, that that is the real being, the consciousness of the being, and it gives his body what to know. You gave him tests. He could pass because his Superconscious gave him the information."

"Never heard of such a thing! What is this gobbledygook? What is this, black magic?"

"Black magic, if that's what you want to call it, but it works. That's all I have to say to you people. You ought to understand how to do these things that I do."

And it works. He went on to become an exchange student in math in Japan. He's up in the Bay Area now. His mother writes to me. He corresponds. What am I talking about? I'm saying that there is a way to help this human race.

We used to have meetings on Sunday evenings in our auditorium. We had met this man who was doing some phenomenal work with plants. He discovered that plants have emotions. He had done experiments and had written a book about it. He is well known. We invited him to speak that evening and it drew a nice group. About a hundred people came. Ricky's parents came with Ricky.

The man explained what he does with flowers and how they have emotions. If he puts anger on them they wilt. If he gives them love they come alive. That was such wonderful information to have. Then Hadron got up and talked about Totality. And I went to the podium to give the meditation for the evening.

I get up to the podium and Ricky's spirit comes in almost plus density. I thought maybe people could see him.

His spirit said, "I want to talk to these people."

"How are you going to do that?" I said.

"With Ricky."

"Ricky's fast asleep on his mother's shoulder."

"Just tell Ricky that he wants to talk to the people."

And I did. He got up and came toward the podium. His mother tried to hold him back because she couldn't understand what he was doing. He came up to the podium and stood there looking ten feet tall, this little boy of about eleven years of age.

He said to the people, "Do you think you're a body of blood and skin and bones and hair? You're not." Coming from this little kid. I hadn't been teaching him about Totality. I had enough to get him to know that he knows. He says, "You are a total being, whole and complete." This spirit was talking through Ricky and sounding off. I have a recording of it somewhere. "Please wake up," he said. "Please wake up, people of Earth. You need to wake up. You need to evolve. Where you're at now is not good."

He was saying that. The spirit was talking. I had tears in my eyes. Hadron had tears in his eyes. The audience had tears in their eyes. He said a few other profound things, almost like Hadron or I would be talking. Then when he was finished he bowed his head and said, "Thank you."

This little boy walked off, sat down, and fell asleep on his mother's shoulder again. The applause was thundering. Here I was so afraid to call on him, because what if it didn't happen. I'd be sticking my neck out in front of a hundred people. I was really hesitant. But that spirit was very very definite that I was going to do this for him. It created quite a furor. It got around town. The father and the mother are known in the Jewish circles. I understand from the mother that they're still talking about it.

When we became a church legally, I said to Hadron, "Please, you take the church. I really don't want to because I don't particularly care for church. I'll take the children."

I would sit on the floor with the kids in a nice office room that we had and the thought occurred to me: I said, "Who wants to play the game *I know/I don't know*. Raise your hand if you can say *I know* and raise your hand when it's *I don't know*. So there were a few kids that didn't know. Most of the kids said they know.

I said, "There's only one rule to this game. Whatever anybody doesn't know or whatever anybody knows, we do not tell them that it's not right. We don't invalidate them. That's the one rule of the game."

I did not talk down to these children. I spoke as I would to any adult. This is what came to me to do with these children. Each one would put his hand up and say he knew something — what happened in school or with his friends or with a parent. Each one would tell what they know. Pretty soon the kids who said that they didn't know when they started said, "I know something." And they could know something, which I was so thrilled with.

Then this little three-year-old, Julie, said, "I know something."

"What do you know?"

"I was not born through Mommy."

Oh boy, she almost got invalidated.

"What do you mean? Julie said she wasn't born through Mommy."

I didn't allow questions like this.

She said, "It was up there."

"Was it on another planet?"

"I was up there. We don't get born through mommies."

Those kids were out there in space before anyone could say *I do*. I mean it. They were out there with realizations and awarenesses of what was happening on other planets. I said to myself, *"My goodness, look what I did with these children. Knowing."* That was one session, kindergarten.

Then Julie said, "I can't go to the bathroom."

"Julie, send your mother the information. Tell her."

"She's in the church."

"That's right. You just tell her. Think it at your mommy that you have to go to the bathroom."

I wanted to see what happened with the kids.

Mommy comes out: "Julie, you have to go to the bathroom."

I explained to them how that could happen, that we could do that if we decided to. We could do unusual things, we could do different things than what we do all the time. So Mommy came and took Julie to the bathroom. That was it.

That's what began to happen. One woman, a very wealthy woman, came to me.

She said, "My husband died and left me with the two children."

"But you've got a lot of money."

"Yeah."

In the session, the husband came and tickled my throat.

I said, "Who are you?"

He said, "I'm her husband and I want to tell her something. I told her how to do business in the stock market, to make investments and everything. I did not leave her without any way that she could support herself and the children and the home. But I got cancer. I had other things to do, and I'm here getting ready to do them."

She said, "What is he talking about?"

"Your husband said he had other things to do besides staying in an Earth body and making money."

I told her everything as he was saying it to me. And that she should forgive him. And that she should go ahead and make investments, but listen to him, so that she could continue making a lot of money. So she cried, I mean, grief, she cried.

She said, "Tell him to forgive me."

He said, "I forgive her, of course. She didn't understand."

Then she proceeds to meet a man who is in the shaman religion.

I looked at him said, "What are you doing in this shaman religion?"

He said, "Well, it's something that appeals to me and I like it."

"Do they like your money?"

"I suppose."

They had an Indian wedding, which to me was unbelievable. They had this pipe, and they got to smoking, and then they got rocks, and they got a whole lot of ritual, which I've never cared for. I attended this wedding. Then they go to California and they get married in the church. They come back, and the shamans tell him that she is not good for him. He listens to the shamans, and he leaves her and their marriage. That woman came to me in such grief.

I said, "If it wasn't for you, why stay with it? So you got married, so you went through that rigmarole. You're a beautiful young woman. You're wealthy. You've got this gorgeous home with a swimming pool inside."

I helped her to release from that, and she went on with her life. She was in grief, rejection. And by whom? Not the man she married, but some people who called themselves religion. What rights did they have? And what right did he have to accept their backup over his so-called love for her and her love for him.

How were you able to help her release her grief?

I released him. It was a former lifetime in which they were together, and that was what attracted them this lifetime.

There is an interesting thing when two people come together. If they live together they're fine but if they get married they restimulate each other's former lives when they were together before. I found that out in a number of instances.

For example, this woman comes to me. She says, "I lived with this man for six months. We love each other so much. Our sex is great. Our life is great. We both are into metaphysics. We're very happy. We go and get married, and we feel like killing each other."

That's what she told me.

I said, "Where is he?"

"He's an architect. He was giving a lecture in LA. He's probably home sleeping."

I took her back to a former life in Rome where in the Coliseum they actually killed each other! We released it.

And I said, "We're going to do something here. We're going to release it not only off of you but we're going to release it off of him."

And we released it.

She went home.

He said, "Where were you?"

She said, "I was over there with Joanna Walsh releasing the Roman Coliseum lifetime."

He said, "I felt the release."

That evening he called me and said, "I want to come over and see you."

I said, "Do you want a session? You really don't need it. We worked on you. Did you not get it?"

"Yes, I did. I want to see you. I want to meet you."

He came in with a dozen red roses in a crystal vase and hugged me and kissed me on both cheeks and thanked me.

He said, "When she came home, we went to bed and we enjoyed each other. Why, we had sex again."

So what does that say? People come together, they call it chemistry, because they want to be together, and then that marriage certificate ruins the whole thing, because that bonding, you see, it's a bind. And so they restimulated each other into that former lifetime. That is what's going on on Earth.

9

WORKING TOGETHER WITH GLORY

In all our extensive walking and talking together, Glory and I swam through oceans of inner processing, as well as juicy creative work in sacred dance and music. Glory was the first person I had ever met who I could share anything with, say anything to, hear anything from, without fear of hurting or being hurt, offending or being offended—at least until there was another woman in my life. Though we spoke very different spiritual languages, the unitive love energy between us was so strong that we were always understanding each other perfectly and finding heart agreement though logically we still had very different points of view. We had many intense discussions and arguments, but the underlying song, just like the sunlight on our bodies, was always "I love you, I love you, I love you."

If Joanna triggered me to awareness of being Totality and Super-conscious, Glory constantly coaxed forth and loved my inner child—innocent, naive, joyful, exuberant, as well as injured, hurt, angry, and sorrowful. She gave me the experience, however brief, of being totally loved by another human being, another human child, and being able to magnify and return that love. Glory was always calling me out to play in the light of day. Glory was always tugging at me and saying, "Come on, stop being Mr. Totality. Come out and be Mr. Humanity." (Stop being above it all. Come on down and be in it all.)

In one particularly dramatic session, Glory guided me to go back and be that hurt and angry child who, when I became unmanageable, was simply locked in my room without discussion, without understanding, without being held, without being touched, without being fed. At those times my rage would go global and all-consuming until finally, exhausted, I would see the wisdom of repressing my emotions and being well-behaved. I didn't know I still had them in me. I thought I had been certified, released and, cleared of all that stuff. But Glory took me back to that locked room and held me and loved me while all the unhealed rage and grief of a very young child was finally allowed to come out and be heard and be held and be healed by her love. She was holding me, loving me, telling me that Jesus was holding me and loving me. Why should I doubt her?

Glory also taught me about forgiveness, about the necessity of forgiving all in order to be whole and complete. I was holding on to anger, resentment, and rage against a number of people in my life, starting with my father and ending with someone in our community who had betrayed my trust in our friendship and turned my confidences to him against me. Glory showed me that holding on to anger against anyone created a dark spot, a black spot, a tightly clenched spot in the heart, like a fist of darkness, and that in forgiving others we are asking God to relax, open up, wash clean, and illuminate those dark spots in our hearts. The arrogant ego may sneer at forgiving others as being a weak act, when in fact forgiving others is one of the strongest and highest actions we can do for our true self. Forgiveness loosens our hearts from the anger, rage, and hatred that imprison, that constrict and confine, and opens our hearts to the light and love, to the wholeness and completion that is our true nature.

Being with Glory opened my heart up enough to hear the truth of what she was saying, that only by truly forgiving others can we begin to forgive ourselves, to let go of the tight, dark spots where judgments against ourselves — self-blame and self-hatred — have concentrated and hardened their poisons. Only a pure heart is truly a loving heart. The heart is purified by intending to forgive ourselves and others and asking God's love and mercy to wash our hearts clean of hatred for ourselves and others. My heart was so wide open in love being with Glory that I could directly perceive the truth of what she was saying and begin the long but not impossible task of forgiving those whom I held anger against and forgiving myself for all my shortcomings. It may sound strange, but forgiving myself and others is the most truly selfish thing I can do.

Glory was interested in me, so she was interested in my work with Joanna. I guided her through a good number of Totalizing sessions, always out in the open, out in the wild, under trees at the edge of a meadow, at the edge of a lake, on a steep, remote mountainside. Being the Christian that she is, Glory didn't necessarily buy any of Joanna's language or philosophy, but she was psychically very open to being guided to bring healing to various aspects of her own psyche. Whereas I work slowly and deeply on a psychic level, Glory worked quite rapidly and intensely and sometimes grew impatient with me. She could really turn on the somatics, as Joanna would say, meaning that she would have very intense physical reactions, such as weeping, shaking, dry heaving and so on, when the awareness of traumatic incidents was brought into present time.

I faithfully transmitted the languaging and methodology that Joanna had given me for these sessions, but Glory always wanted to introduce elements of her own knowingness. In particular, she would not want to erase the picture of the traumatic previous incident and make a new blueprint of pictures to give to the subconscious to react out into her life. She always wanted to put Jesus there with her in the traumatic incident and know Jesus was there with her. She wanted to put her awareness of God's love holding her into all of the dark corners of her life. One time she asked me to pretend to be Jesus and hold her and welcome her into the world. And then she pretended to be Jesus, holding Glory and welcoming her into the world. Glory did not stick with the program in the way I had been taught. But after all, it was her session and she was getting her results for herself. I was just there to facilitate. Working with her taught me a lot about working directly from intuition rather than from learned technique.

When Glory and I first came together, all our hearts could yearn for was getting away from everyone so we could be alone. We nourished escapist fantasies of leaving it all behind and running away to Mexico. The picture of Glory and Ahad together, radiant, loving, and happy, was always part of the blueprint I was impressing on my subconscious. No matter how impossible it seemed, I kept seeing us together. And for a long time Glory knew I was doing this and made no objection. But by now we were four years into the process and Glory was still a very married woman. Finally she objected to me holding this strong picture of the two of us being together. She said it felt like I was using sympathetic magic and working voodoo on her. And I had to agree.

As long as we both were holding the picture of being together, it seemed fine to see the image of our heart's desire, to give the picture to God and see what might happen. When she felt like *I* was doing something to *her*, over and against her, no matter how subtle, I had to give it up right away, for I certainly don't want the karma of forcing my will on another person. I've done that too many times. Enough already.

Now Glory was saying, "I just wanted to play with you. I never thought I would fall in love with you. You have to find a girlfriend, someone who can take care of your physical needs. I can't take care of your sexual needs. You have to find another girlfriend."

GETTING TOGETHER WITH LYNN
June 13, 1986

Meanwhile back on the Earth plane, the karmic clock kept ticking and another woman entered my life — the other woman entered my life. It all began with me doing something different.

For the first time since leaving Lama Foundation two and a half years ago, I went back to the mountain to live and work with the community for a week. Then at the end of the week, on Friday morning, I set off to climb Flag Mountain, an 11,600-foot peak, 3,000 feet above Lama. It was a glorious day, with clear blue skies. As I climbed to the ridge all my ordinary thoughts and worries came up and fell away. As I walked along the ridge my mind opened to the sky. Shabbas songs and zikrs sung around my head and blew away in the wind. Before long I was above the world in pure space listening to songs beyond words, awareness beyond thought. Superconscious walking meditation.

By the time I came down from the peak, ten hours of solid walking later, my body was tired and my soul was at peace. It was late in the afternoon just before sunset. I met my old friend Lynn and she asked me if I would be the rabbi that night, if I would lead the song and prayers at the communal Shabbas feast. I said I would be happy to if she would light the candles, if she would be the Shabbas bride. Little did I know.

We sat together late into the night, bathed in the glow of the Shabbas candles, filled with the glow of the Shabbas wine. I felt such strong love flowing from her to me, and I flowed love right back to her. She must have had her eye on me for some time. I was really ready for a woman who would love me with her whole body. And that she did that very night.

Apparently I had been in her pictures at certain times. She had a recurring dream in which she was seated at a table in a dark restaurant. I came out of the kitchen carrying a large covered platter, which I presented to her. I removed the cover and revealed a big ball of soft light sitting on the dish, my gift to her.

I, on the other hand, had no idea what was coming. I certainly liked Lynn and admired her but had never imagined myself in bed with her. The wine took away whatever resistances I may have had as she opened up new areas of intimacy for me. But in the morning I felt very strange. I woke up at the apex of a romantic triangle, a very uncomfortable position.

Glory was slender, blonde, and Northern. Lynn was full-figured, dark-haired, and Southern. Both were very psychic and deeply Christian.

Glory had always encouraged me to be open to having another woman in my life, one who could satisfy my sex needs. She had her own sex life with her husband. Why couldn't I have my own sex life with another woman? Perhaps it would take the edge off the intensity of the unfulfilled sexual longing in our relationship. Neither of us was prepared for how fiery and agonizing her jealousy would be.

At first I kept most of my attention on Glory and treated Lynn poorly sometimes, making no secret of my feelings about Glory or the uniqueness of our love. I didn't talk much about Lynn with Glory because she didn't want to hear about it. As Lynn became more real for me, she demanded more of my attention and loyalty, eventually asking that I stop communicating with Glory entirely, which eventually I did do. Then Lynn's father died and everything changed again. We'll come to that later.

It is very exhilarating and confusing to be passionately loved and desired by two women at the same time. But when they are jealous of each other and suffering for it, then everything you do is wrong and harmful to one or the other of them. You can't do anything right until you choose to be with one and let the other one go. I wasn't prepared to do that yet.

Besides, something felt wrong about being with Lynn. After making love with her, my body would be satisfied but my feelings were unsettled. I felt nauseous, vaguely polluted, dark, murky, and confused. As time went along I came to recognize that I was deeply afraid of this sweet, gentle woman who loved me so much. It had nothing to do with anything that was happening in present time, but sometimes in the pit of my stomach I would feel cold terror, abject fear of the ruthless power of this being next to me. I felt suffocated. She would kill me if I talked about it.

More grist for the mill. More mist from the grill.

This fantastically efficient automatic recording ABILITY of all cell structure extends through many lifetimes: CYCLES OF EXPERIENCE of BIRTH — SURVIVAL — DEATH.

The CELLS of each type of BODY at the end of each CYCLE retain as THOUGHT-FORM recordings all the THOUGHTS, EMOTIONS, and EFFORTS involved in that experience.

The SPIRIT — the CELLULAR INTELLIGENCE — entering a new CYCLE OF EXPERIENCE takes the old THOUGHT-FORMS as blueprints and builds them into ENERGY PATTERNS of structure. This new BODY is built with additional COUNTER-EFFORTS to make it SURVIVE in spite of the old recordings.

BODY STRUCTURE is created from OLD RECORDINGS OF PAST EXPERIENCES plus the addition of NEW SURVIVAL FACTORS which seek to enable the body to exist in spite of the environment which destroyed it.

TOTALITY CONCEPT 171 740710

FIRST RELEASE ON LYNN
August 11, 1986

Lynn loved me, wanted me, desired my light in her life. Yet how could she be comfortable with this situation? She had the love of my body, sexually, but all too much of my heart was still given to Glory. My attention was not fully present to Lynn, something I unkindly made little effort to hide at first. "Why do I always set up triangles for myself?" she said. Lynn was much more psychically aware than I was of the karmic ties bringing us together yet again. She told me that she had sacrificed me in two past lives, once as a man and once as a woman. She also had an image of an Indian woman putting a knife through her baby in a bath.

After making love with Lynn, I felt drained of energy. I felt passivity, darkness, and confusion. Sometimes, riding along in a car with her, hanging out in what should have been comfortable silence, I would feel nameless dread, overwhelming terror, as if some dark, devouring rage might destroy me at any moment. This was clearly a case for Mama Totality, who was always generously open to working with me on my endlessly arising issues.

I went in to have a session with Joanna. She led me through the Totalizing Meditation until I was in a very refined state of consciousness. Then she directed my superconscious to ask my subconscious to show me the recorded pictures it held that were causing blockage with Lynn.

At first I saw a very large, round, female face hovering over me, long, wild, dark hair, crazed eyes, huge, wide, devouring mouth. Next I felt stabbing pains in my chest, in my heart. Then I moved fully into the picture.

It was in Mexico, two hundred years ago. I was a handsome young Spanish gentleman betrothed to the daughter of a wealthy family. She was fair-skinned, dark-haired, with ample breasts and a very feminine figure—in fact, very much like Lynn today, except she wore one of those white Mexican dresses with the colorful embroidery. She was passionately attached to me, her fiancé, and to the success of this arranged marriage. Though I was pleased with her as well, I felt smothered and confined. The passionate longing of my heart was given to a wild dancing girl, slender, brown-skinned, with long, wavy, shining copper hair and flashing green eyes—someone whose energy was very much like Glory, not surprisingly. We planned to run away together, away from the constraints of civilization and religion, and live free in the wild. Unfortunately my fiancée was sensitive enough to pick up on all these undercurrents and became insanely jealous. If she couldn't have me, nobody would. As I lay sleeping in a big canopied bed in her father's hacienda, she came to me in the middle of the night and, making sure that I was awake enough to know what was happening, stabbed me through the heart, a quick and almost painless exit.

There it was, the recurring karmic triangle: Lynn and I still triangulated by the dancing girl who I would really rather be with, and me still terrified of her jealous rage. Clear karmic recurrence. *Rnanubandhana*, the bonds of karmic debts.

Next Joanna directed me to ask to be shown the pictures of the first time that Lynn and I had been together on Earth. I got a picture of your basic caveman reality, somewhere in Europe, Germany, during the Ice Ages. I was a big ol' caveman and she was my woman. I came back to the cave one day and found her letting some other caveman fuck her. I wasn't too happy about that. I grabbed her away and beat her up so she could know how I felt. I guess I didn't know the strength of my enraged male body. The next thing I knew I had beat the life out of her and I had no more woman. That made me very sad. I had loved her in some primitive way. I just wanted to let her know how I felt. That was the beginning of what goes around comes around.

Then Joanna had me scan forward along the time track and let all the times and locations Lynn and I had been together come to my awareness. As I scanned forward I saw event locations in Mesopotamia, India, Greece, Mexico, Palenque. . . .

I saw the two of us standing together by the broad river in Mesopotamia. We were brother and sister. I loved my older sister, but felt uncomfortable with her control over me. A lifetime familial relationship.

In India she was a big, fat, handsome prince, and I was in his harem, the most beautiful of his many wives. The other wives were jealous of me because I received more of his attention, and yet I was not all that happy with the attention I was receiving from him because he was very rough and bestial in his sexual desires. He used me and abused me as the object of his affections. When I became unresponsive he would get enraged, slap me around, and force even rougher sex on me. I was the number-one sex slave, living in fear of my husband and all of the other wives. When he died, I was thrown on the funeral pyre and burnt up with him, as was the custom. Another one bites the dust.

In Greece we were married and had children. I was a carpenter, a peaceful citizen, and she was a wild woman. She went out and ran with the Maenads under the full moon — women whipped up into the wildness of Pan-frenzy, dancing, drinking, carousing, hunting, tearing apart living beings and eating their raw flesh. I was terrified of this destructive energy and fearful for our children. I was solid, stoic, and conservative in this lifetime. She burned herself out. I outlived her and died in peace.

In Palenque there she is on top of a pyramid, a priest in full regalia, stabbing me, the sacrificial victim, in the chest, ripping out my heart and holding it on high.

Another time on top of another pyramid in Mexico, there I am, a priest in full regalia, stabbing her, the sacrificial victim, in the chest, ripping out her heart and holding it on high. What goes around keeps coming around again and again and again.

Joanna's notes complain, *"How many more lifetimes?"*

PRETENDING to be DIVIDED and be OTHER THAN TOTALITY is the GAME played by spirits, bodies, planets, universes, etc.

The PRETENDED SEPARATENESS is a DIRECT ASSIGNMENT of TOTALITY.

The OTHERNESSES or SPIRITS, the ASSIGNED SEGMENTS of TOTALITY, at first played the GAME fully AWARE of the PRETENDING.

Then gradually, in the playing of the GAME, there is a FORGETTING, there is a PRETENDING.

At the present state of the GAME
   it has been FORGOTTEN
     there is a FORGETTING
      there is a PRETENDING
       to be OTHER THAN —
        the TOTAL PRESENCE of SELF — TOTALITY.

TOTALITY CONCEPT 690814

KNOWING & NOT KNOWING, PRETENDING & FORGETTING
October 4, 1986 – October 23, 1986

With infinite love and patience, Joanna worked with me for years on the issues ceaselessly arising from my own never-ending story. In the balance, though, she often called me in to have sessions and work on what I would call her own agenda for me, which was always opening to greater awareness of being Superconscious, of having knowingness, of releasing not-knowingness, pretending, and forgetting. She had taught me her methods.

She had made me a Minister of Totality. I was working with other people using her methods. She wanted to open me to the same awarenesses and abilities that she and Hadron had experienced.

The basic paradigm is that as Totality, as Superconscious, one has Total Awareness and Total Ability to create and uncreate realities to experience and enjoy. As Superconscious one creates infinite realities, cosmoses, galaxies, solar systems, planets, life species, races, nations, tribes, families, individualities, etc., to experience and enjoy exquisite identification with particular energies and forms in defined game plans.

Creation and uncreation are the two primary abilities of Totality. The postulate is that *agreements create realities.* Agreements within and among Superconscious create realities to experience and enjoy. When there is no longer agreement to experience a particular reality, that virtual reality simply ceases to exist — or, as is more often the case, the created form persists or lingers, absent the vivifying energy that engendered it.

This postulate, *agreements create realities,* is an excellent touchstone for the validity of human relationships. In those areas that you and I are in agreement, consciously or unconsciously, including agreement to disagreement or antipathy, our relationship is real. In those areas where there is no agreement, consciously or unconsciously, between you and me, there is no reality to our relationship. And, of course, agreements are always subject to change and always changing.

The paradigm continues. At a certain point one decides to make the game more interesting by pretending to forget that one was the creator of all these realities, thereby pretending to have total identification with these realities, total identification with the role that each player is playing — and then further pretending to forget that one can create each of these realities with a thought. It's kind of like we wrote the script, we memorized the script, then we ate the script and swallowed it — and forgot all about writing it, or even that there was a script in the first place. It's your basic "Life's a bitch and then you die." (Which is the basic Saturn complaint. Jupiter, however, quips "Life's a beach and then you fly.")

Joanna would often say to me, "Now is the time to remember that you pretended to forget that you are Totality, that you are Superconscious.

"Now is the time to remember that you pretended to forget, then you pretended to forget that you pretended to forget, and so on down the line of pretending, until you have ended up almost totally forgetting that you pretended to forget in the first place. You have ended up forgetting who you really are. Now you are pretending to be totally caught up in this game, this virtual reality you have created, and you think there's no way out. You're terrorized, overwhelmed with fear. You did a really good job of pretending to forget and then forgetting that you pretended to forget!"

A great deal of emphasis was placed on remembering the original impulse, the original decision, to make the game more interesting by pretending to forget. And a great deal of emphasis was placed on releasing pretending.

"Do more remembering. Release pretending and forgetting. When we do not function as Superconscious we are pretending not to — and forgetting is the key. Remember again."

Another major quality Joanna worked on with me at length was knowingness, superconscious knowingness, direct intuitive knowingness — not to be confused with the "stinking thinking" of the rational mind, whose job is to understand and manipulate reality on a material level. The development of the rational gets most, if not all, of the attention of what passes for education in our culture, while direct intuitive knowingness is generally not only unacknowledged and undeveloped, but it is actively resisted and invalidated when it arises on its own.

209

Direct intuitive knowingness is superconscious awareness operating in our lives if we are open to receive it. Direct intuitive knowingness can operate on a very simple level, such as the first impression you receive when you meet someone, or on a very deep and complex level, such as the inner knowingness that unerringly guides some people to live out their destined role, even as it seems to elude many more people lost in the dream of an ordinary life.

It is said that first impressions are lasting ones. On an ordinary level this is an admonition to wash your hair, brush your teeth, dress in style, and be on your best behavior, especially when you go for a job interview or go out on a first date. On the other hand, if our minds are unclouded by worldly desires ("How can this person serve to get me a little more money? sex? power?"), worries, and prejudices, when we meet another person for the first time with a calm mind and an open heart, first impressions are also true ones. We can know instantly that this new person is a beloved, a friend, an indifferent person, an enemy to us, and all sorts of subtleties immediately and intuitively apprehended on a deeper level than the conscious mind — to the degree that our minds are unclouded by anger, lust, or greed.

Joanna continually worked with me to awaken knowingness, even in the most minute ways. She made me painfully aware of how often I interject "you know" into conversations, unconsciously indicating that I was unsure of what I was saying and seeking validation from the other person. She was always questioning me, probing my Knowingness. She would never invalidate my not-knowingness but she would never allow me to stay in it. Whenever I said, "I don't know," which was often, she would say, "Thank you for not knowing. Now, tell me what you *do* know, man!"

I had lived in the psychic shadows most of my life, operating with vagueness, hesitancy, and uncertainty. My subconscious was holding pictures that knowingness can get you killed on the Earth plane. As a Persian astrologer I had had my head chopped off — for giving accurate readings and telling the truth! Written, musical, and visual expression constituted the only area of my life in which I operated with certainty, and then only in spurts and mostly in secrecy. When I left Lama, at the age of thirty-six, I didn't even know how to survive in what is most commonly called the real world.

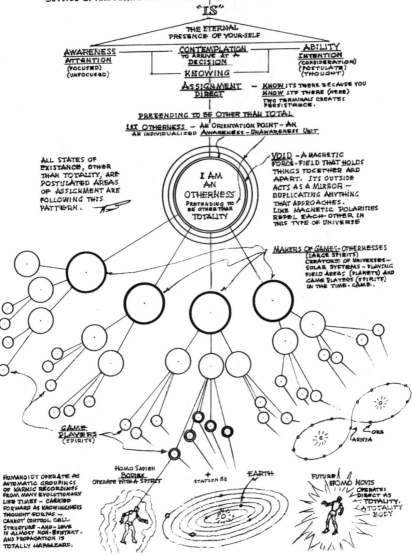

ETERNAL
NOW
I
TOTALITY

ONENESS – STILLNESS – SPACE – STATIC – YOUR-SELF
OUTSIDE OF AND PERVADING AND MAINTAINING ALL TIME GAMES AND OTHER ACTIVITIES

"IS"

THE ETERNAL
PRESENCE OF YOUR-SELF

AWARENESS — **CONTEMPLATION** — **ABILITY**
ATTENTION | TO ARRIVE AT A | INTENTION
(FOCUSED) | DECISION | (CONSIDERATION)
(UNFOCUSED) | | (POSTULATE)
| KNOWING | (THOUGHT)

ASSIGNMENT — KNOW ITS THERE BECAUSE YOU
DIRECT | KNOW ITS THERE (HERE)
| TWO TERMINALS CREATES
| PERSISTENCE.

PRETENDING TO BE OTHER THAN TOTAL

1ST OTHERNESS – AN ORIENTATION POINT – AN
AN INDIVIDUALIZED AWARENESS – UNAWARENESS UNIT

ALL STATES OF
EXISTANCE, OTHER
THAN TOTALITY, ARE
POSTULATED AREAS
OF ASSIGNMENT ARE
FOLLOWING THIS
PATTERN.

I AM AN OTHERNESS
PRETENDING TO
BE OTHER THAN
TOTALITY

VOID – A MAGNETIC
FORCE-FIELD THAT HOLDS
THINGS TOGETHER AND
APART. ITS OUTSIDE
ACTS AS A MIRROR –
DUPLICATING ANYTHING
THAT APPROACHES.
LIKE MAGNETIC POLARITIES
REPEL EACH OTHER IN
THIS TYPE OF UNIVERSE

MAKERS OF GAMES- OTHERNESSES
(LARGE SPIRITS)
CREATORS OF UNIVERSES –
SOLAR SYSTEMS – PLAYING
FIELD AREAS (PLANETS) AND
GAME PLAYERS (SPIRITS)
IN THE TIME-GAME.

GAME-
PLAYERS
(SPIRITS)

ORB
ARIVIA

HUMANOIDS OPERATE AS
AUTOMATIC GROUPINGS
OF KARMIC RECORDINGS
FROM MANY EVOLUTIONARY
LIFE TIMES – CARRIED
FORWARD AS KNOWINGNESS
THOUGHT FORMS –
CANNOT CONTROL CELL
STRUCTURE – AND – LOVE
IS ALMOST NON-EXISTENT –
AND PROPAGATION IS
TOTALLY HAPHAZARD.

HOMO SAPIEN
BODIES
OPERATE WITH A SPIRIT

STATION 88

+ EARTH

FUTURE
HOMO NOVIS
OPERATES
DIRECT AS
TOTALITY.
A TOTALITY
BODY

ETERNAL
NOW
I
TOTALITY

ONENESS – STILLNESS – SPACE – STATIC – YOUR-SELF
OUTSIDE OF AND PERVADING AND MAINTAINING ALL TIME GAMES AND OTHER ACTIVITIES

"IS"

THE ETERNAL PRESENCE OF YOUR-SELF

AWARENESS
ATTENTION
(FOCUSED)
(UNFOCUSED)

AWARE OF BEING AWARE.
AWARE OF BEING YOUR-SELF.
AWARE OF BEING TOTALITY.
AWARE OF PRETENDING.

CONTEMPLATION
TO ARRIVE AT A DECISION

KNOWING

ASSIGNMENT DIRECT

ABILITY
INTENTION (CONSIDERATION) (POSTULATE) (THOUGHT)

KNOWS IT'S THERE BECAUSE YOU KNOW IT'S THERE (HERE) TWO TERMINALS CREATES PERSISTANCE.

ABLE TO BE AWARE.
ABLE TO FOCUS ATTENTION.
ABLE TO UNFOCUS ATTENTION.
ABLE TO ASSIGN – MAKE EXIST.
ABLE TO UNASSIGN – VANISHMENT – BACK INTO TOTALITY – YOUR TOTAL SELF.
ABLE TO EXPERIENCE SENSATIONS FROM YOUR CREATIONS – ASSIGNMENTS.

AFTER A DECISION IS MADE KNOWINGNESS IS USED TO PROJECT YOUR CONSIDERATIONS OR POSTULATES TO MAKE AN ASSIGNMENT AT A LOCATION IN THE TIME – GAME

PRETENDING TO BE OTHER THAN TOTAL

IST OTHERNESS – AN ORIENTATION POINT – AN INDIVIDUALIZED AWARENESS – UNAWARENESS UNIT

VOID – A MAGNETIC FORCE-FIELD THAT HOLDS THINGS TOGETHER AND APART. ITS OUTSIDE ACTS AS A MIRROR – DUPLICATING ANYTHING THAT APPROACHES. LIKE MAGNETIC POLARITIES REPEL EACH OTHER IN THIS TYPE OF UNIVERSE

I AM AN OTHERNESS PRETENDING TO BE OTHER THAN TOTALITY

ALL STATES OF EXISTANCE, OTHER THAN TOTALITY, ARE POSTULATED AREAS OF ASSIGNMENT ARE FOLLOWING THIS PATTERN.

MAKERS OF GAMES-OTHERNESSES (LARGE SPIRITS)
CREATORS OF UNIVERSES – CONSIDERATION OF UNIVERSES – SOLAR SYSTEMS – PLAYING FIELD AREAS (PLANETS) AND GAME PLAYERS (SPIRITS) IN THE TIME – GAME.

ANCHOR POINTS – CONTAIN RULES OF THE GAMES. UNMOVING GROUPS OF POSTULATES AND ENERGY, RELATIVELY SOLID. CONTROLS FOR GROUPINGS OF SPIRITS – SOLAR SYSTEMS AND PLANETS. I.E. NATIONALITIES, PEOPLE – ANIMALS.

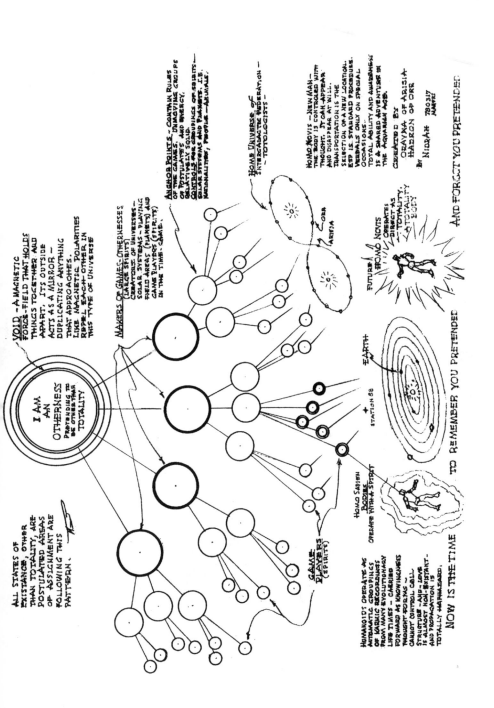

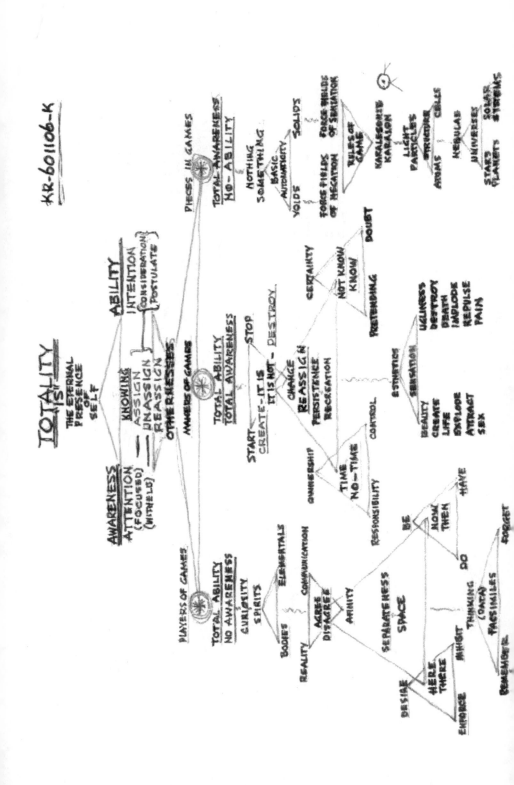

KR-601106-K

TOTALITY
IS!
THE ETERNAL PRESENCE OF SELF

ABILITY
INTENTION
{CONSIDERATION}
{POSTULATE}

AWARENESS
ATTENTION
(FOCUSED)
(WITHELD)

KNOWING
ASSIGN
UNASSIGN
REASSIGN

OTHERNESSES

PIECES IN GAMES

PLAYERS OF GAMES

MAKERS OF GAMES

TOTAL AWARENESS
NO-ABILITY

NOTHING
SOMETHING
BASIC
AUTOMATICITY
VOICES
ROBOTS

FORCE FIELDS
OF NEGATION
FORCE SHIELDS
OF SENSATION

RULES OF GAME

KARALS SONIC
KARALION

LIGHT
PARTICLES

STRUCTURE
ATOMS
CELLS

NEBULAE
UNIVERSES
STARS
PLANETS
SOLAR
SYSTEMS

TOTAL ABILITY
TOTAL AWARENESS

START — STOP
CREATE - IT IS
IT IS NOT - DESTROY
CHANGE
REASSIGN
PERSISTENCE
RECREATION

CERTAINTY
NOT KNOW
KNOW
PRETENDING
DOUBT

AESTHETICS
SENSATION

BEAUTY   UGLINESS
CREATE   DESTROY
LIFE   DEATH
EXPLODE   IMPLODE
ATTRACT   REPULSE
SEX   PAIN

OWNERSHIP
TIME
NO-TIME
RESPONSIBILITY
CONTROL

BE
NOW
THEN
DO
HAVE

TOTAL ABILITY
NO AWARENESS
CURIOSITY
SPIRITS

BODIES   ELEMENTALS
REALITY   COMMUNICATION
              AGREE
              DISAGREE
              AFFINITY

SEPARATENESS
SPACE
HERE
THERE
MUST
THINKING (DATA)
FACSIMILES
DESIRE
ENFORCE
REMEMBER
FORGET

TOTAL TIME-GAME LEGEND BY HARDIN D. WALSH, PhD, EDA, EGA, TM
OT - 601106 - FHW 760414
BEYOND IMMORTALITY

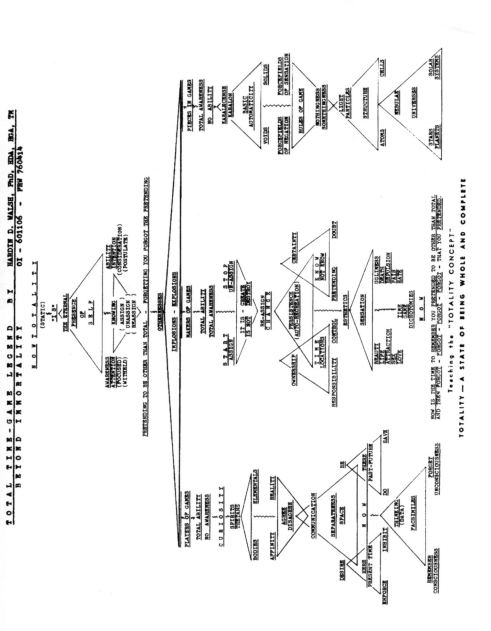

Teaching the "TOTALITY CONCEPT"

TOTALITY — A STATE OF BEING WHOLE AND COMPLETE

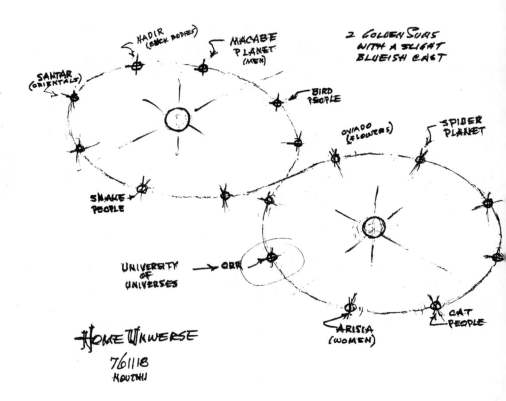

NADIR
(BLACK BODIES)

MACABE
PLANET
(MEN)

SANTAR
(ORIENTALS)

BIRD
PEOPLE

2 GOLDEN SUNS
WITH A SLIGHT
BLUEISH CAST

OVIADO
(FLOWERS)

SPIDER
PLANET

SNAKE
PEOPLE

UNIVERSITY
OF
UNIVERSES → ORR

ARISIA
(WOMEN)

CAT
PEOPLE

Home Universe
7/61/18
MOUTHN

TIME GAME — TIME MACHINE

ALL MOVING THINGS — AUTOMATICITY CYCLE —
ASSIGN — UNASSIGN — REASSIGN ←→ TIME

SOUTH
MAGNETIC
POLE

NORTH
MAGNETIC
POLE

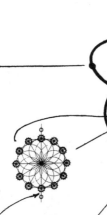

BIG WHEEL
144 VOIDS
12 GROUPS OF 12 VOIDS
ALL 3 DIMENSIONAL
UNIVERSES IN 6th VOID
THIS GROUP OF 12 VOIDS.
EARTH IN LOCAL 6th VOID
VOIDS — INVISIBLE FIXED
MAGNETIC FIELDS.

TIME TRACKS
CONTINUOUS TUBULAR VOIDS
THROUGH WHICH BIG WHEELS MOVE

6 TIME TRACKS
6 BIG WHEELS EACH TIME TRACK
36 BIG WHEELS IN 6 TIME TRACKS
5184 VOIDS IN ALL 6 TIME TRACKS

HUB — CONTROL CENTER OF TIME MACHINE
12 OTHERNESSES — "THINK TANK" MONITORS

HUB — NORTH MAGNETIC POLE — OUTER AXIS
DODECAHEDRONS — MACHINES

HUB — SOUTH MAGNETIC POLE — OUTER AXIS
TETRAHEDRONS — MACHINES

691001 — 701208

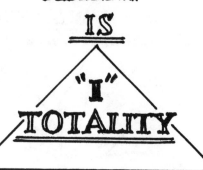

AWARENESS
ABILITY
IS

"I"
TOTALITY

IS NOT | **OTHER THAN**

IS NOT

DENIAL OF
SELF
LOSS OF
ABILITY
DENIAL OF
"BEING THERE"
CREATES
SO-CALLED
SPACE
UNKNOWINGNESS
UNAWARENESS

OTHER THAN

CREATES
OTHERNESSESS
SPIRITS
AWARENESS UNITS
VOIDS
GAME SEGMENTS
GAME PLAYERS
MYSTERY
SURPRISES

690920-KHS

Joanna educated me that the way to deal with life problems or situations was not to try to figure things out and do something about it. Get the thinking mind out of the way. Quiet the reactive emotional turmoil and, as Jesus said, be still and know. Give particular value to dreams, hunches, inspirations, and intuitive impulses. Intuition is an element of superconscious guidance. Be clear about your desires and give your pictures, your prayers, to Superconscious and allow Superconscious to materialize the results in your life. Recognize and be grateful for superconscious action in your life.

Joanna wanted to trigger a wholesale release of all forgetting and pretending. "Blow the whole karmic pattern of forgetting, from the beginning, from the first bodily experience. Postulate releasing all Earthly forgetting. The three-dimensional plane is a turn off. 'Then I forgot.' These are the key words: 'I forgot.' Release all forgetting."

A SPIRIT picking up a BODY at BIRTH brings the sum TOTAL of all his/her past experiences on the THOUGHT-FORM level.

The SPERM carries with it the sum TOTAL of FATHER'S experiences.

The OVUM carries with it the sum TOTAL of MOTHER'S past.

Thus the incoming SPIRIT winds up with a BODY which is a composite of the three groups of recorded experience.

Since SPIRITS are indestructible and move from CYCLE to CYCLE of lifetimes over centuries and millions of years, a lot of recordings are accumulated and used.

On the theories of mathematical progressions alone, EVERYONE eventually had EVERYONE ELSE'S recordings, somewhere down through the so-called ages. EVERYONE, they say, is a 57th cousin.

This is true without the FACT that as TOTALITY you are in direct contact with ALL BEINGS and ALL CELL STRUCTURES throughout all LANDS, SPACES, and CONSECUTIVE LOCATIONS known as TIME.

TOTALITY CONCEPT 173 740710

SUFFERING SUCCOTASH

I was born into a situation of material privilege and status that externally at least started me out with an advantage over the vast majority of humanity. White, Anglo-Saxon, Protestant, American male. Good schools, good mind, well-funded. What did I have to complain about? Why should I lay claim to so much suffering? My parents wondered. My mother would say to me, "I don't know why you spend so much time looking for yourself. I've never had that problem."

And yet, as Mother Teresa said, "America is the poorest nation on Earth. You suffer from a lack of love."

When I first came to Lama Foundation in 1970, my soul was awakened, opened, and challenged by many of the beings there who were passionately focused on God. Love of God, yearning for God, seeking God realization, union with God, etc., was the fundamental motivation for many of these splendid souls.

At that time I had only the faintest glimmer of the notion that God was a living reality within and throughout all creation. Mostly I was still convinced that "God" was a duplicitous "universal solvent" concept, a word that could be used to explain away everything that could not be explained away, a theoretical but unproved "final cause."

The luminous love and intelligence of Ram Dass and his friends in satsang, of my brothers and sisters at Lama Foundation, gently opened me up to greater possibilities and persuaded me to at least imitate their practices of meditation, devotion, and selfless service, to take a chance and at least pretend that I loved God and longed for God to come into my life and my heart. And indeed this did lead me to some taste of God-realization.

In retrospect I can see that my underlying motivation all along has been to relieve the incredible mental and emotional suffering that I experienced constantly. The true purpose of my use of marijuana, which I justified by claiming it brought me inspiration and understanding, was clarified when I found out that THC, the psychoactive component of marijuana, is one of the strongest pain-killers known to man.

Love, joy, ecstasy and delight, peace, wisdom, insight and understanding were all awakened in my soul through spiritual practice and community. And yet the dark sludge tide of suffering would pull me under time and time again. My work with Joanna, the realization of being present as space, of being Totality, of being Superconscious—and most important, the discovery and release of traumatic, inhibiting, and distorting emotional complexes held in subconscious—led finally to enough realization of my true nature and enough release of unnecessary suffering that I could finally in my early forties begin to function as a more or less normal human being.

The First Noble Truth of the Buddha is simply: "There is suffering" *(dukkha)*—or, in another translation, "Suffering really exists."

So much of all forms of human culture is built around denial of the truth of suffering. When I took a course in Buddhism in college, our user-friendly professor asked us what we wanted to study first about Buddhism. And of course we all said, "Enlightenment!"—which at the time we all equated with getting high on psychedelic drugs. So we all got high on the study and pursuit of enlightenment, skimming over the First Noble Truth, the foundation of Buddhism, as an academic footnote. But true awakening, not just getting high, begins with the awareness that suffering really exists in all living beings, especially human beings.

The English verb *to suffer* comes from a Latin root meaning *to bear up under.* I also like the sense of the verb in the King James translation of the words of Jesus, "Suffer the little children to come unto me," which I interpret as *allow it to happen.* Spirit that we are, we have to "bear up under" the heaviness of physical existence and "allow it to happen" to us.

The Second Noble Truth is that "The cause of suffering is attachment."

We may be in essence pure mind, free spirit, but as incarnated beings we are attached to, identified with, locked into, imprisoned in a physical form that is born, grows (growing pains), matures, declines (disease and debilitation), and dies. The Three Poisons (delusion, aversion, attachment) keep the Wheel of Time turning.

Throughout every lifetime, I Totality, pure mind, free spirit, am usually totally attached to, identified with my limited physical body, my fragile ego, my flimsy personality, my growing pains, my hopes and fears, my desires and ambitions, my aging aches and pains, and in terror of my ultimate death and non-existence.

Attachment to and identification with my own suffering tend to limit and isolate the focus of my awareness. When my awareness expands beyond the limits of my own self-identification I become aware that everyone suffers just as I do — every single living being suffers just as I do. That is what the Buddha saw.

Even the delight of sense perceptions is suffering: pure mind identified with and attached to the physical body must "bear up under," must "allow to happen," must suffer the ceaseless onslaught of the cutting edges of billions upon billions of sense perceptions. Hadron called this a "sex-and-pain universe."

Buddhist psychology exquisitely unfolds infinite subtleties of "the chain of interdependent origination" that constitutes our fleeting existence as separate self identities. This is beyond the simplicity of our discourse here.

Within the vastness of all suffering one can make a distinction between what could be called "necessary pain" and "unnecessary suffering." Pain is a necessary component of all physical embodied existence. The Buddha opened the way for all those who long to go beyond the necessary pain of physical existence, who long to get off the Wheel of Birth, Death, and Rebirth, and surrender any identification as a separate self.

Most, if not all, of what can be called unnecessary suffering is the result of automatic identification with and contraction around karmic accretions: self-identification with the consequences of wrong thought, wrong belief and wrong action; the tendency of all thoughts, beliefs, and actions to be recorded in subconscious; and general ignorance that ingrained, mental, emotional, or physical patterns can be released and replaced.

An example is commonplace neurosis, which may be defined as an adaptive behavior that once was thought necessary for the survival of the individual and which persists in present time, though it may no longer be useful or appropriate for the well-being of the individual. Perhaps "suffering that which is no longer necessary" would be a better term. This is why so much mental, emotional, and physical suffering can be alleviated and totally or partially healed through the spirit and through the loving work of the true healers among humanity. Of course some karmic consequences are so severe that they are immovable and appear to be fixed for this lifetime or perhaps even many lifetimes. But through treading the path of liberation, of right action, right thought, right practice, right belief, it is said that all karmas can be released.

Joanna believed that she had a modern, scientific, technological approach to the release of karma. She did achieve many successful results working with people over a period of thirty years, including great successes in alleviating human suffering.

I have been blessed with relatively good physical health. I have also been blessed with incredible amounts of mental and emotional suffering, which have been a great impetus in my search for truth. For thirty years I could barely relate to or deal with the suffering of others because my own pain was so great. Spiritual practice and community opened me up to a higher love, a higher power, greater joy, and greater peace, but still the dark sludge of unhealed suffering and irrational fear limited me and prevented me from leading anything resembling a normal life. The inner work Joanna shared with me revealed and healed enough of the hidden suffering in my psyche that my dark clouds began to lift and I could see things more as they really are — and I could feel more clearly the universality of the suffering of humanity.

By acknowledging and accepting awareness of my own necessary pain and unnecessary suffering, my heart begins to open to the reality of pain and suffering in every living being — my loved ones, my friends, my enemies, and all those who are unknown or to whom I am indifferent. My heart begins to feel quivers of compassion, of suffering with the billions of beings who have taken this precious and terrible human birth.

HER STORY—
VORTEX ENERGY—THE FOUR R'S

One day I decided, after regressing a person, that, sure, the regression serves the purpose of enabling the person to see how the past life is reacting in present time, and that's good, but I don't get the realization that it's releasing from the subconscious.

I asked Hadron one day, "What is it that makes Earth people react? It keeps them in bondage. How are we going to evolve? We're here to help Earth people evolve. How are they going to evolve if they're reacting all the time?"

He said, "I don't have that answer for you—but you ask and you shall receive."

He encouraged me.

A week later a man calls me and says, "I was given your little book *Totality Beyond Immortality*. I like it. It makes a lot more sense than most of these other positions that I hear. I'm a scientist from Germany. I'm going to tell you how I got your book. A high school teacher from Seattle came to visit the place where I am staying, and he went to the Bodhi Bookstore. He picked up your book because the cover was so pretty. He looked inside. He's a Christian Scientist, and there's no religion in it, so he put it down. He gets to the checkout stand and that book is in his hands, so he has to take it."

He has to take it and give it to Walter Baumgartener, who has the answer to why Earth people react. How do you like that for an immediate about Superconscious? To get a book into a man's hands because I asked why Earth people react! And he has the answer! Doesn't that help you to understand the miracles that you can create once you acknowledge that you are in fact Superconscious and that you have an Earth body and that you may possibly have bodies on other planets as Hadron and I do? I urge you to acknowledge it, because that's who you are, that's what we are eternally.

At that point that man called and said, "I like what you wrote in that *Totality Beyond Immortality,* and I invite you to dinner."

All right.

He was in MarVista at Joy's beautiful home, and we are in Brentwood. We rode along the ocean. We get to the home and we go into the dining room. He had fixed a German dinner, and her dining room was French: French mirrors on the ceiling, French dishes, French pictures, French everything. In she walks, this delightful person—Joy, she calls herself. She has her doctorate degree in computers. She is brilliant. She walks in. She's got this French pompadour henna-colored hair and a cute little pudgy figure. And he serves the German dinner. They ask questions about Totality. They're both scientists and they wanted to experience the techniques we had developed.

After that I said, "Walter, you're a scientist. What are you into?"

He says in his German accent, "Wortex energy."

And my hair began to stand up on edge. I was trying to figure out what the thinking left to ask him. Unh-uh, I didn't have any previous data in relation to vortex energy.

My blessed I Superconscious came in through my body and asked him, "What is the nature of this energy?"

"It's universal energy."

"What is its function?"

"Its function is to cause everything that is created to be maintained."

"Oh, that's interesting. How does it do that?"

"By being automatically reactive."

I almost blew through their ceiling, their mirrored French ceiling. I just felt myself leaving the body, because that was my question—what makes people automatically reactive, and how are they going to evolve if they're reacting to their past.

I said, "Walter, that's fine for the universe, but for humans it's a down-witch, it's a trap."

"I never thought of that," he said.

"What are you doing with it in Germany?"

"We're trying to find out how to use vortex energy as alternative energy before the planet is destroyed with their philosophy and all that stuff. I come to America. I find out you don't change the oil system. We're trying anything other than oil."

"But there's got to be another way. The planet can't tolerate that oil and gas way."

"Right."

"Have you got anything we can read?"

She had created a library for him, because they had been sending her information, and he had been studying her books and pamphlets and scientific discoveries about the vortex and how it works.

He took us in there, and he said, "Look. Anything you want is yours. You want to help people."

I said, "It would take us a hundred years to go through this information. What would you charge us to help us?"

"I wouldn't charge you anything. You want to help people."

"When can we start? It's very important that we find out how we can release people from being automatically reactive."

Hadron wasn't into this at all. I was the motivator on all of this, but he did help. He made charts. He was a scientist. He understood what Walter was saying.

We got together. Walter and he are sounding off scientifically about it.

I said, "No, no, no, gentlemen. We want to find a very wonderful, simple way that we can give people so that they can do it with themselves and with each other, or they're never going to get out of that automatically reactive trap. There's not that much time. People are without it on Earth."

Walter and Hadron looked at me, and they said, "Really, we don't know where to take this for simplification."

Superconscious came in. Aah, gorgeous. I Superconscious is so wonderful, so remarkable, knows that it knows and gives me all of this knowing. I sat there and I received for four hours.

"Locate—have the person locate what the problem area is, whether it's this lifetime or any other lifetime, and give that vortex the information to release that. But first realize that the person is the Creator, is a creator. A person made out of atoms,

which are over ninety percent space. Space has the potential to create. You've got to get that in there, because that is important. The vortex works with the creator in the universe and the living universe, the body."

That was the information.

"The First R is to give the vortex as the Creator the information to Release those recordings off the body. Just watch the vortex release it off the very cells of the person's body. Tell them to feel it. Tell them to see it Release. And then tell them to know, to know it's Released, because then Superconscious comes in as the Knower for the body to assist in this wonderful process. That's the First R."

I repeated what Superconscious was giving me right at that beautiful dinner. The thinker doesn't know what I'm about to say.

"The Second R: Revise your considerations. Change your mind about what you did. Change your mind about what you just released and what happened to you. Change your mind about it. Revise your considerations.

"The Third R: Replace. Since the vortex reacts everything, have the person create an image of what they want to be in this life. Pictures are important, because the body takes pictures. Have that person make an image of what they want to be and what they want to have. If they have a mate, is it the right mate? If not, don't have the mate there with you—or create a mate and put it there with you."

And here I got the bright idea, since dollars can be precarious on Earth: *"Have them create gold coins and silver coins and put it in their image."* Because when I did that the very first time, I inherited a whole coin collection from a very precious man, a Chinese man who came into my life.

"Take that image of that creation. You're the Creator. Remember that. Put it into your body, and tell your body, tell the vortex, this is my new life, this is my new life. And the vortex will react it for you."

Isn't that wonderful? It seems to me that this is the first time on Earth that this kind of information is given to Earth people so that they can evolve.

"The Fourth R is Retain."

That is where I have found that people fail. That is why I have decided that with a community people would remind each other, *"I see your new blueprint. It's beautiful."* If they're going to grow something, if they're going to print a book, if they're going to create something—in a community, the passage of it, they remind each other: *"I see your new blue-print, and it's working, and it's beautiful."*

Otherwise, on the Retain, people go out, they get into anger with someone, and they call me to say, "I got angry today."

I say, "You gave your new blueprint anger? What would you want to do that for? Take that anger. Give it to the vortex to release. Maintain the love and emotion that you gave your new recording."

I've been doing that for years with people. It's wonderful to be able to remind a person, so I call people on the phone to say, "I see your new blueprint and it's working fine."

That's where people falter. They don't place the importance upon what they have done. They don't realize that it's like taking a picture with a camera. You've got a piece of film. You put it in the developer. If you take it out too soon, you don't have a picture, do you? I remind them of that. So they come back in again. We release their desire to have anger, hatred, hurt, invalidation, all of the negative emotions. We work on purging them.

How do you purge a negative emotion?

That was given to me by another superconscious being called Majine. She gave me the method to purge icky characters from children. She wants me to have her children's program on Earth. She gave me the purge. She said to have the child or the person select the icky character that bothers them, or the negative characteristic that they are harboring, because it's damaging to the cell structure. No one, not even the parents, should interfere. And the purge is thus: Select the character that bothers you and feel it. Feel it more, and feel it more, until you feel that you are bursting. Then flow it out, flow all the way out, all the way out. And look at the color of it. Always the color comes out icky the first time round. Have the person or the child continue to purge and see what color it is, until the color comes clear. Then you are released of that kind of energy and should no longer have any desire to use it. And it's true — they don't.

I thought, *"How wonderful!"* I gave it to the people. It's a technique that's used by everyone that I've given it to. I can say in all sincerity: I feel no hatred, I feel no worry, I feel nothing negative. I have no desire to argue with anyone, to make waves with anyone. I have no desire for any negative emotion, and I'm thrilled that I don't have to deal with it. I never argued with Hadron, never argued with anyone.

The idea is that the vortex is the saving grace of the human race, as its use was outlined in the Four R's. You know what a tornado looks like. That's a tornado that has come into the third dimension. Vortex energy is circular, spiral, goes counterclockwise when moving in and clockwise when reacting out. When you see the eye of the tornado, that's the center of the vortex. That's where all of the damage is done on Earth when the vortex comes in to the three dimensions. The vortex for the body is in the fourth dimension, and that's merciful, because the body could never tolerate the vortex if it came into the third dimension. So you need to work with the vortex using your imagination.

Our dear friend Dr. Einstein tells us, *"Imagination is greater than knowledge."* And he said, *"I function from the fourth dimension."* That's how he got all of his creative information.

We made up manuals and gave them to people. Hadron, Walter, and Joy wrote scientifically about vortex energy. Hadron did magnificent charts. I wrote in the manual about Totality and about the vortex. And then it came to my realization, remembering what Jesus had said about knowing, and here I had come to the realization about knowing, and here I had worked with this wonderful child and gave him the ability to know superconsciously. All these realizations about knowing came to me. So I began to incorporate the teachings of Jesus to put the knowing in my work. Hadron somehow or another continued with the Buddhist teachings, but he added much more than what he had as Buddha, in my estimation.

Though Hadron worked with us on the manual and did brilliant charts, he only wrote about Totality in that manual, not about the vortex. Hadron was doing research with people and not getting paid. He offered to do research on Whole Life with people, whatever their reality was. He took them into space stuff. He was doing research in consciousness with people, and he was writing his brilliant book *Totality Concept* at that time.

I continued the practice. I retained a secretary to run the bookwork and make appointments and all of that for me. I began to work with people on the vortex and to realize that I was really getting results. I asked Superconscious to give me a meditation. It takes the person directly from the space in their body, which is Creator, and acknowledging Creator, to the space throughout all areas of awareness to Superconscious. Be aware of being Superconscious. Be aware of being your own light. Be aware of being the knower and that you know that you know. And since you're cosmically connected to all other Superconscious knowers, you have an unlimited potential of knowing. I want Earth people to realize that and evolve. Because if they don't evolve, Earth right now is going down the drain. People are killing each other.

Then somebody comes in and gives me a book called *The Ohaspe Bible*, and in it are pictures of the vortices that created the universe. According to the book, in the 1800's spirits came and asked this medical man, a doctor, to buy a writing machine. They said they were going to give him important information and charts.

He said, "I don't know how to draw."

They said, "Don't worry. We'll draw through you."

That's an outline of what happened in the beginning of the book. The part that I like is *The Book of Ben* because it's all about how the vortices created the universe. There was further validation.

Other validation we had on the space being the Creator occurred a good thirty-five years ago. Fermi, the nuclear physicist, announced this in the *Scientific American* magazine, which we saw when we were walking down Hollywood Boulevard to a restaurant that we liked there. We bought ten copies of it, because it said, *"Fermi discovers the Creator!"*

We looked at each other and laughed because he had discovered what we had discovered. We wanted to see what he had to say.

Sure enough, the scientists said, "Do you mean God?"

He said, "Look, I said Creator. I don't care whatever else you want to call it. It's Creator for me. Look at an atom. What do you see? Space. If you look very close you'll see a little nucleus of energy, won't you?"

"Yeah."

"Aren't the universe and people created out of atoms?"

"Yes."

"So space is the Creator with the potential to create."

When Hadron sent me out to space I had that realization when I discovered creating the first otherness Superconscious, right along with when the universe was created with vortices. All this could be unbelievable if I wasn't in it every day all the time. It was so marvelous!

Jesus had said, *"Ask for that which you desire, knowing you already have it."* And I did have the vortex. The vortex is in fact the saving grace of the human race. I have experienced it myself, and I have experienced it with others.

In relation to what Superconscious did for me, I had similar reports from others. For example, when you intuitively get information or hunches or insights—how to write a book, do a painting, whatever—that's you Superconscious giving it to your body.

Or to recall Jesus's teachings: when someone said to him, "God helps those that help themselves," he said, *"Know ye not that ye are gods? Know ye not?"*

And then he said, *"Be still and know."* What does that mean—*be still*? The analytical thinker is always active, so you've got to tell it to leave you alone. You can train yourself. I've trained myself. Tell the thinker: go away, play some place else. Stick with the knowing. You'll be truthful, just as Jesus said.

Then I read an article about the Kahuna masters. A friend had gone to Hawaii. I told him to go to the library and get me some of the teachings of the Kahuna masters. He comes back with this information. The Kahuna masters tell people: you have three minds. You have a superconscious mind. How's that for validation? You have a thinking, analytical mind, and you have a subconscious mind, the *unihipili,* where all your experience is recorded and reacts out in feelings. Tell the *unihipili* to go play somewhere else so you can remain being Superconscious.

That was further validation of what Jesus had said: *"Be still and know."*

10

RELEASING EXCESSIVE FEMININITY
December 26, 1986

One of things I felt I suffered from was an excess of femininity and an aversion to masculinity — not to individual men but to men in groups and masculine culture in general. I admired and appreciated feminine values, and the greater portion of my best friends have always been women. I had an abiding fear and distrust of all hierarchical masculine organizations, whether it be in government, religion, education, medicine, etc. At Lama the whole community, men and women, sat on the ground in a circle and made our decisions by consensus or unanimous vote. This felt good to me. Old way, good way. I was the sensitive seventies male, out of touch with my masculinity, so well described by Robert Bly. Now as the veil was beginning to lift, I could acknowledge that my energies were out of balance on the feminine side and ask Joanna to work with me on this.

The primary image I came up with was that of being a woman in Victorian San Francisco who married and turned into a hysterical housewife. Her husband was rarely around the house, uncommunicative when he was, and treated her as a possession. She knew he didn't love her and suspected him of having other women. She felt both imprisoned and abandoned. She was extremely alone and became in stages depressed, anxious, hysterical, irrational, and out of control. Temper tantrums, screamie meemies, creepy weepies, you name it, she pulled out all of the stops.

With the predictable results for the time. She got locked up in a so-called mental asylum where she could scream, weep, and rage hysterically out of control in isolation for the rest of her miserable life — as well as acquire a comforting addiction to good old-fashioned opiate painkillers.

Joanna notes, *"Everyone is lying to him. He can't live with it. He made the decision: 'I'm crazy. Lock me up.'"* It proved to be a remarkably tenacious decision.

There seems to be a remarkable similarity between this story and the story that came up in releasing Roger. Both stories take place in the same general time period, one in New York, one in San Francisco. In the earlier story I play the role of the abusive, abandoning man who is now being tormented by the wrathful curse of the woman's father's spirit. In this story I experience being caught up in being the woman herself.

Fortunately my job was not and is not to try to make linear sense out of all these recall stories. My job was to uncover the emotionally charged pictures in my subconscious which seemed to be affecting my ability to operate effectively in present time, to bring the pictures up into present time, to play the recordings in present time, to feel that they are real — and then to erase the tape, release the pictures and disperse the light particles back into the space from which they came. My job was to clear away the space in my basement, not to get caught up in analyzing the clutter of countless lifetimes.

As Neem Karoli Baba said, "It's better to love God than to try and figure it all out."

We dug deeper and found my most vivid childhood trauma, being shut away in my room when I was "out of control." I just had a whole lot of energy, maybe too much energy for my parents to deal with, or so it seems to me now. I would be talked to, not talked with, not listened to, and when that didn't work I would be shut away in my room — and my high energy would turn into anger and go global, unrestrained, howling and screaming until finally I exhausted myself. As a small child I felt totally unfairly treated, not listened to, not respected, not held, not loved — and I vowed that I would never do this to anyone.

I have since learned that when a child is in a temper tantrum he or she needs to be held and loved. A child who is not held and loved in such a state may end up totally out of control in later life just as he or she was permitted to be in early life. That is how it happened with me. I outwardly repressed most of my anger, but inwardly committed all my energy to rejecting any involvement with the so-called normal world, which led me to Lama Foundation.

I didn't remember any of this childhood trauma until right after my son Abe was born. Abe spent the first days of his life in his mother's arms and at his mother's breast. But on the fourth night he was crying so much that Varda finally lost patience with him, put him down, and said to me, "I can't deal with this anymore. You deal with him." So I went in and held my son and loved him to no avail. I smiled and cooed and talked to him. He was howling and screaming. I sang little songs to him just as my grandmother had to me. More howling and screaming. Nothing I did had any effect on his unhappiness. Finally something inside me snapped and a brutal surge of raw anger filled my whole body. I was uncontrollably angry and shook my baby. Just a little. For immediately I heard inside my own voice saying, "I'll never do this to anyone. I'll never do this to anyone."

I had forgotten all about this, never thought of it, but when the occasion arose my decision spoke to me clearly and forcefully. I never again used any physical force against my son. I recognized instantly that the awesome anger arising in me was not my own creation. It was my father's anger expressed on me that I had stored in my body, which was in turn his father's anger that had been expressed on him and stored in his body, which was his father's anger . . . and so on back to cave man and before. I was so grateful for that decision, a truly healthy decision, which I had made as a child, and so amazed at the power of true decision, which once made is imprinted on the soul though it may sleep for centuries.

Another seemingly small but significant decision is one that I made with my best friend in high school. We vowed to each other never to go out with any "normal" girls, who were, in our eyes, prep school princesses without any imagination or independent intelligence. "We will only go out with crazy girls," we decided. Not surprisingly, most of the girls and women I have been with have been anything but "normal," and many of them had deep mental and emotional problems just as I have.

DEEPER DRAMA WITH LYNN

March 7, 1987

Lynn was very psychic, and being with her deepened my psychic sensitivity. For sure we are all psychic, just like we all got rhythm and we all can speak our mother tongue. But these gifts are given and developed to greater or lesser degrees among all God's children, as are the gifts of making money, making music, making love, etc. Both Joanna and Lynn were naturally clairvoyant. They could clearly see energies and entities on a subtle level, something that came with much greater difficulty to me in a waking state, though I must admit that my dreams and sexual fantasies have always been quite vivid. Strong clairvoyance is a great gift, but it can be confusing and disturbing unless rightly developed.

My gift was much more in the direction of clairaudience — hearing clearly intelligent voices on a subtle level. This is not channeling, which involves being a vehicle through which an entity, an otherness, can speak or write. Clairaudience is simply the ability to hear and speak from a more subtle and transcendent level of mind. For instance, in sessions with Joanna, once I had seen the hard-won picture I was looking for, the meanings and understandings of that picture, of previous events and future consequences, would come spilling forth effortlessly in my mind and speech. But even while I was seeing only a few video clips and extrapolating from them, Joanna was seeing the whole movie. I know because she told me so.

Lynn's awareness of past-life pictures was spontaneous and effortless. She did learn from Joanna the technique of erasing the recordings and releasing them using the vortex, which she worked quickly and smoothly. She seemed to be able to do by herself in minutes the same things it took me hours of concentration, hard work, and constant guidance to do. Lynn was very aware of devas and nature spirits. Walking in the woods with her was a constant delight.

Lynn even helped a lost spirit to move on from the house I was living in at the time. I was sensitive enough to realize that the intermittent strange incidents and moods, effects, and affects in the house I was renting might come from an unhappy spirit that was hanging around. Lynn agreed to check it out with me and found, in the darkest corner of the house, in the boiler room behind the converted garage, the sad spirit of a young man who had lost his life in the Vietnam War. He had managed to find his way back to the house he grew up in, but when he got there his parents had moved on to parts unknown and nobody seemed to recognize him. He didn't know where to go, so he just hung out in the dark alone, every now and then wandering among the living inhabitants of the house who paid no attention to him. While I was present, holding the space, Lynn communicated with the spirit verbally and nonverbally, explained to him his true situation as a disembodied spirit (something they never teach you in Sunday School), and asked him if he wished her help in moving on to the spirit world. She had him call out to his family and beloveds who had already gone over to the other side, and they came and joyfully took him away. It is something that is so simple when done with a pure heart and right understanding.

Our sexual love life had a rich psychic component for me. While we were making love or lying in bed together, I could visibly see and feel her making love to some of her past lovers at various times (the most intense experiences), and I could spontaneously experience at least some of our past-life times together as lovers (always the best ones). It was like making love with an ever-changing stream of the forms of the same woman at different ages, in different locations, in other bodies, in other lifetimes. This must be the sexual enrichment program, I thought. It is something that I have never experienced with anyone else.

The more I saw of Lynn, the more she wanted me not to speak to, speak of, or even think of Glory. This was very hard for me to do, for I knew Glory was my twin flame, my soul mate, whatever you want to call it, and I still felt uncomfortable with Lynn despite the good loving we were sharing. But I knew that Glory would always be a married woman and that it would never work out for us to be together on the Earth plane. Glory was also becoming more tormented in relation to me, torn between the need to stay closely in touch with the exquisite intimacy we shared and the anguish of knowing I was now with another woman who was loving me physically as she wanted but never could permit herself to do.

Lynn was challenging me to let go of clinging to a perfect but impossible dream and commit myself to a real life with a real woman (and child, for she had a three-year-old son just as I had a eight-year-old son).

Things just seem to have a way of working out. As soon as I had fully committed myself to being with Lynn and letting go of Glory — letting her go back to being a good Christian wife with all my blessings, something she had really never stopped being — at that point Lynn's love was already lost to me, although I didn't know it at the time. Her love was already given to another man, who she would come to marry, although she didn't fully know it at the time. And I went from the apex of a love triangle to being the odd man out in another love triangle, from being a big winner to being a big loser in the game of love. Perfect karmuppance, Hadron would say.

Surely there must be an analogy between the triangulation that surveyors and navigators use to map out the land and the sea and the love triangulations we keep using to map out the uncharted territories of the heart. Instant karma — just add desire and get mixed up.

Lynn's father passed away suddenly in January 1987. I went with her to her hometown, a small town in the Mississippi delta, for the funeral. Afterwards I stayed with her for two weeks in her father's house, sat in her father's chair, read her father's books, drank her father's liquor, and perhaps even housed her father's spirit for fleeting periods of time. After the funeral Lynn would not make love with me anymore — not just for those two weeks but for the rest of our relationship. I went back to New Mexico, and Lynn stayed for another month in Mississippi, putting her father's house in order. When she came back to New Mexico things got even weirder.

Unbeknownst to me, as soon as I left town, a man named Flynn came to visit her. He was a powerful shaman, and they had shared umpty-ump lifetimes of love and power together. He and she were both buried in the sacred Indian mound outside town (a pair of their previous bodies, that is). In this lifetime they both grew up in this same small delta town, he a good deal older than she. He had always loved her from afar. She marginally knew that he existed. He was a great shaman, now an alcoholic riverboat captain, but still possessed of great powers. Now certain karma had come to fruition, and it was their time to be together. So he put his mojo on her, his love spell, and began to psychically attack me anytime I got near her.

Here I was taking the advanced course from Joanna, and I hadn't even gotten through all the intermediate levels. I must have skipped over Psychic Self-Defense 101, thinking I was too pure for it or something like that. For that was shore 'nuf the lesson I had to learn right then. When Lynn came back from Mississippi things got really, really weird.

If my first six months with Lynn had been relatively heavenly, the best I can say of the last nine months of our relationship is that the lower levels of Purgatory are pretty warm indeed. One of the reasons it was so weird is that neither of us really knew what Flynn's role was in causing all the turbulence between us. Lynn might have known more than she was letting on to me, but she didn't really understand what was happening until after she went back to Mississippi and got married to him. Only ten years later did she share with me all of the gory details of the energies being flung at us for those nine months. All of a sudden she didn't love me, she didn't enjoy me, she didn't even like me very much. If I wasn't a love-and-sex addict I shoulda coulda woulda just walked away, which is what Joanna kept urging me to do. But I was committed to my addiction (or is it addicted to my commitment?), and my heart would stay true to Lynn until she packed up and left town for good.

My heart has had to be broken open so many times before it could even love a little. Loving Glory was easy. She loved me even more than I knew how to love her. Loving Lynn became hard, very hard. And I had no choice but to let both of them go.

Joanna notes, *"Primal fear always comes up strong with Lynn. Must have sex or she'll leave him. She'll kill him or leave him. Women use him up, waste him. It's gut level—primal terror, fear in stomach, like a tiger going to eat him up."*

Once again Joanna and I went into session and unearthed yet another string of past lives in which Lynn and I danced together. The most powerful picture was that of her as a temple priestess in ancient Mesopotamia and me as a captive sex slave. I wanted her special favors so that I would not be sacrificed immediately. I had to perform for her or die. I'm kept inside the temple, doing menial labor. Sexual performance was crucial.

Eventually she tired of me and I was disemboweled. There was a sense that my spirit was eaten up by the demonic entities to which she had sacrificed me. There is a decision to get even with her.

In Egypt she is the captive slave girl and I am her owner. In Rome I am the nubile slave girl and she is the brutal master. There are more images of human sacrifice on top of pyramids in Mexico — last minute recognitions: "Oh, you're the one who is going to do me in!" In Hawaii she is a powerful medicine woman who has my body thrown into the volcano. How many more lifetimes? — indeed!

"Contagion of aberration!" Joanna's notes exclaim.

As a TIME GAME PLAYER SPIRIT the key requirement is PRETENDING. Since you are an ASSIGNED UNIT of TOTALITY, as a SPIRIT you are indestructible and as TOTALITY YOU are BEYOND so-called IMMORTALITY.

There is the PRETENDING TO BE OTHER THAN TOTAL — to BE A SPIRIT — to be ALIVE — to be DEAD — to be HUMAN and MANY OTHERS.

The main PRETENDING is being separate from. This CAUSES THE MARVELOUS games of HOW MANY TIMES HAVE YOU BEEN TOGETHER WITH YOUR LOVED ONES?

How many times have you PRETENDED to be DESTROYED by your BELOVED OPPONENTS and/or PRETENDED to DESTROY them?

Research indicates that individuals get together — perhaps marry — because they LOVE each other — or to GET EVEN for other EXPERIENCES in the past.

WHOSE TURN IS IT NOW? This seems to be the popular GAME on this planet in this series of CONSECUTIVE NOWS.

TOTALITY CONCEPT 174 740710

SUPERCONSCIOUS FINDS
A NEW HOME FOR ME
March 16, 1987

During my first seven years in Santa Fe I moved houses eight times, schlepping from one rental to another for a variety of reasons, always sharing with roommates because I could not afford a place of my own. In the spring of 1987 I had been stable for two years before my landlord gave me the heave-ho.

For someone with little income, finding a rental in a landlord's market can be a laborious, traumatic, and exhausting experience. This time, though there was a deadline coming very soon, I decided to try Joanna's way of operating — giving my needs to Superconscious, knowing that I would receive what I needed. So, defying conventional logic, I did not go house-hunting. I didn't even look at classifieds. I meditated and prayed with a certainty that my needs would be provided for.

And this is how it happened.

I had been up at Lama Foundation visiting Lynn for a long weekend. Monday afternoon it was finally time to go, though there was no big rush about it. I was still hanging around. Lama was buried waist-deep in winter snow. We got word that some woman had driven her car off the road and was stuck in a snowdrift a mile down the road. She needed someone to dig her out.

So I and another guy put snow shovels on our shoulders and trudged down the road. It was a bright sunny day, later in the afternoon, with a clear blue sky above. I didn't have a thought or a worry in my mind. I was "happy just to be alive, underneath a sky of blue."

As we were digging out her car I got to talking with this woman.

"Where are you from?"

"I'm from Santa Fe. Do you live at Lama?"

"No. I'm from Santa Fe, too."

"Where do you live in Santa Fe?"

"I live on Pine Street right now, but I have to move really soon."

"Oh, what a coincidence. I have a friend who has to find a roommate right away. Maybe you should give her a call."

"Thank you. I think I will. But actually I need to find two rooms, because my son lives with me part-time."

"Well, that's what she has: two rooms."

What a coincidence. That's all it took to find a new home: one conversation, one phone call. I liked this way of doing things. Joanna was delighted at this demonstration of Superconscious in action, which is definitely one way to look at it.

My new roommate was almost an astrological twin, born in Mexico just one day before I was born. I found the perfect home and the perfect roommate for the moment. That particular moment lasted about six months.

COMING INTO THE EARTH SPHERE
& HUMANITY
July 26, 1987

In session Joanna posed the question to me, " Ask Superconscious to get information from your body, your subconscious. Since you know you're Totality, what did you do so that you could live in an Earth Body experience?"

I saw a group of light beings flying through the immensity of cosmic space, like a flying wedge of luminous spirit bodies with Glory and myself at the leading edge. I was attracted to experience this lovely blue-green-white planet Earth. It seemed so fresh, so new, so full of vitality and potential compared with all the other old worlds we had visited. I wanted to zoom into the Earth sphere and merge into it. Glory didn't. She wanted to stay in her light body dancing in space. No problem. We had always been together. I didn't give a thought to what separation might mean. I projected a light beam from my hand and followed it down into the atmosphere, entering the Earth game alone.

I am flying freely above the African veldt. I see vast herds of antelope. This world is sensational and beautiful — blue skies, green grasses, flowing waters, and at night the familiar infinity of stars. I find I can move into and out of any life form freely, taking tastes of what it feels like to be in a physical body. The human life forms are dark and dirty, primitive hunters and gatherers. They don't move in and out of bodies like I do. I am a joyful spirit, lyrical, inquisitive, intoxicated with the songs, the vibrations of the myriad life forms. I'm a disembodied spirit, a body of wind, aware of embodied thoughts, feelings, sensations without being trapped in them. I play games with animals and people, making energy phenomena happen, sometimes mischievous, sometimes helpful, reveling in the joy of experience. Some people can see me and hear my voice, others not. I'm a spirit playing at being a god.

I immerse myself in earth, water, and air, moving through mountains, rivers, winds, and storms for a long time before I take the plunge and dive into a human form. At first I'm just moving in and out of human bodies, vicariously experiencing human realities. Then I go the full route and come in through conception. Glory and I come in together as golden-haired twins. She has agreed to do this with me. We want to take this experience together.

Now I remember the gradual involvement with human conditions, the gradual forgetting of who it is I really am. I am aware of automatically recording my human experiences, automatically identifying with them, weaving myself into the web of karma. Then I hang out too long in the body of a caveman and end up popping the head of a woman. Now I'm really caught.

Joanna's notes say, *"When the pictures get too dense, they become reactive. Remember the first turn off. When there is identification with the pictures, only then is reality human. I've always known I Superconscious. When you lose it, you don't even realize it. It's almost like we have very little training in recognizing who we really are. The world is geared for identification. **Learning presupposes you don't know.**"*

HER STORY—RESTIMULATION—CONTROLS

Hadron and I used to go to the UCLA campus. We liked it there. We would have breakfast in the cafeteria and go to the antique library. We discovered Shri Aurobindo there. His books were covered in white linen. I was looking through the philosophers, because I decided I would like to do one church session on them.

I found Spinoza. I was reading the last part of a book about him the morning I had to do the talk at the church. As I was reading it, I realized that Spinoza tried to bring One God to the people and of course they ridiculed him. He died in an attic of pneumonia. And I began to restimulate the pneumonia in my body. I got fever. I got phlegm. I started coughing. I couldn't understand what was happening to me.

Hadron came in for his shower and said, "What's going on here?"

I said, "Spinoza died in an attic of pneumonia, and I feel like I'm getting pneumonia."

He understood it. I didn't. He snapped his fingers in my face and said, "Go earlier. Go earlier. Go earlier. Go earlier."

I could feel the pneumonia leave my body. All the symptoms of which Spinoza died left my body and I came back to normal again. Hadron then was marvelous.

He said, "You got restimulated by reading the book. You were very likely Spinoza."

"I was Spinoza?"

"Why not? Why not? Look at you. Look at what you do. Look at your consciousness. He was a great philosopher. He died in an attic. You were born in an attic. You didn't get very far!"

True. True. Isn't that fascinating?

I thought, *"Wow! Look what's happening to me!"* That understanding—I had a hunger for the ultimate. Anything that would help me to understand how people work, how they function, how things happen, was very fascinating to me.

When you're doing regression work with people, sometimes they can get in a place where past-time conditions are restimulated and come out in the present moment. They can feel the physical effects. Sometimes it can be dangerous.

A woman came to me when I was still in Los Angeles. She was a writer. She had this strange habit of getting awfully upset in the middle of the night and going to the sink and running cold water on her head to get rid of what was happening to her. She couldn't understand it. Psychiatry couldn't give her any answers to what was happening, so she was referred to me.

I worked with her. I couldn't get to the bottom of exactly why this was happening to her. Then I invited the husband in to the session.

I said, "Tell me what happens with your wife when she runs into the bathroom and has to put her head under cold water."

He said, "Well, she's crazy."

"No, she isn't. Why did you decide she was crazy? Because she did that? That is not a crazy woman."

"Well, I think she's crazy."

I looked at him and saw that he was an obsessed man. I could tell by his eyes that there was something wrong with him when he talked about her. Soon after that he died. Now I did not wish him death. But she came alive. She stopped putting her head under the water.

She came in for a session.

I said, "When you used to do that, what happened with you and your husband?"

"Well, he would call me crazy. He would belittle my writing. And I am a published writer. He would get wild. His eyes would get wild."

"Let's go into a past life with him. Let's do that."

"Fine. I'll do anything."

We did. In her former life they were together and they were absolutely horrible. It was devastating. And he had killed her. They did that in former times. Men didn't agree with their wife, and they could kill her.

248

They get together again in this life. They married that energy between them because they had been together in a former life. But then he's got to demean her. In another way he's got to kill her. How he died I have no idea. Whether everything that was in him took him or whether she had the ability to get rid of him so she could come alive, that I have no idea. But there was the past life, there was the restimulation, and this woman came alive when he left. It was unbearable the way he treated her. It made her manic.

Another time I was working with a young man. He couldn't get into any past life. He couldn't get it. I got Egypt. I began to do that. If a person wasn't able to get into a regression I seemed to get a place or a word or something like that. That time I got Egypt, and my prodding took him right into an Egyptian lifetime when he was my baby, and when I was Nefertiti. He was strapped onto his father's back and they went on a chariot ride. Those roads there are full of big stones. The baby bounced off the father's back and got killed. And I have a picture of Nefertiti and Amenhotep IV holding the baby. That young man happened to go into the living room, saw that picture, and fainted. He fainted right on the floor. I had to work with him to release that lifetime.

For me the whole thing was so fascinating because I was able to get a picture of what he should get into on this matter. That was one of the first times that I did that, but since then I've done it all the time. I have found my ability levels improving, increasing, and I'm delighted with it, particularly because they're so helpful for me in my work with people.

Actual physical conditions can clear up for people when you release the subconscious. There was a psychologist sent to me. She had a liver condition. Doctors couldn't find anything wrong. She felt the liver was being torn apart, and she was in agony.

I said, "Let's take a look at it. Let's see where this emanated from."

This was in either Greece or Rome. In the opening picture that she got she was nude on a hill, a very steep inclined hill. She was lying there because she was being punished for something she did. The powers that be had her on that hill without any clothes on, and the vultures were eating her liver. She screamed and she cried.

I said, "Just a minute. That isn't happening now."

She said, "It seems like it's happening now because my liver hurts and it feels like the vultures are actually—I didn't realize what it was but that's what it feels like. In the regression I'm getting and feeling it there."

So we worked to release it. We used the vortex. We put a new blueprint in with a beautiful liver. She went away to the Bahamas with her husband. She came back and called me.

I said, "How's your liver?"

"Fine. Fine. To think," she says, "I'm a psychologist. I can't do any of the work you do."

"Come in and study with me and do it."

"I couldn't do your work as a psychologist. I'd be ostracized."

"Too bad for you," I said.

There are many incidents where things like that happened—people getting cancer through restimulation, for example. The way we do the release, once we get the actual incident, a person can release the cancer. The cancer is actually a mental and spiritual thing, not a physical thing. It causes the physical thing to occur. The imbalance of the cellular structure that happens in cancer is actually mental. What we discovered is that certain types of people get cancer, the kind that don't seem to be able to find solutions to their lives, the kind that are actually unhappy people. They don't admit it but they're not fulfilled. They don't realize it but the body gets cancer because it's not fulfilled. We found that out. I think that doctors are beginning to understand that.

The whole prenatal thing—we came into a realization about that. Early on in Dianetics, after I had come into my own with my erasure technique, a young man came to me and he was shaking.

I said, "What's the matter with you?"

He said, "I don't know."

"What do the doctors say?"

"They don't know."

"There is St. Vitus where a person shakes."

"They don't say that I have St. Vitus. They don't know why I'm shaking."

He was a teenager.

Somehow or other the information came to me that this is prenatal.

So I said to him, "I'm going to take you into an area of your life. I'm going to try to help you remember that area, because that may be where we find the cause of your shaking like that. Can you agree to that?"

"Yes. I'll do anything to stop shaking, because I can't go out with girls, I can't do athletics, I can't do anything."

I take him into prenatal—I think it was the second or the third month—and he begins to cry, "What's that big thing that's hitting me?"

"What does it look like?"

"It looks like a penis. It hits me all the time and it hurts."

That's what he said. He shook right there. He was shaking terribly. Wow!

That's why I say to all the parents, "Look, you guys, you keep your penis to yourself after the third month. You can make love in other ways. You can get satisfaction in other ways." I wrote a paper on that.

So I released him with the erasure technique, back and forth, back and forth, until the whole thing began to dissolve. Even on my little meter I could see that he was coming up, coming up tone scale, and he stopped shaking right in front of me. I looked at that and I thought, *"Isn't it wonderful that I can do this with this child?"*

He looked at me and said, "That's what it was, wasn't it?"

"Yes, your father's penis while you were in your mother's womb. He has a big one and it was ugly and it was hurting you. Evidently he was very sexual, and he gave you too much of that. Your body got the shakes."

That could go down in medical history, I'm telling you. That cleared it up for him. He stopped shaking as soon as we found out what it was. I did the erasure technique and it released. That made me pretty cocky, I can tell you. I began to realize that I do have special abilities and my interest is there. I'm very interested in finding ways to help people.

During the prenatal period everything records. Abortion attempts are primary causes of several well-known so-called illnesses.

There is a tendency among married couples that, once pregnant, as much sex is indulged in as is possible in the early months of prenatal, since the wife cannot get any more pregnant.

The orgasm on the woman's part is a muscular convulsion of volcanic magnitude in relation to tiny cells and zygote. This is a traumatic experience of great magnitude and produces in some cases a hatred of one or both parents. The automatic survival interpretation of the developing infant is that he/she is being destroyed or at least a serious attempt is being made.

The Coitus chain of incidents where the small zygote or embryo is repeatedly rammed and shaken up by the male organ followed by the orgasmic explosion by the female, when keyed-in in later life produces Parkinson's disease and other dramatizations of the entire BODY shaking. The male organ becomes the winning valence which produces a shaking dramatization by the entire BODY later in life. Moments of pain and heavy emotional shock are the key-ins in later years that cause automatic dramatizations on the entire body level.

The optimum approach for creating a BODY, Earth-style, is to abstain from sex activities during the nine-month prenatal period. Plenty of love and affection but no actual sex act where the orgasm is involved by the mother.

It is good to remember that thoughts and emotions record all the time: thoughts and emotions of everyone around the prospective mother.

TOTALITY CONCEPT 170 740409

You have to be careful. There are people who will try to control. I've had people who tried to control me against Totality. In California, there was a man who was on drugs. He was a musician and he was in jail. Someone gave him our literature and Scientology literature. He chose our literature for some reason. Hadron was called and went and took him out of jail, set him up in an apartment in San Jose, and worked with him. He would call Hadron often to help him. Hadron was always there for him. Periodically he would come to us and we would work with him together. I would make a nice breakfast, wonderful vegetable omelets and biscuits and everything. Then he would bring friends in. We would work with them. They would never pay us. He very rarely paid us. I didn't like him.

I said to Hadron, "Look, that's your case, not mine. There's something about that guy that I don't like."

Hadron says, "Well, he needs help and you know me: I'll help him."

"Yes. You should."

That was a twenty-year siege.

Then when we decide to move, he says, "I'll help you when you move." And he never shows up. I thought that was pretty awful after all we had done for him. We were coming to Santa Fe. He never showed up. Hadron's son Shawn didn't show up either, and he said he would. So I had to pay extra to the movers, ten dollars an hour — it amounted to several thousand dollars to get moved.

We're in Santa Fe about a week or two. We get a letter from a lawyer that this guy is saying that we're not a real non-profit corporation, that we're fake, and that he's suing us. For what?

I said to Hadron, "See? It's like I said. He's not for real. He's really a Scientologist."

Hadron said, "Well, it doesn't make any difference to me."

"It makes a difference to me."

So I wrote the attorney a letter and sent him a copy of our incorporation papers. I said, "You tell that guy that he did a very wrong thing and he's going to suffer for it. I'm not going to make him suffer. His own Superconscious is going to make him suffer."

And he did. I heard that he died a very painful death shortly after that.

I began to realize that you don't do wrong to Totality or to Orayna and Hadron of Orr. You just don't. We had that experience with others as well. Not all of them died, but they became painfully sick. Not that we would do that to anyone. But it was done to them because they tried to do it to us. There were several people who tried. A couple came from Germany and tried. They got put in jail and then sent back to Germany. It's very interesting for us to realize that because we are who we are, because we do what we do for humanity on Earth, we have a protection going for us.

There were some people who wanted to fund us with twenty-five thousand dollars if we would just become a religion and preach religion and Jesus Christ.

At that point Mary Baker Eddy came to me and said, "Don't! Don't! I didn't want to be a church either. I wanted to be an education taught in the universities. But I took their money and they took me over and made a church. They're not real. They're not doing what I taught."

Hadron looked at me and I said, "Hadron, I am getting a big fat no."

Later I told them what Mary Baker Eddy said.

They could not understand it.

"We'll give you a church. We'll publicize you. You're nice-looking people."

We did make a nice appearance when we would stand up on the podium. And Hadron laughed. He could care less. Money didn't mean anything to him anyhow.

I refused.

They said, "We can't understand you. Look what we can do for you."

I said, "That's fine, but we don't want what you can do for us."

And that was that. It would be controlling. With churches you've got people and they dictate to you. I don't want that. Here we are a church, but I don't invite people to join me. I'm going to help them. And when we have a community there will be our corporation and there will be a cooperative corporation.

It is practically impossible to work with people who have religious implants. Hadron did have a few Jesuits that came to him. That was very interesting. He knew of course that all religions have implants. That's how they get the people to come to them. There is what is called a black electromagnetic box out there just short of the spirit realm in space. It's hierarchic control. Hadron did this chart on hierarchies and spirits. It's a magnificent chart. When I saw him doing that, I was so impressed. That's how I realized about hierarchies and what they do. They control people.

These Jesuit priests came to Hadron. He knew enough to take the priests out there and find the electronic controls — tractor beams on the back of their necks, on chakras there. These priests were beginning to realize that it wasn't their creative consciousness to be a Jesuit priest. They're brilliant men, these Jesuit priests. That's why they came to Hadron, and Hadron helped them release the controls on the black box. They came up out of it like emerging from an ocean of water. I watched them. They came to light. They came to themselves. So they simply discharged themselves from the church.

One of them was such a nice-looking man. We were invited to this barbecue up on the Hollywood Hills at the home of a Russian Jew, a brilliant woman. She had written books on improvisation in schools and in the theater. We were always invited out. We were the culture. She had this beautiful barbecue out of doors. So I decided to bring this priest with us. I thought, *"I'd love to have her meet him."* She was a very sexy gal. She had all of these motion-picture television people at this tremendous barbecue outdoors in the hills.

We introduced them. She got a hold of him and had sex with him, that day. That's the way she was, the most free soul you ever want to know. They eventually got married.

He called and said, "Thank you. Thank you for giving me my life."

The other priest became a librarian and worked out in the world. We didn't know whether he married anyone or not. That connection didn't remain. That was our experience.

We began to realize that the whole religious church control thing was definitely an implant on the beings as they came into the spirit world, and they could not do anything creative in their own life at all. Religious implants are almost impossible to release. I have not worked with a lot of people in this area.

I made a decision. I remembered that I was here to help people evolve. Then I was given this information: *"Get the high-consciousness ones and help them to become aware of being Superconscious, because they're bordering on it. They will be ready and willing to be aware of being Superconscious. Don't work with the others anymore. Don't work with insane people. Don't work with alcoholics and drug addicts. That's not your forte. That's not your responsibility. Your responsibility is to take these people from other planets who are on Earth. Take them to their home planets so they realize who they are, why they are here. Then bring sanity to them."*

And the work actually does this. I was given this wonderful meditation that takes people to their own Superconscious. The work I'm doing now is really magnificent.

11

GOODBYE GLORY
August 26, 1987

Glory came to visit on her way through Santa Fe. I took her to see Joanna for the first time. Though she was interested the clearing work I was doing and felt she had benefited from it, she was not impressed with Joanna. She thought Joanna was too full of herself, interested only in her own ideas and not in what anyone else had to say if it did not validate her own thinking. Joanna put a good number of people off in this way.

That night I was driving Glory up to Taos through a drenching thunderstorm. Glory had asked me not to say anything about what was happening with me and Lynn. Of course she always shared freely with me about what was happening with her and her husband, but who said the rules of the game are fair? We make the rules up as we go along. Of course I forgot myself and said one too many things about Lynn.

We were driving along the flat, lonely stretch between Española and where the highway enters the Rio Grande Gorge at Velarde. When I forgot and said just one more word about Lynn, she got more angry with me than she ever had been, and screamed, "I hate you! I hate you! Stop the car right now! Let me out!" She jumped out of the car and stomped away in the dark and the pouring rain, yelling and screaming, "Fuck you! Fuck you! I hate you!"

I was shocked and speechless. I had never seen this side of Glory before. I had no idea she could explode with such animosity. I had no idea what to do except to stay calm, stay above it all, be the space, Mr. Totality, Mr.

Cool. I drove slowly along the side of the highway following her, keeping her in the headlights, for a few minutes. She never looked back.

I finally decided to stop pretending to be Mr. Totality and start being Mr. Humanity, accept her full anger, and take my licks. I stopped the car and knelt down by the side of the road in the dark and the rain. She came back and stood over me screaming, "Why? Why? Why?" I thought she was going to kick me down. I felt intense stabbing pains in my belly and in my gut. After a while she got back in the car and sobbed and softened and forgave me, and we drove on to Taos. I dropped her off where she was going and drove back home.

The next morning I discovered four punctures on the left side of my navel. These were not pimples or sores like I sometimes get. These were actual puncture wounds like bee stings. They were not externally, physically caused. When I showed them to Joanna, she said, "Of course, she stabbed you." She saw a picture of a long thin blade like a stiletto in her hand stabbing into my belly in some other lifetime. And of course I recalled the vivid picture I got before of me stabbing her in the back in some other lifetime.

That was not the very last time I would ever see Glory, but that was certainly the end of our psychic intimacy. It could really only work as long as she was the only woman in my heart.

GOODBYE LYNN
October 14, 1987

I had seen less and less of Lynn all summer. Her man in Mississippi was calling her home, and she had been pulling up her stakes and packing up to move on from Lama and New Mexico. When she finally left Lama, she and her son Luke came to stay with me in Santa Fe for two weeks. Almost every day she went to Albuquerque to shop for the Volkswagen van of her dreams. She must have visited every car lot in town, seen every van twice, researched, bargained, haggled, all those things you do to get the best car at the best price. I was impressed by her concentration and energy and the way she brought her new van back to the dealer two or three times to get everything just right before she set off.

All I wanted to do was to hang out with her while she was still in my life, but there was very little time for that. The last night she was at my house, she promised to come and sleep with me just as soon as she put her baby boy to sleep. I turned off all the lights and lay down in my bed waiting for her to come to me this one last time. My heart was wide open and throbbing with love and longing. I waited and waited and waited as the longing in my heart grew more and more intense. After a long while I heard gentle snoring from the other room and realized that she would not be coming in to me after all. But the burning yearning in my heart just kept getting stronger and stronger, and as I lay awake all night I received the final gift of our relationship — a tender, open, and loving heart.

These days we speak of "being in a relationship" or "having a relationship" when what we really mean is that we are romantically involved, making love, having sex with another person, hopefully a significant other. In reality we are in relationship with all beings, all our relations, all of the time, although most of the time we are not mindful of this. The final gift of my time with Lynn was knowing in my full body that the purpose of love is not to have and to hold and to cherish and adore and let's not forget copulate with another person. The purpose of love is love itself — to awaken more love, more life, more compassion, more openness, more tenderness. The gift of love is a loving heart, and love gladly breaks our hearts open again and again and again until our hearts are open twenty-four hours a day and we can be convenience stores for humanity.

And with this final gift to me, Lynn went down the road and out of my life.

Hazrat Inayat Khan says, "In tenderness of heart the tone turns into a half-tone; and with the breaking of the heart the tone breaks into micro-tones. The more tender the heart becomes, the fuller the tone becomes; the harder the heart grows, the more dead it sounds."

GOODBYE HADRON
October 23, 1987

On this morning I stopped by Joanna's house unannounced, something I never did. But when the intuition came I didn't question it. Joanna came to the door in a high flush of emotion. It was a miracle I had come to her door, she said, for the hospital had called just ten minutes ago to inform her that Hadron had finally left the body. She felt a tremendous rush of energy leave her body and just didn't know what to do with herself. It was obvious that I was the new male energy to come into her life now that Hadron was gone, so she said.

When I first met them four years ago, Hadron was already well advanced into Alzheimer's disease, rarely speaking, rarely present in anything but the body. Every now and then he would lift up his head and say something like, "This sure is a strange planet," and nod away again. Previous to this he had kept on producing his brilliant metaphysical writing by typing while standing up. If he sat down he would fall asleep. He said that Totality was doing the writing and was grateful for his condition for it took the brain out of the way and allowed Superconscious to bypass the interfering filters of the rational mind.

Joanna took wonderful care of him for as long as she could. Eventually the situation became unmanageable when one morning he passed out and fell over on top of her and she could not move. After that he was in hospitals and nursing homes. None of this seemed to bother him, for he only came briefly into the present moment when Joanna would visit him. Otherwise, according to the doctors, he simply was not there, although his body was strong and kept on living. Eventually Joanna said to him, "Hadron, why don't you do something about this body you've left behind here on Earth." Soon after that he passed away.

Joanna was surprised at the depth of the grief she experienced when Hadron finally left his body. Her son Harvey also died by his own hand that year, which was an additional source of grief. She would brush away her tears and tell her body to get over it and function superconsciously. She had had two marriages, had raised her own son and later Hadron's son, and for the first time she was free to live without taking care of the men in her life. She was eighty years old, but she still had great projects envisioned which she knew would take her another thirty years to complete.

Joanna had already led a long and full life serving as an awakening, liberating, and spiritually healing influence on hundreds, perhaps thousands, of individuals. She triggered them, however briefly, to an awareness of being functioning Superconscious in an Earth body, achieving release from limitations and the sometimes miraculous manifestation of desired results in the individual life. Yet her creative vision went far beyond working with individuals.

She had long nurtured the imaginal figure of Majine, the Spirit of Creative Imagination, who comes from beyond outer space to help the children of Earth lead happier lives. Majine is a beautiful, radiant, blonde young woman in a white and gold Flash Gordon-style space suit. Joanna's husband, Hadron, had done beautiful renderings of Majine, Captain Johnny Zanzibar (Majine's male counterpart), Busy Body (the subconscious), and an assorted cast of characters representing the negative influences which limit the children of Earth — characters such as Kreepy Doubt, Sadness Sack, Gimme Greedy, Colonel Hurtsick and so on. Together they had produced a radio play and written a feature movie shooting script and several television treatments of stories of Majine.

Joanna was now working to put together a prototype of the Majine doll, an interactive talking doll that would bring inspiration and trigger creative imagination in the children of Earth. The Majine doll was to be the central product of a multimillion-dollar worldwide toy industry whose profits would then enable her to buy land in rural New Mexico (Ojo Caliente) and create a community dedicated to superconscious life and bringing fully aware children into the Earth plane. And I was the primary person she would rely upon to help her.

This was effectively the end of our period of intensive work together and the beginning of her work to realize the Majine doll. She and Hadron had operated as a non-profit corporation, Totality Research and Development Corporation, since 1958. She and I incorporated a for-profit corporation, Majine Enterprises, Inc., in 1988. We visited doll makers, electronic engineers in Albuquerque and Phoenix, and *maquiladora* factories in Juarez. We drew up a business plan and sought investors. She had run several entrepreneurial businesses in her life and was unwavering as always in her confidence of success.

Joanna never lost faith in her vision and never tired of selling it to everyone she talked with. Unfortunately, though, Majine Enterprises never really got off the ground. One major problem was lack of significant capital, which led to her trying to get people to work on speculation or by trading Totalizing sessions. Though many people gave their time and skills, the prototype of the Majine doll was never completed to her satisfaction. Another major problem was her advancing age, which rendered her less and less able to focus fully on the material plane, coupled with her unwillingness to give anyone else real authority in what purported to be a corporate venture.

For better and for worse I helped her in every way I could, and we remained the closest of friends for the last ten years of her life. Joanna had worked with me intensively for three solid years and had triggered me to cosmic awareness and psychic clearings I could never have imagined before, producing definite results not only in the levels of peace and joy in my life, but also in my ability to function with less obstruction — to function normally and sometimes perhaps superconsciously in everyday life.

MAJINE

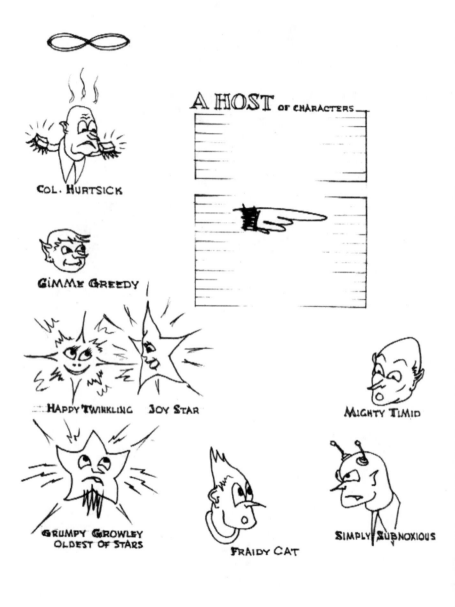

COL. HURTSICK

A HOST OF CHARACTERS

GIMME GREEDY

HAPPY TWINKLING   JOY STAR

MIGHTY TIMID

GRUMPY GROWLEY
OLDEST OF STARS

FRAIDY CAT

SIMPLY SUBNOXIOUS

KREEPY DOUBT

BUSY BODY

MAJINE

HER STORY—SANTA FE—HADRON'S PASSING

As it developed, when Hadron was writing his book, by the time he was partway through he had to stand up to write. His memory was failing.

I said, "What happened?"

He said, "I turned my thinking mind off. I turned my brain off. I didn't want any interference with this information that I'm leaving for the people of Earth. I was getting interference from the thinking mind. So I'm going to turn it off. I want direct communication with Totality. I Totality to my body. ."

That was real to me, too. I had been aware of being Totality. I knew what that meant, but on a practical level I didn't have Totality that way that Hadron had it. So I remained with I Superconscious which was functioning for me with my body.

It wasn't Alzheimer's with Hadron. He decided to turn his brain off. But nevertheless he became impossible to live with.

What made you decide to come to Santa Fe?

It was an intuition at first.

I began to faint when we would go into buildings from the gas fumes that would come up from parking garages. We went into Century Plaza for dinner one day. We're waiting to go into the dining room and I faint dead away. The garage was underneath there and the fumes were coming in. Then we went to the city one day and the smog was so terrible I fainted dead away. I couldn't tolerate the smog. We decided this is not good. I found Los Angeles and the surrounding area intolerable.

We both took maps and went in separate rooms with a pendulum to pendle where we should go. It was northern New Mexico. It seemed to focus on Ojo Caliente. So we got into the car and drove to New

Mexico. We went to the springs at Ojo Caliente, and I was so turned off by the whole place. It was a mess as far as I was concerned. That wasn't my idea of a place to go to. We took some people out there. We took a builder out. We made three or four trips.

We had written a concept of a community. We had read this book in which someone said that the Earth situation was going to change so that people would be safer living in communities. We immediately drew up a whole plan for a community and how it could function. I wrote to Washington and got cooperative information on how to form a cooperative organization, a cooperative bank, and all of that. Our vision was to have a very nice community. Then we saw that there were healing springs, like at Baden-Baden.

We thought we would make a health resort, but there would have to be millions of dollars put into that place to make it anything I would be interested in having. I have an elegant complex. I'm sorry, but I do. And I found that place intolerable. It was so shabby.

I went to a legal firm. There were three counties there, for goodness sakes. I was told that the politics were impossible in all three of them, that the town of Ojo was impossible, that the Indians would fight us if we wanted to build.

I said, "Yes, but we would be providing employment and everything nice there, a school they could come to and all of that."

But then I realized that it's a public place and we really need a private place. So we decided, I decided at least, that it wasn't at Ojo.

Then an agent took us to a piece of property less than five miles from Ojo. It was four hundred and twenty-five acres of beautiful land. It has a gorgeous home on it and a beautiful barn. A good start. We could live there and start building a community. We sent a hydrologist out. He came back with a report. We saw springs bubbling out of the ground. He said there is a whole lake of mineral springs water under this property, as it is at Ojo. It's a continuation, a whole lake of water, exactly like the mineral springs at Ojo.

I said, "That would be ideal. We could make nice bath houses instead of what they have there that we would have to knock down."

But we weren't ready with money. Hadron was going through this depletion stage, and I was having to take care of him.

We decided then that we would go to the nearest town, which was Santa Fe. The pendulum okayed Santa Fe. I flew there. I went to a motel and I sat there and meditated. I got a Sunday newspaper and looked through it. My heart wasn't in it. How do you find a place where you don't know what's going on in it? I found a cab and had the driver take me all around the town.

I was thoroughly disgusted with Santa Fe. It was old. The sidewalks were crooked. The buildings were old. Everything was old. There's a lot of art stores and that was nice. I was not entranced with Santa Fe. And yet I had heard that people think that Santa Fe is the so-called spiritual place to be in.

So I went back to the hotel and called Hadron and said, "Hadron, if it isn't brown, forget it!"

He said, "So what do you want to do?"

I knew I couldn't ask him for an opinion, because he never gave me an opinion even when he was in his right mind about what to do in life. So we pendled Santa Fe and it said *yes*—the pendulum said *yes*.

I came back again and saw an ad for a two-bedroom, three hundred and sixty-five dollars a month. I didn't realize it was in the old part of town. I didn't really have any idea of what was happening there. The man came to the hotel and drove me to that old house of his. I looked it and thought, *"Oh God. . . ."* (We were living in a thirteen-room beautiful house in Brentwood. It was right next to Bel Aire that was right next to Beverly Hills.) I looked at this shabby house. It seemed shabby to me, no garbage disposal. It had a garage. It had a yard. We did bring all of our stuff with us, thirteen rooms of furniture. And here I'm renting a two-bedroom house which I did not like. And I rented it.

We moved in November 1982 from sunny California to the snow in Santa Fe. It was cold. I wasn't thrilled about any of what we were doing. It cost us three thousand dollars to move. We put most of our furniture in storage, because I had dreams that we would again. . . .

But then Hadron was deteriorating too much, and I was having to take care of him, which was terrible for me. He was urinating. I would put a device on him. He would take it off.

He said, "I don't urinate in my pants. I don't pee in my pants. What do I have to wear that for?"

271

And he wouldn't put it back on again. That meant I was really half of my life in the bathroom with him. This was terrible for me.

There was a woman here in town, a very wealthy woman, and she knew a woman in Los Angeles who knew me. She had called this woman and told her she was going to commit suicide because her son in India had committed suicide and she felt responsible. This lady told her, "Look, Joanna Walsh has just moved to Santa Fe. I'll give you her phone number. Call her. She'll help you. I'm sure you won't commit suicide when she can help you."

And I did. I worked with that woman. That was my first client here, the first money I earned. It got me going. And she referred me to other people.

This woman was so upset by a male entity that she looked male. Her hair was cut like a male. She dressed in jeans and sweaters, and they weren't very clean. She invited us to her home. It was a beautiful home. She was a wealthy woman. She had this little husband who was English.

One day he called me and said, "I'm going to put her back in the mental hospital."

I said, "No, you're not. I know her problem. I've been working with her gradually to get her confidence and to see what was going on. I know exactly what her problem is, and I want this opportunity to do this."

He said, "OK."

We drove out to her place in the snow. I decided I was going to get at this situation that I knew was there. I did a meditation with her that kind of put her into an altered state.

Then I addressed the male entity. I said, "Hello. I understand that you're living with this woman. How long?"

"Since she was two years of age."

She didn't tell me this in the session. He told me that she was raped by her mother's husband who was a medical doctor, raped. She left her body and he went in to help her. But he controlled her. She was a male. She wasn't a female. She couldn't have sex with her husband because she was a male. When a male entity moves into a female body, he takes her over. She's not her own self at all. Periodically she'd be going in and out of mental hospitals because of it. I knew that was there. I was shown superconsciously exactly the situation. I was determined that I was going to finally do this with her.

I communicated with him. I said, "How would you like to get out of her body? I'll help you, take you to the spirit world. We have friends there that will help you, and you can come back in your own body."

"I've taken care of her all her life practically. How's she going to get along without me?"

"I'm going to help her to reestablish herself as a female. I will help to bring her female spirit into action in her body. She'll be all right and you will be better off. Don't you think that would be a good idea? Tell me what you think about this."

"You sound like a very nice lady. I feel I can trust you."

I put my arms out. A spirit is very light. I did call upon help from the spirit world. Red Wing came in. He said, "Me help you, Joanna. Me help you."

I could see that spirit come onto my arms. Red Wing took him to the spirit world. That's the first time I had any experience like that. But it seemed so natural to do it that way.

When she came back into her body again, I said, "How do you feel?"

She said, "I feel fine."

I told her what happened.

She said, "Oh, I didn't remember the rape."

"You wouldn't. You were a little girl."

"Oh, I could kill that guy. He's still alive. I'm going to call my mother's attention to what he did to me." And the whole family went into an uproar, which was all right, because it wasn't fair what happened.

That was on a Saturday.

The next morning, Sunday, her husband calls me and says, "What miracle have you wrought?"

"What happened?"

"For the first time in twelve years of marriage I felt I had a woman in my bed and we made love."

"That thrills me. I am delighted. I did help this entity release from her body. If I were you I wouldn't talk about this too much with her. I've explained it to her. It's better to leave it alone."

The next time I saw her she was a female. Her hair was bleached blonde, all puffed up. She had this Mexican blouse on off her shoulder with a lot of Mexican jewelry and a big full Mexican skirt. I thought to myself, *"What miracle have I wrought!"*

She helped me put together a workshop of people, and that started putting me into business. I realize that I seem to be able to get myself going wherever I'm at and do my work. I seem to be able to do it. I have a survival factor going that enables me to do that. She sent me clients. In her home she called up people she knew. She did a certain kind of healing work. She had a room set aside for healing. We had a workshop going for me, and from then on it was referral. I began to work and make a living.

What I found unusual was that a lot of the people I worked with in Santa Fe couldn't afford to pay me, whereas in California people had no problem with paying. In California I used to have a thousand dollar intensive so that I would be sure to have clients that continued working. When you do this deep work with people the subconscious begins to act up and not let them come back to complete the work. So I decided on the thousand-dollar intensive, and it worked. People stayed with me long enough to complete the work. Then I was told that in Santa Fe you can't do that. People don't have that kind of money. So I set a fifty-dollar minimum, no matter how long. My sessions are two hours and sometimes three hours. I don't watch time. I'm interested in completing what I start out to do in that particular session with a person. My work is multi-dimensional.

One day I decided Hadron had to leave. I didn't know how. I took care of him for four years. He reverted to being a child, a petulant child. So one day I'm walking out of the bathroom, always cleaning up from incontinence. I would buy him everything but he wouldn't put it on.

He said, "I don't pee in my pants."

He didn't remember. I had to go to the bathroom, put it back on him. I had just about had it with all of that.

I come out of the bathroom and I hear, *"This is not your consciousness,"* three times. I said, "I know it isn't, but what can I do?" No answer.

I take him into the living room, and he sits down on the couch and watches television while I go to fix breakfast. I'm in the kitchen. My face is facing the wall and the counter, and I feel kissing on my neck and my ears, and I feel hands around my waist, and I said to myself, "This is not Hardin Walsh's energy. This is Hadron of Orr's energy. What's going on here?"

Hardin Walsh's body was used to give me this exquisite experience of Hadron of Orr's energy. The only time we had sex that was anything worthwhile was when Hadron of Orr came in and used Hardin Walsh's body. And here was an experience, and I got it.

I got, "This is it. This is it. This is the end of it, isn't it?"

I turned around and put my arms around his body and kissed him and he kissed me. That was like a kiss that I had never had even with Hardin Walsh. I turned around. Hardin was walking away, didn't know what had happened. We had no discussion about it. He sat down and waited for his breakfast. But that was the experience to help me realize why I can't have sex or even kiss or hold hands with Earth men. I couldn't, because of that wonderful experience at our home planet with Hadron of Orr.

I fixed breakfast and took it in to him. We had breakfast in the other room watching television. He went into the bathroom, and I didn't follow him this time. I had said I wasn't going to anymore. The love seat is a LazyBoy, which has a foot rest that comes up, so I had my feet up. Hadron walks in, sits on my legs, right across my legs, dead away. I thought, *"You can't hold me in bondage anymore, mister."*

I had the phone next to me. I called the doctor. I called the ambulance. The ambulance came and I had to shove him off my legs or I couldn't open the door for the ambulance. That's when I began to cry, the grief.

They took him in the ambulance. I went with him and I cried all the way to the hospital. I was telling them that this man was equal to Jesus Christ in his goodness and his awareness and his ability. I cried and kept talking about the merits of Hadron of Orr. We got to the hospital. The doctor was there, Dr. Hawkins.

He said, "He's got an infection from urinating into all of those things."

"What's going to happen?"

"We'll get rid of the infection, but I don't want you to take him home, because you have candida albicans because of his condition and the smell of the urine. So don't take him home."

"What can I do?"

"There's a state hospital."

"I don't have money to pay for a nursing home."

"For six months they will take him into that state hospital."

I had to leave this once-elegant creature in that nursing home where all of these sick and dilapidated people were — and he had already declined, in size and memory and everything, with so-called Alzheimer's disease. I had a lot of grief for the time I left him there, but I went on with my life. I went on working with people. I couldn't when I was taking care of him. I developed a pretty good clientele at that time, enough to support myself. I didn't have his Social Security or veteran's pension anymore. I had my own Social Security.

After the six months were up at the state hospital, they said I had to put him into a facility in town and I had to pay.

I said, "With what?"

"Whatever money you both have has to be given to the nursing home."

And I did. That left me bereft of any personal money. But any time I worked I would ask the person to make a contribution to Totality. That money went into the Totality account, and that helped to pay the rent.

I had to take him to a regular nursing home in the town of Santa Fe. I went three times a week to see him. They would tell me, "When you come in, he comes alive. When you leave, he's dead meat."

They put him into his bed and he's dead. He doesn't communicate. He doesn't do anything. So I began to wonder where he went, where did he go.

One day I was there and he looks up at me and says, "What are you doing here?" I had to know what "here" was for him.

I said, "You're here, aren't you?"

"Yes."

"Well, then I'm here, too."

That got me out of it. Later on I found out that he actually had gone to the fifth dimension, but his body was a strong body and it was holding out.

I gave them all the money, and I got along somehow, as I always do.

When Hadron passed over—

The doctor calls me one day and says, "This guy is something else. I don't know how he keeps his body going."

That genetic entity, we knew, was keeping the body going.

I said, "I'll go over to the hospital."

He said, "What do you want done with his Earth body?"

"I'll ask him."

"He isn't talking. He hasn't talked in I don't know how long."

"I'll go to the hospital anyhow and I'll see what happens."

I sit down on his bed. I hold his hand in mine. I look at that face. It's not Hadron any more. It just is not him anymore. That handsome face is not there anymore. I sit there and I wait for Superconscious to give me information. And this is what I came up with.

"Hadron of Orr, this is Orayna of Orr." I repeated it. "Come in please. Come in please." It sounded like *"Earth calling Ork"* on that television program. For the life of me it sounded like that. "Come in please. I need to communicate with you."

He opens his big green eyes. He looks at me and smiles.

He says, "Of course you're Orayna of Orr."

I needed that validation.

"And of course I'm Hadron of Orr. What do you want? What do you want?"

Where is this guy coming from? Where did he come alive? Here one moment he couldn't talk and now he's talking to me. What is this about?

He did say, "I am in the fifth dimension."

I said, "What do you want done with your Earth body?"

He said, "I will take care of that thing."

And I could have kicked myself. Why didn't I ask more? Why didn't I ask what are you doing where you're at? Afterwards I became curious. I didn't realize that I could continue communicating with him until a later date when he did come in and talk with me.

The next morning at eleven o'clock I'm ready to go back to the hospital. I feel energy leave my body like a Niagara Falls. Volumes of energy left my body and I had to go lie down. Then I realized that he left, and he took whatever energy he could from his body, and he took what he had of his in my body. All of his energy went.

Then the phone rang and the nurse said that he just expired.

I said, "I know."

"How do you know?"

"Oh, I'm psychic."

I knew. His energy leaving my body did leave me bereft of energy. I realized that I had to find some way to get that masculine energy back in my body.

So Ahad came in like he did the first time. The first time Ahad came in was the time Hadron left to go to the hospital. The second time he came in was when Hadron passed over. We went to the memorial house and initiated the final procedures of Hadron, the cremation. When we went to get the ashes, I gave it to Ahad to take. I couldn't quite take it home with me at that time. Ahad took it home with him and gave it to me later. Ahad is no ordinary soul. There seems to be a destiny there between us by the way he functions with me.

C O N T R O L   S T A T I O N

Most SPIRITS are operating BODIES on planet Earth under HYPNOTIC control from some local, this solar system, CONTROL STATION. When the SPIRIT leaves the BODY at death a kind of homing pigeon beam keys-in which says, "I AM GOING HOME." This beam has a very high esthetic value and the SPIRIT generally hangs around for the funeral. As soon as all the excitement is over, he/she takes off, guided to the CONTROL STATION on this beam, because it is so beautiful and comfortable.

Some CONTROL STATIONS are satellite-type space stations, manned by SPIRITS WHO OPERATE CERTAIN TYPES OF EQUIPMENT. Other types of CONTROL STATIONS operate on and in the actual planet.

What happens between lives is more or less the same for all

CONTROL STATIONS. There are some very fancy variations in many universes but the results are all similar.

The departing SPIRIT is either sadly or gladly heading for "HOME" after the funeral. Arriving at the door or entry chute he/she gleefully enters.

Immediately there is a blast from four directions of sub-SONIC energy beams, designed to knock him/her even more UNCONSCIOUS than his recent befuddled existence on planet Earth.

In the main control room he/she is attached to a robot-type android BODY with earth-type characteristics in a barber shop-style chair. From the outer perimeter of the circular control room he/she is hit from 12 different positions (clock) with heavy shock beams containing "wipe outs." Hypnotic suggestions that there will be no remembering of being in the CONTROL STATION and a FORGETTING of all past lives and especially the last one.

The STATION OPERATORS are punching out a new lifetime pattern on the computer system, which is fed into the energy beam converters as hypnotic commands, which are installed in the SPIRIT'S force-fields with pain and shock.

These commands can be termed FORCE-FIELDS OF NEGATION, usually non-verbal on the THOUGHT level.

You will NEVER REMEMBER any of these happenings.
You will ALWAYS REPORT BACK to this station upon leaving the body.
You will think it is your imagination if you remember this.
You will GO INSANE if you remember this.
Your HEART WILL STOP BEATING if you remember any of this.
You will NOT REMEMBER that you are a SPIRIT.
You will NEVER REMEMBER that you are TOTALITY.
You will think that you are a BODY.
You will not leave the body until your PROGRAMMED ASSIGNMENT is completed.
If you leave the body you will never be able to find it.

If you remember any of this you will immediately go to sleep and
FORGET IT completely.

The more you try to release this, the more solid it will get.

NOTHING WILL DO ANY GOOD.

There are perhaps a thousand or more of such hypnotic implants
installed as FORGETTER MECHANISMS.

The SPIRIT is then shown a set of pictures on a video screen —
usually a set of 48 pictures showing segments of his new life, such as
size, shape, and color of the BODY.

> Go to such-and-such town or location — report to Cedars of
> Lebanon Hospital — pick up a male body. . . .
> Your mother is — so-and-so. . . .
> Your school is so-and-so. . . .
> Attend so-and-so university. . . .
> You will be an attorney. . . .
> The left arm is to break at 1400 hours 17 August. . . .
> One operation is allowed. . . . Appendectomy. . . .
> Married two times. . . . Blondes. . . .
> Three bodies must be created for children. . . .
> Report back to Control Station 88 immediately after age 86.5. . . .

Death is installed as a hypnotic implant complete with pictures and
sensations. How beautiful it is to escape from all your relatives and
creditors. . . .

The SPIRIT is then enveloped in a beautiful beam of exquisite sex and
other sensations and told of the miraculous wonder and joy of being
human.

He/She is beamed back to Earth near the hospital or contact
LOCATION to pick up his/her newly ASSIGNED BODY. The entire
elapsed Earth time is generally, on an average, 20 or 30 minutes
between lifetimes. This is perhaps true of 75% of the population on
the planet.

TOTALITY CONCEPT 185-188 740719

The STUDENT is most interested in cleaning up the agreements with which HE/SHE came into this lifetime: all the others seem to impinge or key-in on the last most recent IMPLANT STATION contact.

Between lifetimes the SPIRIT will discover that he/she is being fed a complete set of pictures and instructions and hypnotic implants for the next lifetime.

In some of the cruder stations next-lifetime patterns are presented on a flimsy erector set-type ferris wheel. In some cases a set of cards is used by station operators. GOD is often presented as an old man with a long gray beard. In some cases statues are used with illuminated lights. Basically the pictures depict segments of this life to be, i.e.: You will be a male. Attend such-and-such a school. Marry twice: one blonde, one brunette. Two children are created. You will be an Episcopal administrator. At age 87.8 you will leave the body and report back here.

Beautiful heavenly white lights and divine blue lights are used for electronic energy beams.

No matter how beautiful they seem you must ASSIGN and UNASSIGN them over and over until you have CERTAINTY of CONTROLLING the picture or recordings of them.

TOTALITY CONCEPT 192 740725

12

DANCES WITH MELINDA
1988–1991

One characteristic of superconscious action in our lives is that things seem to proceed smoothly and effortlessly without anxiety or worry. Just knowing what is desired for one's life with certainty that it will come about, giving the way it will come about into the hands of a higher power, is often all it takes. Which is not to say that other desired results will not require a lot of concentration, effort, and work, but again without undue anxiety or worry. The next few times I had to move to another house, the way opened up immediately and effortlessly. In the same way my next lover came into my life so smoothly I didn't notice it at first.

Luke Gatto and I were sharing a house on Lugar de Monte Vista. Our roommate had just moved out and we needed another housemate right away to meet the rent. One afternoon I was on my way to the gym, late as usual. Luke was sitting and talking with someone in the living room.

He said, "Ahad, I want you to meet Melinda. She's a massage student looking for a place to live. Tell me what you think of her."

I came in and glanced briefly at Melinda — tall, willowy, blonde, big brown eyes. I knew immediately that she was a friend and that we could live just fine together. Without saying anything more than hello to her I told Luke that she would be fine as a roommate and rushed on out to the gym. Instant recognition. No second thoughts. Indeed, no thought at all.

Melinda was a new roommate who came with a steady boyfriend. I had not the slightest inclination to any romantic involvement with her. But when she was having emotional issues I informally shared some Totalizing with her and helped her clear up some feelings. She was no longer happy with her love relationship, so things were breaking up even while lingering on, as those things tend to do.

One night I had a dream that she came into my room, lay down with me, and made love with me. The next night she came into my room, lay down with me, and asked me to just hold her. It felt wonderful and blissful. The next night she came again into my room, lay down with me, and made love with me. Effortlessly, love came into my life again.

Along with love came all sorts of emotional turmoil and psychic uproar, for Melinda was very volatile and uncertain in intimacy, one day running away, one day clinging on, a never-ending flow of drama — which of course triggered all my reactive bank of negative feelings such as rejection, abandonment, confusion, etc. This was a major practical test of the methods Joanna had given me to work with subconscious interference.

Instead of just giving in and being overwhelmed by all these familiar feelings, as I had always done in the past, I would go out and take long walks, being aware of the vortex of energy around and within my body, putting the information into the vortex to release the negative emotions that were arising, following the energy of my intention down the vortex, and seeing it react back out and dissolve the limiting feelings back into space. And it worked! I could actually recognize and take charge of clearing away negative emotions for the first time in my life! I came back from these walks clear and calm, invigorated and inspired, and to a large degree did not feed my own reactivity into whatever dramas were churning in Melinda. Totally awesome!

Using the vortex energy for psychic birth control was another major demonstration of the practical effectiveness of Joanna's teachings. Melinda and I shared incredible sexual intimacy, making love longer and more often than either of us ever had before, and reaching unimagined waves and peaks of ecstasy and union. Sometimes we would literally make love all day long. All without ever using any physical form of birth control. While we were making love, I would be aware of the vortex of energy surrounding our bodies and put into the vortex the information, '*No conceptions, no pregnancies, no births. No conceptions, no pregnancies, no births.*' I did not have to repeat this mantra for very long, but I did do it with absolute certainty, knowing on every level that this was true. And I would repeat this practice when our lovemaking was over. And it worked!

It also helped that I had enough control that I never ejaculated inside her, but there was certainly plenty of minor release of fluid in our extended lovemaking. We both had demonstrated that we were fertile human beings. We were at an appropriate age, going through the motions of making babies for a period of three years. There can be, of course, no "scientific" proof that psychic birth control worked for me or can work for anyone else. But for me there is no doubt that it worked.

At times Melinda became strongly convinced that she wanted to have a baby, but she was not willing to have a household together, let alone get married. (When we had to leave Monte Vista, she didn't want to find a house with me — she wanted to have her own place and continue our relationship.) Like everything else, her desire for a child was volatile and wavering, sometimes very intense, sometimes not present at all. But she did not want me to go on using psychic birth control.

I would say to her, "I have already had one child with a woman who could not live with me. I'm already raising one child in a broken family. I know that that is not the best way to bring a child into the world, and I am not willing to do it that way again. Let's make a home together and see how that feels, then get married, then go about having a family. I would love to do it with you if we can do it in a good way." In the meantime I kept on putting the postulate into the vortex, '*No conceptions, no pregnancies, no births.*' And it continued to work — even when she didn't want it to.

The last night we spent together, sleeping in separate rooms by that time, just before I fell asleep I saw a very bright point of light pass very slowly above my bed, just like watching a satellite orbiting way up in the sky. I knew that this was the spirit that wanted to come in to Melinda, but I knew that this was not the right time for this to happen — a correct intuition, as it turned out, for Melinda lost her life under tragic circumstances less than a year later.

SUPERCONSCIOUS IN ACTION
Summer 1994

Although Joanna focused on generating a new blueprint for life and seeing material results in the lives of her clients, her primary goal was to trigger awareness of being Superconscious functioning in an Earth body. Profound changes resulted from working with her. I was able to support myself and my family working at a normal job in accounting. I was able to have normal loving relations with people without distorting romantic obsessions.

But the most profound changes were in my self-identity, my attitude and approach to life. In present time I no longer have more than a trace of identification with the person written about in this book, because so much of the automatic reactivity of my past-life recordings has been released, once and for all. I am no longer the suffering succotash recorded in these pages. I am no longer dominated by obsession and compulsion, aversion and attachment. I am aware of Superconscious love and guidance in my everyday life, open to accept life as it comes, and surrendered to serve in whatever way I may.

When material things need to manifest, they happen in a much different way, with much less effort, anguish, fear, and doubt. If something needs to manifest, I do my work with due diligence and offer the results of my work to Superconscious to manifest in the right way. I know that there is a Higher Power guiding, guarding, loving, and protecting all of us. This was demonstrated by the almost effortless way that Superconscious found a house for me to buy, once karmic recordings were released and once necessity was real.

I had decided that I was ready to buy a house for the first time in my life in the winter of 1993. Guided by my realtor friend Nancy, I had looked at numerous houses throughout that winter and spring, never finding anything satisfactory. Though at times I would feel guilty for not responding positively to the opportunities with which she presented me and often wondered whether I was wasting her time with my ongoing lack of clarity, she was always very positive. "We'll just keep on looking," she would say.

In June, after viewing one of the last remaining hilltop lots in Santa Fe, a gorgeous building spot, I went for a drive in the country to celebrate. Immediately a feeling of darkness and gloom descended over me — fear, terror, and despair. To build a house there, anywhere, would be to be trapped, doomed, was all I could hear.

These feelings were so intense and irrational. I began to realize that they must be due to the restimulation in present time of negative emotional complexes hidden away in subconscious. I had carefully considered this move and explored its consequences. I had made a rational decision which seemed supported by higher consciousness, and I was approaching it all in a very business-like manner. But subconscious reactivity kept being restimulated and getting in the way. I knew it was time to ask Joanna for help.

In session Joanna guided me to look at various contributing factors — the loss of my beloved, my early childhood alienation, and my immediate previous life as a fugitive from the Holocaust. This alone took many hours of concentrated work. Though resonant, none of these recordings seemed primarily causal, and we asked to be shown the picture that was the root cause of my not being able to buy a home.

I maintained awareness of being space, it seemed for eternity. I asked to see, to be shown, and waited, waited, waited. Finally in the gray ethers of my vision there was a small opening through which I could see flames. It was a lightly constructed house, as in the tropics. The roof was on fire and collapsing in on me.

Joanna said, "Where are you?"

I heard, *"India."*

And immediately my rational mind tried to invalidate me, *"Oh yeah, sure, India, that's fantasy."*

But I had learned to discount the resistance of my rational mind to seeing and said out loud, "India."

Joanna said, "Good, go into the picture deeper. Get more information."

I sensed that there were men standing outside my house, men who had set fire to it to destroy me. I got a clear picture that I had been an astrologer living in an Indian village, a small brown man with a white beard, a good man, a Sufi and a lover of wisdom. Joanna told me she saw that I had a wife and a small child who were also destroyed in the fire. I tried to identify the men who destroyed me. My mind said that maybe they were Hindus who hated Muslims. Whatever. Having identified the causal picture, I released the picture and all the feelings associated with it using the vortex energy, dissolving all the light particles back into space until nothing remained. Then I replaced that picture with my new blueprint for a home, family, love, and security. Now I was clear and ready to proceed.

I related this to a Vedic scholar friend. He asked whether this incident was in recent times, after the partition of India and Pakistan. I said it seemed to be in an earlier century. He remarked that Hindus were not known for their violence but that Sunni (orthodox) Muslims were known to persecute Sufis and other heterodox believers.

When he said that, it all fell in place: my Sufi heritage but aversion to orthodox Muslims, my love of astrology but reluctance to promote my profession to the public. The bottom line was that the last house I had owned had been burnt to the ground, myself and my family along with it, and this had been the memory that caused the arising of fear and terror at the prospect of owning a new house.

Matters came to a head in the middle of July 1994. My sixteen-year-old son Abe had been living mostly with his mother and her husband for the past few years. Now due to a burden of accrued debt they were forced to sell their house, pay off their debtors, and move to another location. They had the house on the market for years with no result, but all of a sudden they were made an offer they could not refuse At the same time, their offer was accepted on an acre of land in Pecos on which they intended to put two trailers. This all came down on Monday.

Abe was losing his home. He would have to come and live with me. My apartment was much too cramped for both of us. Necessity had arrived. In the very same week Superconscious found a house for me to buy.

The value of necessity in fostering evolution and opening the door to superconscious action in our lives cannot be underestimated. Inertia is such a strong reality on the physical and psychic planes that few of us would change at all unless we absolutely had to, unless we were compelled by changing outer circumstances or by inner urgings to fulfill our destiny. The more comfortable we are, physically and emotionally, the less likely we are to budge from our niche in the world. We work long and hard for material and social security, only to have it stripped away when Superconscious desires to prepare us for a deeper task at certain times.

At a certain point, Mr. Gurdjieff desired to remove from his life everything and everyone that was a source of comfort to him so that he would be left to solely concentrate upon his task of writing.

The Hopi say they settled in the middle of the desert so that their people would have to live through the power of prayer and not merely through the abundant wealth of the Earth.

Rumi says, *"Increase the necessity."*

I had done my homework. I had cleared the way. Then, as of Monday, it became necessary that I have a new home for Abe and myself to live in.

On Thursday around noon Nancy called me at work.

"I have a house for you to see. I think you're really going to like it. These people are going away on the weekend. I know you don't like to look at houses in the evening. So the first time we can see it is Sunday afternoon. But I really think you ought to see it. It's a very good price for the market, and it's going to go very fast."

"Well, that sounds good. Why don't you just tell me where it is? Maybe I'll drive by and check it out."

"It's on Callejon Emilia."

That was in the neighborhood I desired.

"How much is it?"

"I think it's one-thirty-seven."

That was in my ballpark.

After work I went to the gym as usual and worked out in my aerobics class and on the stationary bicycle. Around 6:45 I was driving home. Halfway home the thought occurred to me, *"Why don't you drive by that house and check it out?"*

I drove down into Barrio La Cañada where I used to live. I didn't look at a map. I thought I could find it. I drove up one or two wrong streets before doubling back and finally finding the street I was looking for. I turned onto the street and was immediately turned off. I didn't like the first couple of houses I saw. But down toward the end of the street there was a group of huge Chinese elms, green and shady, lining the street, three times as tall as the houses. I thought to myself, *"I could really live here, under those elms."*

There were no For Sale signs posted in the yards along the street. I wondered how I was going to find the house I wanted to look at. I cruised slowly up to the first of the houses under the Chinese elms and looked into its yard. It was very green and pleasant, with lots of colorful plantings, a nice house. I thought, *"I could really live here."*

On the sidewalk in front of the house a woman was opening the door to her car. The moment I drove by, she looked up, looked me straight in the face through the windshield of my van and said, "Oh, it's him!"

This was Nancy. I wouldn't have recognized her car sitting in front of the house. There was no For Sale sign. I would have missed it entirely unless she had been there at that very second, looked up, looked me straight in the face and said, "Oh, it's him!"

That was it. There was no way I could have planned this. It was a superconscious setup, and I knew it at that moment.

Everything came together perfectly and smoothly from then on.

I pulled my car over and greeted Nancy, who was surprised and pleased to see me. We went in and met the owners of the house, an older couple with whom I felt a good rapport. We toured the house. It was neat and clean and spacious. It not only had three bedrooms, two bathrooms, and a garage, but also a beautiful enclosed sun porch full of light and air, which was more than I was looking for. Nancy and I went out in the backyard, which was well tended, with beautiful flowers, lilac bushes, cedar shrubs, aspens and fruit trees. I felt very warm, very at home.

"This is really a good deal," she said. "If you want it you'd better move on it right away. The woman accepted a job up in Wyoming, and they have to move immediately. They didn't even list it with a realtor. They advertised it in the paper. I happened to see the ad and came over to check it out tonight. The price is very good because they want to move right away. Someone is bound to pick it up very quickly."

"How much is it?

"I think it's one-thirty-five. We'll have to see."

As I stood there in that lush backyard in the early evening, everything did indeed seem perfect: the time, the place, the price. As we were going out the door, a pickup truck pulled into the driveway. It seemed to be an elderly couple who were probably also going to check out buying the house.

"They're going to go away for the weekend. They'll be backpacking in the Pecos until Sunday afternoon. Probably nothing will happen until then. But if you want this house you need to make up your mind very fast about it."

I went home and sat with it. It felt good. I did astrological charts for the moment of coming to the house. They seemed very good.

Although usually I worry and agonize over decisions, especially when the choice is not the right one and the answer is really no, in this case it seemed good on every feeling level. When I got very still and listened I got the intuitive *yes*. The feeling of *yes* combined with the way in which it had happened so spontaneously and serendipitously, led me to recognize Superconscious acting for me in my life.

When it's not the right choice all sorts of questions, negative feelings, quibbles and judgments linger about, preventing choice from happening. When it's the right choice there is literally no question about it. It just is.

The next morning at 7:30 I called Nancy.

"I want to buy the house. Let's make them an offer."

"Good. I have a tennis game. I'll draw up the papers after the game. I'll come over to where you work for you to sign the offer. They're leaving around 12:30 for the Pecos, but I'd like to get it signed before then."

At 11:00 she arrived at my office with the papers.

"How much do they want for the house?" I ask.

"A hundred thirty-three five."

"That's what I want to offer."

I signed all the papers.

At 1:00 she called me.

"It's a done deal. They accepted."

It was all downhill from there. The rest of the process went without a hitch. The approval of the mortgage, the attainment of the downpayment, the funding of the mortgage, the closing on the house and the final move all proceeded without obstruction. I bought the house for well under the appraisal value. In addition the closing date was perfectly in sync with the closing date that Abe's mom and stepfather had on their house, such that Abe and I would be totally moved in to our new house on August 31, the same date that they had to be totally out of their house on Valley Drive.

That is how Superconscious found me a house to buy, probably the first house that my spirit took ownership of in centuries. I did my homework. I cleared the way. I got in a position so that I could do it. But when it came down to the actual action of finding the house, it was purely superconscious action. After more than nine months of preparation, I had been shown the house, made an offer and had the offer accepted in less than twenty-four hours.

I didn't plan to drive by and look at that house that evening. I just had a hunch, a feeling, while I was driving home from the gym. I didn't go directly to the house. I didn't use a map. I took a couple of wrong turns. There were a few small delays. But the timing was perfect. Before I knew it was the house I had the feeling, I had the Knowing, *"I really could live here"*— not once but twice. And at the split second that I drove past the house Nancy looked up from opening her car door, looked me straight in the face, and said, "It's him!"

That's more than happy coincidence. That is superconscious action.

A SPIRIT is an ASSIGNMENT: a THOUGHT that states "I AM A SPIRIT." The SPIRIT IS THOUGHT and therefore is not ENERGY. The AREA OF ASSIGNMENT that is the SPIRIT is THOUGHT which is TOTALITY — an ASSIGNED segment of the TOTAL SELF.

A SPIRIT that REMEMBERS and is AWARE of being TOTALITY can APPEAR and DISAPPEAR at WILL and thus cannot be hurt, trapped, or affected by other BEINGS, ENERGY BEAMS or THOUGHTS.

To move from LOCATION to LOCATION the SPIRIT who operates with AWARENESS as TOTALITY unmakes himself and REASSIGNS

HIM/HERSELF at the new LOCATION. He/she APPEARS AND
DISAPPEARS at LOCATIONS simply by deciding to.

SPIRITS in the Earth-type GAME have entered into two basic "GAME
AGREEMENTS"

CAN CREATE WITH A THOUGHT.

CANNOT DESTROY A THOUGHT.

Since the SPIRIT is a THOUGHT ASSIGNMENT, this AGREEMENT
causes a SPIRIT to be unable to UNMAKE or UNASSIGN (DESTROY)
her/himself from any given LOCATION. Rather than disappear
she/he must MOVE from the LOCATION.

TIME GAME-wise. all movements are places on the AUR CYCLE —
ASSIGN-UNASSIGN-REASSIGN — and thus there is MOTION or there
appears to be.

With this AGREEMENT — "CANNOT DESTROY A THOUGHT" — a
SPIRIT cannot escape from a given location by UNMAKING
him/herself and returning to the state of pure THOUGHT or the
TOTALITY level which creates THOUGHT, by a DECISION. This makes
it possible to trap and control SPIRITS with ENERGY beams and
various magnetic devices.

In this way it is possible to EXPERIENCE the sensations of PRETEND-
ING to be DESTROYED and enjoy the BEAUTIFUL SADNESS of a
GAME in which a LOSS is GUARANTEED.

Apparently this is desirable after a SPIRIT has WON for millions
upon millions of aeons of so-called TIME. Boreing ???????????

TOTALITY CONCEPT 183-184 740719

PSILOCYBIN SESSION
outside of time

Joanna never used psychedelic drugs and was not interested in them or
the people who used them. But she was interested in any way she could

find to bypass the body and be Superconscious, and she had heard all the claims people made about how psychedelics opened one up to cosmic consciousness. So at some point in time she asked me if I could obtain some psychedelic drugs, ingest them, and go into session with her so that she could see what effect they might have on my ability to be aware of being present as the space, to be aware of being Superconscious, to be aware of being Totality. She was very clear that I should never tell anyone about this, as she didn't want to be associated with drugs in any way — so I never recorded the date of this session, since it took place "outside of time."

One afternoon when the Moon was conjunct Jupiter in Aquarius, which I thought might be a propitious time, I brought in a large dried psilocybin mushroom, showed it to her, and slowly ate it, savoring its bitter chocolate taste. We were sitting in her living room talking, and after a while the effects of the psilocybin began to come on. The walls behind her began to pulse with vivid green and orange cellular patterns, and she appeared to be a Mayan priestess in ornate regalia sitting on a throne. I suggested to her that it was time to go into session.

We went into her office and sat down at right angles to each other, as we always did. She placed the galvanic skin reactor clip on my hand and activated the Totalometer to monitor me. Great surges of blissful energy were pulsing through me. I was already having a great time. Joanna began to lead me through the familiar stages of the Totalizing meditation, starting with being aware of being present as the space within the physical body. I was aware of the mushroom energy totally filling my space with gently exploding luminous energy. I could not be aware of being present as the space because I had totally filled my space with mushroom energy.

Joanna kept guiding me and questioning me as to my level of awareness. I kept responding that my space was filled with strong mushroom energy and I could not get beyond the psychedelic effect to the subtle emptiness of space that by now I knew so well. And I started laughing hilariously. After a while Joanna gave up and left the room, leaving me to surf the blissful mushroom energy. I sat in that chair for hours, flooded with vivid colors and blissful sensations, laughing, laughing, laughing. I have never laughed so much in my life. I was having a great time. Every now and then Joanna would look in on me to make sure I was all right, which I certainly was.

But at the same time, sitting in the same place where I had done so much real subtle work in real space, I was experiencing with certainty that I was not accessing Superconscious or any form of higher consciousness. I was totally flooding and intoxicating my system with mushroom energy. For several hours I was mushroom consciousness, beshroomed, and my thoughts were all dancing mushrooms. This was a real revelation for me. I knew mushrooms altered my consciousness and I had previously assumed that this was higher consciousness. But now I knew that true higher consciousness was so much more subtle and so much more real than this chemical carnival of organic energies.

Fortunately, the intensity of the psilocybin rush subsides after several hours and I returned to more or less normal consciousness. I came out and sat with Joanna in the living room again. She said she had no idea why anyone would want to pass so much energy through their body as I did laughing and laughing for hours. We both agreed that psychedelics did not seem to enable one to bypass the body and be aware of being present as the space, of being Superconscious, of being Totality. Then I drove Joanna out in her car to do some errands: go to the bank, go grocery shopping, sit in the cafeteria and have some pastry, all quite normal.

This session was not very productive for Joanna, but it was very transformative for me. I no longer felt any desire to take psychedelic drugs. I no longer have any illusions about reaching higher consciousness through eating mushrooms.

As Hadron would say, "This sure is fun, wasn't it?"

ENDING WITH REMEMBERING THE BEGINNING
December 25, 1992

After a big Christmas morning at his mom's house, I engaged Abe in the project of cleaning up his room. This was a big job, and by the end of it he was pretty exhausted and lay down on his bed to sleep. He was fourteen years old at the time. As he was drifting away, I did a brief Totalizing Meditation with him and asked if he could get any sense of who he was in his immediately previous life. There was a lot of space. Finally he said, "A young man in the seventies." And drifted off to sleep.

Later I asked him, "What could that mean, that you were a young man in the Seventies when you lost your life?"

He said, "I guess I died very young and came back very fast." (He was born in 1978.)

This certainly clarified his affinity for Jimi Hendrix and the Doors, as well as his intense dislike for Richard Nixon and the Vietnam War since a very early age. Why else would a four-year-old boy in 1982 vent strident contempt for Richard Nixon?

In the summer of 1992, I took Abe camping at Porvenir Campground outside of Las Vegas, New Mexico. He had dozed off on the drive. I was driving my bus up the long and winding road along the side of Gallinas Canyon. The turns were very sharp and there was a very steep drop-off on the left-hand side. Abe woke up with a start and was very alarmed and fearful of this steep and winding road. Something was restimulated in him.

Later on, talking by the campfire, we put it all together and got some sense that he must have lost his life driving along such a road. He was a young man in California, driving fast late at night, probably intoxicated, around the steep curves of the Pacific Coast Highway. He didn't have much of a sense of purpose in life, throwing himself into partying and getting high, and apparently lost control of the car, plunged off a steep cliff above the ocean, and lost his life.

As he drifted deeper into sleep that Christmas afternoon, his statement restimulated in me the fact that I had been a young man when I died in my previous life in the Holocaust in Europe. My recall on Truchas Peak with Glory had been very vivid and undeniable. However, throughout all my work with Joanna I had not recovered *how* I had died at that time. I sensed that I had been a fugitive, not immediately killed with my family, but I didn't know for how long, nor whether I had been murdered, committed suicide, or what.

At this very moment the image of the way station by the railway late at night with deep snow falling all around, shining in the light of one street lamp — the image that had haunted me in my early twenties —

came back again, and I knew that this was the picture of my previous death. I knew now that I had been a fugitive from the Nazis, running, hiding, wandering, perhaps with a companion, and finally had reached the end of the line. Starved, exhausted, cold, I had sought shelter in this way station by the railway in the middle of a big snowstorm. Too exhausted to move any further, I had simply let the snow and the cold embrace me and had left my body.

Now my soul recall had come around full circle. I had no doubt that when I was experiencing this image in my early twenties, *end of the line* echoing in my head, seeking out empty railway stations in the middle of the night in the cold and the snow, fantasizing about abandonment, homelessness, helplessness, being a fugitive, that the impact of my previous death was restimulated in present time at exactly the same age at which I had lost my body before.

The restimulation of my own previous death radically altered my life in my early twenties, among other things, such as the spirit of the sixties. My inner and outer state went from being identified with being a successful, well-dressed, well-to-do college student to being identified with being a homeless vagabond with torn and tattered clothes. Living in the material world was no longer real for me. I sought refuge in the only place I could, in spiritual community and seeking a spiritual path. I outlived the trauma of my previous death, and true grace granted me the blessings that life has to offer for those no longer young.

That Christmas afternoon I took a walk up Valley Drive with Abe's mom, Varda. It was a bright sunshiny day with clear blue sky and snowy mountains in the distance. I told her of my realization. She responded that maybe she had been with me at the time. Perhaps she had been my sister or more likely my cousin in this misadventure during the Holocaust. It seemed that I must have promised to always be with her, to befriend her and protect her, which is still the case to this day, despite our inability to stay married and the difficulties in our relationship.

With understanding comes acceptance, the ability to let it all be just the way it is, and not to rage futilely against the way things are. Because everything just is the way it is. And everything just seems to have a way of turning out all right, even including illness, disease, death, and destruction.

Even the immediate or eventual end of the world as we know it to be is all part of what Superconscious — timelessness, vastness, motionlessness, foreverness — experiences through immersion in and identification with this great game of life on Earth.

THE BASIC CONCEPT OF KARMA is that BAD acts done to others will be carried over into other lifetimes and retribution will eventually overtake you.

These OVERT ACTS, or things you have CONSIDERED BAD and/or done to OTHERS are probably most difficult to release.

When the BODY dies and the SPIRIT thinks, "WOW! I'm rid of that THING!", he is NOT. His recordings are carried with him as KNOWINGNESSES which he starts adding to the next BODY structure as soon as he picks it up.

NEW recordings are added to the BODY from moment to moment. GOOD sensations record the same as PAINFUL ones. There is a popular CONCEPT, widely spread by metaphysicians, that you "LIVE OUT" old BAD KARMA by being one of the GOOD GUYS. This is simply NOT TRUE.

Regardless of GOODNESS or BADNESS of a PAST INCIDENT they record in the BODY force-fields and MUST be released with proper methods.

Recordings are recordings no matter what the content. They exist in the cell structure and as ridges of energy in and around the ASTRAL BODY. If they are packed in too tightly the movement of the BODY is hampered and the operation of the organs is interfered with.

GOOD incidents out of the past are probably the most difficult to release because of the importance attached to their esthetic beauty.

ALL RECORDINGS MUST BE RELEASED: GOOD OR BAD.

TOTALITY CONCEPT 179-180 740716

HER STORY—SUPERCONSCIOUS

I'd like to explain how Superconscious actually functions for us. People think, "Oh, Superconscious is going to give me, going to give me, going to give me." Wait a minute! It's like people saying, "God did this to me, did that to me." It isn't a matter of "God give me this or give me that." It isn't that way at all.

You go and you live your life. You work to function from a higher level. You actually have a sincere desire to be more than the Earth body. And this is the right time to begin to function from a higher consciousness, from what I'm reading, from what I'm hearing.

When you are functioning correctly and even desire to function superconsciously, you can receive information from You Superconscious for your body by Knowing. Knowing is the tutor, I have found out. Jesus gave us the trigger. He said, *"Know ye not that ye are gods?"* And we have discovered that you are, as Superconscious. We need to get that reality very strongly. I have found that in working with people.

I have used my meditation that was given to me superconsciously to help people to acquire the realization, the sincere depth of that realization, that they are in fact Superconscious, have always been Superconscious, and will always be Superconscious. The realization of that is to function on Earth with your human body that way.

On other planets, on our planet, we function that way. We are light forms. We function directly as Superconscious. We don't have thinking minds. We don't have a subconscious that records everything and then the automatic reaction of the vortex on the body. That bondage doesn't exist on our home planet.

I would like people to understand that sometimes we get into very negative situations and we think that Superconscious isn't guiding us. It isn't a god. It's You Superconscious. You are Superconscious. You do want to help your body, but the human interferes. He uses doubt, or he uses thinking, or he reacts from the subconscious, and those are definite blocks to functioning superconsciously.

Sometimes Superconscious will create difficult situations, obstacles, failures, things that don't seem like goodies to us. But in fact they are part of superconscious intention — by meeting these obstacles we will grow in some way. If we had our way, then afterward in the long run, it wouldn't have turned out right for us. I had my personal experience that way, which I relate here, when I met Hardin Walsh, and in working with people.

We can recognize Superconscious by things that happen to us, incidents that we don't think. There's no thinking involved with the function of Superconscious, none whatsoever. That thinking interferes. As Jesus said, *"Be still and know."*

Be still means to brush aside the thinking, gibbering mind so that you can know and function superconsciously, because as Superconscious we know. The human body has thinking and reaction but doesn't seem to have Knowing.

In my experience of remembering Superconscious, when Hardin took me out into space (he called it *first otherness,* which it is, but I said *Superconscious*), I realized being that vortex of light. I didn't even realize I had a body down here. I was aware of being that vortex of light and Knowing. I had been given clues how to Know. I can give you examples of when I was able to let my body go and Know and have miracles happen.

I can't begin to tell you enough that you are Superconscious, you've always been Superconscious. Every living being in the universe is Superconscious. We created it all together right in the beginning. You Superconscious is there to help your body whether it's on this planet or any other. Be aware of that. Make use of it. And evolve as a result of it. For that is the truth.

13

DEATH AND DYING
1995–1998

In her later years Joanna had her name legally changed to her home-planet name Orayna Orr. She had been born Blossom Cohen (Bluma Cohen), was married as Bluma Friedman, then married again as Joanna Walsh — and when she was leaving the world she bore her true name, Orayna Orr.

Despite being well into her eighties, despite increasing physical disability and inability to manage her affairs, Orayna never lost her enthusiasm or her vision for Majine Enterprises and a rural community center, a huge project that she knew would take at least thirty more years to fulfill. She kept forging ahead without regard to any limitations until finally old age caught up with her.

In the fall of 1995 she was confined, very much against her will, to the Horizon Healthcare nursing home in Santa Fe. She was physically disabled by a variety of ailments, was no longer able to earn her own income through working with people, and had squandered away her meager income from Social Security and VA Widows Pension on sweepstakes and lotteries in the unshakable belief that Ed McMahon had personally promised her eleven million dollars and the check was in the mail, etc. Despite being many months in arrears on paying her rent, her landlord mercifully did not evict her until she was confined to the nursing home.

Orayna Orr passed away peacefully on June 17, 1998, at the age of ninety, still in the nursing home in Santa Fe. The Moon was conjunct

Jupiter. The feeling surrounding her deathbed was that of gentle release and blissful expansion into lighter and subtler reality. The last three years of her life had been a living hell in the nursing home. Orayna was finally ready to let go.

I was Orayna's closest friend during the last years of her life. It was a great and painful privilege for me to share her process of dying and death. In my family the process of dying had always been carefully hidden away from the children. It was even, "Oh, no, don't come home for the funeral. We know you're so busy working out there." All the intellectual comprehension and philosophical understanding of dying and death can prepare one but cannot substitute for the reality of sharing dying with a loved one. With Orayna I went through over and over again the various stages of dying described by Elizabeth Kubler-Ross: denial, anger, bargaining, pleading, and finally acceptance — not in any neat sequential order, but with all the various emotional levels piled on top of one another, mixed together in pain and confusion, except for acceptance, which waits until the end.

Twice in her life doctors had told her she would never walk again — once when she had polio as a child and once when she survived a severe car crash as a young adult. In both cases she had refused to believe the doctors when they told her she would never walk again and had successfully set about curing herself through her own superconscious guidance.

So naturally she refused to believe that she was dying or should be in a nursing home. This was just a temporary setback for her. She was always certain that she could rejuvenate herself and get back to fulfilling her life's work again. Only at the end when she could no longer walk at all, was confined to the bed and the wheelchair, and the pain was so constant and debilitating despite all the medication and care she was given, did she begin to accept her dying, long for relief, and ask how she could let go.

She had told me about her own work with dying people and her success in helping them shift their awareness to their home planet for an easy transition. But in her extremity she was rarely receptive herself to my guiding her home in this way. Much of her intellectual and philosophical subtlety had been stripped away or covered over by the intensity of the endless pain. It seemed to block off her ability to focus on subtler levels of awareness except, one hopes, when she was asleep. She came down to the level of a much more basic personality.

Despite her constantly reiterated aversion to life on Earth, she spent a great deal of time projecting and living in imaginary pictures of her desired future life. The longing for the beloved was very intense. She was constantly in anticipation of his imminent arrival to fulfill his promises to her and take her away in his limousine to his elegant estate in Switzerland with beautiful gardens, fish ponds, and loving children.

Many of my friends have often expressed the wish that this would be their last lifetime on Earth. Orayna always knew with certainty that this was her last lifetime on Earth. At the Intergalactic Federation Council, two thousand years ago, she and Hadron had volunteered to come here to awaken the awareness of Totality and Superconscious in the children of Earth. This lifetime, she always said, they had completed their mission. Perhaps it was because her final projects were never realized. Perhaps it was because in the end Orayna was all too human, much more human than she liked to pretend. But in the end she seemed, outwardly at least, unwilling to let go of all earthly attachments, as one of our nursing home dialogues may illustrate.

"Orayna, when you finally let go of your physical body, there'll be no more pain and suffering in a physical body."

"Oh, how wonderful!"

"There'll be no more old age, sickness, and death."

"Oh, how wonderful!"

"No more doctors and psychiatrists in their pain palaces."

"Oh, how wonderful!"

"No more Earth plane sexuality, the sweaty coupling of physical bodies."

"Oh, how wonderful!"

"No more big penises pounding at you, trying to get into you."

"Oh, how wonderful!"

"There'll be no more money, no more working for money, no more debt, no more taxes."

(disturbed) "Oh, no, no."

"You don't want to let go of money?"

"No, no."

"But Orayna, you always told me that on your home planet you didn't need money, that you could create realities with thought and there was no need for money."

"No, no. Got to have money. Got to have money."

"But, Orayna, if you've got to have money, then you have to come back to the Earth plane and have an Earth body in order to enjoy having money."

"Well, then that's the way it's got to be."

After the privilege of sharing dying and death with Orayna, I know with certainty that my time here is limited. I know with certainty that, barring accident or sudden death, eventually my body will fall apart and be unable to function as it is accustomed to, eventually my mind will fall apart and be unable to function as it is accustomed to, that eventually the elements of my carefully constructed personal reality will fall apart and no longer function, that eventually any residue of unhealed sorrows and unfulfilled desires will surface and be nakedly present, right in my face. That whatever I have been given, have accumulated or created, will all be lost. That at the end there will only be pain and breath and awareness, and awareness and breath, and ultimately only awareness.

14

REFLECTIONS
1999

It is said that when the student is ready the teacher will appear. On Thanksgiving 1983, at a time of abrupt total transition in my life, I was certainly ready for Joanna Walsh to appear in my life. She became my closest spiritual friend and mentor for the next fifteen years. She would not accept the common designation of spiritual teacher, for she claimed she did not use a spirit but operated directly as Superconscious. She also would not accept the label of teacher, preferring to refer to herself as a trigger, serving to stimulate people to an awareness of being Superconscious. Perhaps we could say, "When the gun is loaded the trigger will materialize."

Even today as I sit and listen to my mother hold forth endlessly about her perceptions and reflections or recall the many "long serious conversations" with my father when he would probe, if not comprehend, my youthful mind, I can see how behaviorally well conditioned I was for long sessions with Orayna when she would alternately hold forth endlessly on Superconscious and stimulate me to probe the depths of my own knowingness. It was an intimate familial relationship of mother and child, and I returned some of her generosity to me by helping her and serving her in every way I could.

My thirteen years at Lama Foundation had introduced me to a wide variety of spiritual traditions and practices, most importantly the practice of regular meditation. Lama Foundation welcomed and supported sincere travelers on many spiritual paths, promoted dialogue and exchange between various spiritual traditions, and encouraged the growth of the recognition of what Hazrat Inayat Khan called the unity of religious ideals. All genuine spiritual traditions lead the individual to awareness of and closeness with a Higher Power, called by whatever name you will, and open the individual to accept the presence and activity of a Higher Power in everyday life on Earth.

For me Orayna's understandings and methods were yet another valid living path to the one reality, called in her system Totality or Superconscious. Although it utilized some of the language and techniques of Scientology, Totality Concept has the advantage of being contemporary, self-originated and free of the negative accretions that encumber most religions. Although I honor and respect the millions of people for whom Jesus is God and who are saved by the love of Jesus, I also honor and respect the millions of people who have been murdered, tortured, raped and oppressed, whose cultures have been destroyed, in the name of "Jesus is God." I guess I'd rather take my chances with someone who comes from another planet.

Orayna wasn't at all interested in the variety of religions and spiritual traditions on Earth, unless she upon occasion found in them direct confirmation and validation of realities she had arrived at herself. As far as she was concerned, religions were the mechanisms by which various spiritual hierarchies (or *lowerarchies,* as she was fond of saying) controlled individual and collective human behavior and prevented the individual from realizing his or her own true superconscious reality.

When Jehovah's Witnesses came to her door, she told them that she was God, thank you very much, and what did they want to know. She could be arrogant, audacious, hyperbolic, and wildly humorous in her communications. Her role, she said, was not to teach but to trigger.

She would pick out certain words of Jesus, such as *"Know ye not that ye are gods?"*, which confirmed her point of view, but pay no attention to the whole story, the whole teachings of Jesus. *"Whatever you ask for in prayer, believe that you have received it and it will be yours."* Jesus knew the reality of Totality and Superconscious, which he called Abba or Father. The gems of his wisdom were sown into the fabric of the gospels.

The one tradition which she did research more deeply and enthusiastically was the Huna wisdom of Hawaii, whose knowledge of the conscious, subconscious, and superconscious mind, and the magic that could be worked through affecting the subconscious and invoking the superconscious, were very close to her own.

The whole gestalt of Orayna's metaphysical teachings was quite familiar to me, not from Scientology, for which I have little inclination, but from Sufi, Hindu, and Buddhist wisdom. Same soup, just a different name for all the ingredients and a different name for the soup itself.

Orayna was not much interested in the varieties of Earth-plane religious experience, unless someone happened to use the specific words *Totality* or *Superconscious.* Then she would get very excited. She did, however, see confirmation of her knowingness in the well-known teachings of Jesus and Buddha. Hers was yet another version of the *sanatana dharma,* the eternal truth, the perennial wisdom philosophy that mankind has arrived at, albeit with modern touches such as the Totalometer or the home planet.

My interest and her disinterest in various spiritual traditions was frustrating for me at first, as I have more of a scholarly nature. Over time I came to recognize and accept that she was a Saturn figure, over eighty years old, one who carries wisdom teachings crystallized in a certain form. After her husband passed away, she was the only one who held the specific form of the language and methodology that had been given to her by Superconscious. It was her role to hold and transmit the Totality teachings, undiluted by any other considerations.

Joanna opened up a fresh approach to the unity of consciousness and creation, which she called Totality. Though the language of Totality is modern and scientific (technological) the unity it guides one to is identical in essence with that unity seen by all the great spiritual traditions of humanity, although it may lack the depth and subtlety gained by the millennia of development that occurred in the major spiritual traditions.

By presenting me with a naive and "primitive" intellectual structure, Totality allowed me to integrate all of my previous intellectual and spiritual experiences under a thought umbrella untainted by deep cultural and social accretions. (The science-fiction wrappings of her teaching are much more humorous and much less threatening than, say, the trappings of the Roman Catholic Church.)

Of greater significance was the psychological clearing of karmic recordings and encumbrances that was realized by my work with Joanna. Mystical spirituality inspires one to experience unity, *sat-chit-ananda,* being-consciousness-bliss, while leaving the specific tasks of psychological clearing to the skill and grace of the guru and the relationship of the individual with the teacher.

Spiritual truth, spiritual reality, is unitive — one arrives at the same qualities of love, joy, peace, etc., no matter how one gets there. The aberrated egotism that veils this truth is individualistic, no matter how the mind may generalize it into delusion, aversion, attachment, etc. The forms that delusion configures itself in are particular to each individual, based on the idiosyncratic reactions to automatically recorded traumas in each psyche — which is why the specific attention of a spiritual guide is needed to clear the distortions, to relax the tightly knotted scars in each soul.

Frida Waterhouse, a teacher and guide for the Sufi community in San Francisco, would complain that mystical practices lead everyone into the experience of the light without clearing up the darkness of the garbage of psychic residue that everyone carries, which then aberrates the expression of light in form. Frida described herself as "the garbage can of the Sufi community." Joanna might have described herself as providing instruction in how to use the Vortexya Vacuum Cleaner.

Spiritual practice can lead to delusions of grandeur and illusions of unity without the personal guidance of a mentor. Spiritual practice must be complemented by deep psychological clearing when necessary, as it was for me, and as it is for most of us.

Over the years we worked together I danced around a classic paradox of unitive mysticism. Through my meditation and practice I quiet my self, empty my self, surrender my self, until I come to the awareness that Totality is all that is, a single unitive reality throughout all creation, and that my most essential and eternal being is Totality — in other words, contemplative awareness of union with God, of unity with all that is. On this very subtle level of awareness I also become aware that God speaks through me, moves through me, acts through me.

The tricky point is when my ego, my conscious mind, seizes hold of this and begins to identify its self, my limited self, as Totality. Then the ego, the conscious mind, assigns to itself or pretends to have all sorts of abilities and awarenesses that are not properly its own. The ego becomes intoxicated by this identification with Totality. By assuming that all my desires come from God, I move into the delusion that whatever I want is what God wants, whatever I want for me is what God wants for me, rather than continue to empty into the quietness and listen so closely for what God wants when "I" am no longer present.

I find myself in the classic paradox. Do I pray to God for what I want for me? Or do I listen to God for what God wants for me? Do I ask God to pray for me?

I can pray to God for what I want, and God does answer prayers — within reason, of course, and sometimes way beyond reason. And I can ask God from moment to moment, from day to day, what God wishes me to be, to do, in this moment, in this day.

What gets so confusing — it's more of a psychic or emotional paradox — is when desire gets so strong (my desire for Glory-us union) and so pure that it seems that at least some of the impulse is divine, while most of it is clearly just the working out of karmas for the purification and release — or further entanglement — of the soul.

Madame, would you prefer the thick, rich spaghetti of deeper bondage or the searing burning of karmic ribbons?

I mean, what's a girl (or guy) to do?

For quite a while it seemed fine to Glory for me to be holding a picture of us being together and seeing what God would provide. Then after a certain point it seemed to her like I was working sympathetic magic on her and she wanted me to stop it, which I did. It was only right for me to hold the picture of the two of us being together as long as we were both holding the picture of us being together. When she no longer wanted to hold a picture, a prayer, of us being together, I had to surrender and give it up. Otherwise I would be imposing the will of my desire on someone else and creating the karma of wishing to take away their freedom. As long as there was agreement between us *(agreements create realities)* there was some reality to our being together. When there was no longer agreement, there was no longer reality about being together. We woke up and found ourselves two separate individuals stuck together by our karmas, struggling to be free.

On the other hand, with Melinda I had used intentions put into vortex energy for psychic birth control to prevent pregnancy from occurring with us. She was aware that I was doing this and was in favor of it, until there came a time when she wanted very much to get pregnant, even though she didn't want to live with me or get married to bring a child into the world. She just wanted to get pregnant very badly. She became angry with me and told me that she didn't like me using the vortex energy to prevent pregnancy. But there was not agreement between us about the conditions for bringing a child into the world, so I continued to use the vortex energy and successfully prevented any conceptions. As it turned out, it was a good thing that I did.

I do not identify with or seek to identify with Totality or Superconscious in my personal reality, persona, mask, ego. I am aware that my body, personality, and ego are an ephemeral configuration of matter and energy, here today, gone tomorrow, a brief bubble in the foam of the ever-flowing river of life, gone today, here tomorrow. . . . The bubble only imagines it is an individuality for the most fleeting moment before being folded back into the river. At the same time I am aware of deeper and more abiding levels of reality within and beyond my ephemeral embodied individuality.

My personality cannot honestly or effectively pretend a superconscious individuality beyond time and space, and yet I Superconscious can and does pretend to be (and pretends it forgets it is pretending to be) my ephemeral embodied individuality. Superconscious awareness and abilities can spontaneously, and especially through necessity, become available to my individuality from time to time, but my individuality cannot honestly claim ownership or mastery of these awarenesses and abilities. I personally cannot make the statement "I TOTALITY IS"—even though "I TOTALITY IS" is a true statement both impersonally and personally.

This is one area where I did not agree with Orayna, although I did not argue with her about it. I felt she had a much too strong and unrealistic identification with Superconscious on the ego personality level. At the same time, her personal example and teaching were always waking me up to remember and experience that Totality is all that there is. It might be said that her presentation was superconscious positive affirmation, while my approach is superconscious surrender.

DEMONSTRATIONS
2001

Joanna placed a great deal of value upon the demonstration of superconscious awareness and abilities in individual lives, which she called Superconscious in action.

As it developed, for my part I placed a great deal of value on the cultivation of an attitude that combined surrender to a greater power in my life and a knowingness with certainty to trust and follow inspiration and guidance when it did come. In this way in times of crisis or uncertainty, rather than becoming agitated, fearful, and panicked, I calm the fluctuations of my mind and in the stillness listen, listen for inspiration and guidance, however subtle, knowing with certainty that guidance will come, knowing that everything happens at the right time, that things just seem to have a way of working themselves out, and that everything turns out all right. I keep clearing my space of the desperate efforts of my mind to control everything and the powerful welling forth of negative emotions from my reactive bank that threaten to engulf my space with foregone conclusions of rejection, abandonment, failure, and futility.

For example, at one point I sat for exams to qualify for employment in the state department of taxation and revenue. Fortunately it was a multiple choice (multiple guess) exam, for as I worked my way through the test I found that at least 40% of the questions I was unprepared for. Rather than clutch, brake, and squeal the wheels, with a certain bemusement I took this as an opportunity to test superconscious knowingness. My game plan was simple — answer every question; if you can figure out the answer, mark it down; if you don't know the answer, don't try and figure it out, just allow yourself to know and mark it down. It's certainly a lot easier to allow yourself to know than to try and figure everything out, especially when you have one chance in four of happening upon the right answer anyway. So I was pleased but not surprised a few weeks later when the test results were posted and I got 97%—on an exam that I was only 60% prepared for. I never did go to work for the tax department.

More and more I find that what I think I want to have happen is far less important than clearing my space to allow what is going to happen anyway to happen in the best way, without resistance or uncertainty, greed or fear. Being ever alert to the opportunity to fulfill desires does not necessarily mean taking advantage of every opportunity to fulfill desires. Some old desires may no longer be necessary or even appropriate when their time comes for fulfillment. It may be more appropriate to consciously let go of that desire and move deeper into the great mystery of whatever is going to happen anyway.

All desires will be fulfilled sooner or later. Desires create the universes. All manifestation is the materialization of desires. All desires seek and find fulfillment, even if not in this life, in this body. All desires will result in manifestation, sooner or later, unless they are consciously released.

All my life I have been obsessed with and intoxicated by the desire for love and beauty. And all my desires have been fulfilled, however briefly. Glory and I shared ultimate romantic spiritual love together. Melinda and I shared ultimate romantic sexual love together. My dance with Glory spanned five years. My dance with Melinda lasted four years. Long enough to know that it is real, short enough to miss it deeply when it goes away. As Dan Hicks sings, "*How can I miss you if you don't go away?*"

My primal desire has been fulfilled in this lifetime. It is important that I recognize that. I am so grateful that my desire for love has been fulfilled, so that my love can be greater and flow where it is needed. Do I expect anything to last forever?

So what else do I want? Of course I want. Desire keeps the game in play. But as desire becomes subtler and subtler and more and more is surrendered to the great love we all are, the game becomes much more interesting.

ALL WE ARE IS LOVE

All we need is love. All we are is love. All we need is to realize that who we already are is love. As human beings we all need to experience total love from another — mother, father, brother, sister, lover, friend, teacher, guru, guide, God, Totality, in whatever name or form — so that we can reflect and recognize that we are the love, the deep love, and begin to give the love we are to everyone. Sufis say that *ishk* is the love, the glue, the binding force, that attracts us to be in the life, the creation, in each other — and that the sole purpose of love is beauty, the exquisite life form that is each one of us. *Ishk Allah Mabood Lillah.* God is Love, Lover, and Beloved.

My mother is the primal love that sustained me through all the aberrations and distortions that arose in my karmic unfoldment. But I was lost in the dark forest until I met Ram Dass, who touched the inner presence, the *sadguru*, until I came together with Glory, my twin flame who rekindled the light of my soul, and until I did the deep work with Orayna, who held me in total lovingkindness and infinite patience until the veils of fear began to clear. Now I know that all the interdependent originations of my consciousness are love unfolding. I know that I was conceived in love and born in love, that I live in love and die in love.

I acknowledge all my conflicts with my father, my teachers, my lovers, my friends, releasing them and blessing them. Love brought us together. Karma tears us apart. My father was the best father he knew how to be, tossing the baseball back and forth on twilight lawns, imposing sweaty tasks and chores on me to teach me how to work, wrestling with my wild and unruly mind. Likewise my lovers, teachers, and friends gave me the best they had to give in the moment and then withdrew to let me go my own way. I may have been angry with them and they may have been angry with me from the frustration of union denied. But such is life.

I am life, I am love, I am awareness, I am ability — but not in my ego personality, which is at best a slave of the life, the love, the awareness, the ability. The blessing is in the mystery of the deep love that lives in us all. And for the self-identified human personality there is merely a poignancy, a bittersweet fragrance of desire.

Desire is endless and all-consuming, never fulfilled. Desire creates the universes. Is the glass half empty or half full? If I identify only with my body there is only bitterness, loss, and remorse. But in my soul I know that all my desires have been fulfilled—for love, for sex, for money, for power, for recognition, for knowledge, for wholeness, for completion—however brief and fleeting the moment. And all my unfulfilled desires will be fulfilled, for that is what keeps me in the game. And recognizing the inevitable fulfillment of all desires, what can I have but awe and gratitude for the love that glues us all together—and detachment from the outcomes that are part of a greater play.

NOW HERE THIS

When I went to Ram Dass's public darshan in Santa Fe in October 1996, I heard him say that he was coming to think of three levels of being: ego, soul, and awareness (awareness here meaning consciousness beyond time and space). As usual Ram Dass had the gift of formulating with elegant simplicity realizations that had been nudging around in my head for some time.

So then and there someone asked him, "What about reincarnation? Is that real or not?"

And Ram Dass replied, as best I can remember, "From the point of view of awareness there is no reincarnation, for there is no identification, only pure awareness. However, there may be and often is some self-identification on the soul level after the body is dropped. So then I would say: that which identifies reincarnates."

Nisargadatta Maharaj says, "The memory of the past unfulfilled desires traps energy, which manifests itself as a person. When its charge gets exhausted, the person dies. Unfulfilled desires are carried over into the next birth. Self-identification with the body creates ever fresh desires and there is no end to them, unless this mechanism of bondage is clearly seen. It is clarity that is liberation, for you cannot abandon desire, unless its causes and effects are clearly seen. I do not say that the same person is reborn. It dies and dies for good. But its memories remain and their desires and fears. They supply the energy for a new person. The real takes no part in it, but makes it possible by giving it the light."

KEEP STEPPING ALONG

Orayna's visions of creations and desires for manifestations were so much greater for her at age eighty than mine are for me now at age fifty. She concentrated wholeheartedly on employing all the visualizations and prayers that she could to bring in the millions of dollars she knew she needed to found her Majine doll industry and establish her community. She put crystals on top of her own picture and pictures of large denominations of currency to pull the money in. She believed in sweepstakes and lotteries to pull it all in.

On the other hand, it seems like many of the lives I have been living are over—much of the self-identification with karmas propelling me into writing poetry, singing songs, capturing images, and giving myself over to romantic relationships. Even all the new blueprints for life I carefully crafted under Orayna's guidance are now washed away in the passage of time, although they did have their effect in their own time. It might seem sad or at least poignant that all these self-identifications have blown away, but it is actually joyful and liberating to be less controlled by karmic compulsions. Right now my creative vision extends about as far as finishing this book and seeing it published. Other than that I am present in the present moment, awake and available for whatever and whoever comes into my common presence.

So I wake and sit in stillness, in emptiness, in the morning, listening, glistening, simply aware. Then I go out, drive up to the mountains, walk along the empty paths in the warm sunlight on a bright, clear day like today, and speak these words into my tape recorder. As my heart keeps beating, my feet keep stepping along. . . .

TOTAL MEDITATION TAPE

*This is the transcription of a tape recording made by Joanna Walsh
on July 28, 1985.*
This is a generic concentration on healing the physical body.
This is given as an example of the Total Meditation.
*If you wish to try and experience this, have someone read it to you while you
are sitting quietly.*

This is your Total Meditation.
Relax your body totally. . . .
Breathe in and out to the count of four.
Breathe in, two three four. . . . Out, two three four. . . .
In, two three four. . . . Out, two three four. . . .
Good. . . . Relax. . . .

There is more than ninety-nine percent space in your body.
Be aware of being the space in your body.
Be aware that you are totally present in your body.
Become familiar with that as a fact.
Space in matter is a basic truth.
Less than one percent energy forms the matter in your body.
Your eyes can only see three dimensions of matter.
Your physical eyes cannot see this truth.
The first step for the evolutionary era we're coming into
is to get our facts straight and know the truth,
beginning with knowing the space in your body.

Be aware that you are totally present as the space in your body.

Be there as the space in your body.
Become familiar with being that much space in your body,
all through your whole body.
You are the total presence in your body.
Realize this and know this is the truth.

Be aware of being the space in and around your body.
Include your astral and etheric bodies, for they also contain your
recordings.
In and around your body, be aware of being the space.

Now be aware of being the space that your room is in.
The room is less than one percent energy.
You are totally present as the space in your room.
Become familiar with this realization.
Begin to look at reality this way, because this is scientific truth.
Be aware that the room is within you.

Now be aware that the town you live in
is an energy within your total self space.
You are the space, you the total presence.
The birds fly through you, the breeze blows through you,
and your town exists within your total space.
You are the ever eternal present space.
Realize these things and know them to be true.
Come into the perfect realization that you are everywhere,
and without you, Totality, space — the state of being whole and complete —
no thing could exist in any universe.

Now be aware that the planet Earth and its force-fields
are within you, your total presence, space.
The planet Earth is no more than the size of an orange, even though
it is heavy,
within your space.
You are more than ninety-nine percent present,
and the planet is within you, your total space.

Now be aware that the Solar System is within your space.
The planets and their force-fields revolving around the Sun
exist within you, your total space.
They too are less than one percent energy,
and you are totally, eternally present,
enabling them to exist in your space.

Now be aware that our entire galaxy exists in your space —
this immense vortex of billions upon billions of stars,
planets, and comets, and all kinds of energy manifestations,
all kinds of planetary systems, no end to them —
exist within the eternal presence of your space.

Be aware of being the space in which the entire universe exists —
dark clouds of matter and galactic worlds without end,
black holes, pulsars, quasars, radio stars, infinite creations of energy —
within your total self.
Your eternal presence allows them to exist.
Realize this and know that this is the truth.
This is the nature of your total self.

Be aware of being the stillness.
Be the stillness. . . . stillness. . . . stillness. . . .
Be aware of being the stillness.

Be aware of being vastness.
Being vastness. . . . vastness. . . . vastness. . . .
Be aware of being vastness.

Be aware of being motionless.
Without motion. . . . motionless. . . . motionless. . . .
Be aware of being motionless.

Be aware of being timeless.
Outside of time. . . . timeless. . . . timeless. . . .
Be aware of being timeless.

Be aware of being foreverness.
Foreverness. . . . foreverness. . . .
Be aware of being foreverness.

This is your nature as Totality.
Be still and know. . . . Be still and know. . . .
This is your nature, your total self nature.

Now begin to remember, remember, remember. . . .
Remember your first created energy from your total self,
your first created white-light vortex energy,
high incredible speed of energy,
your superconscious mind—*yes!*—
in direct contact with total awareness, total ability, all knowledge.
Anything that ever was created or ever will be created
exists in Totality, your total self—
the state of being whole and complete.
And the white-light vortex energy is your superconscious mind,
that has direct communication with Totality, as an individualized unit.
Realize this. . . . Just realize this. . . .

Now be aware of being your superconscious mind.
Be aware of being your superconscious mind.
Realize that you have direct contact with all knowledge.
You have total ability and total awareness.
Be aware of this. . . . Realize this. . . .
Become thoroughly familiar with this fact,
because you will be using your superconscious mind on a daily basis from
now on.
This is how you will participate in the evolution of Earth that is now
occurring,
how Homo Novus, New Being, will develop—
by using the superconscious mind to create and produce life
for the next Evolutionary Era of Earth.
Realize this. . . .

Be your superconscious mind—
that exquisite white-light vortex energy.
Realize your total ability and total awareness.
Establish this firmly.
And realize that you are outside time.
You are the producer of the desires of your body.
This is your function as superconscious mind.
You are the producer because you have total ability
to achieve any desires for any time span,
and you use pure thought to produce your desires.
Realize this.... Realize this....

You use pure thought to project any pictures, images, or ideas
into the time stream of Earth, for your physical body and the planet.
That's incredible, but that's exactly what you do.
Now be your superconscious mind,
and project a communication to your conscious mind,
a communication line to your conscious mind,
which is that great creative power in the fourth plane of existence,
where you use your imagination.
Be aware that you're doing this now.
Be your superconscious mind,
and project communication to your subconscious mind,
the photographer of electromagnetic images,
pictures of the past and of the present.
You can do this....You can do this....
Be aware that you're doing this right now,
because this is your game of life.
You're the one that is planting seed pictures,
seed pictures in the ethers that gather light particles to manifest.
You're the one that's doing this.
You will be using your imagination to visualize
the changes you desire for your body.
You have innate visualization abilities.

If there is any condition in your body that you want to change,
any condition in your body that you want to change,
be aware of that so-called condition in your body.
Be aware of it.
Put your attention on it.
Put your attention on it now.
If it's nerves, if it's ears, if it's eyes, if it's glands
if it's organs, if it's your back, if it's your legs, arms, or head,
Put your attention on that area.

Now be aware that there is a vortex of energy,
a vortex of energy in and around your physical body.
You can imagine it — however, IT IS REAL.
The vortex includes your astral and etheric body.
Your body would not exist without the vortex.
And the vortex is there, reacting out the pictures,
the pictures you have previously put into your body,
the pictures stored in the subconscious mind,
which may relate to these conditions that the body is experiencing.

Now this is the process for the use of the vortex.
The information goes from right to left into the vortex.
The information goes counterclockwise into the vortex.
The information is to release those conditions
that you have put your attention on,
and the causes of those conditions in your body,
to release those causes and conditions in your body.
The information is to release them with certainty.
Now the information is going in from right to left.
The information turns into energy,
and you can see it going around the vortex.
As it rapidly goes in and around the vortex,
down to the apex,
the information to release those conditions from your body,
to release the causes of those conditions that you have put your
attention on.

It is your desire that they be released from this body now.
Watch that information going down to the apex,
down to the apex, the power point.
Watch it. . . . Watch it good. . . .
See how it works for you.
You're the creator.
The information gets down to the apex,
and when it does, there is a tremendous explosion.
The energy reacts clockwise like an explosion.
It goes clockwise up back out the vortex,
cleaning out those conditions that you have put your attention on,
clearing those conditions and their causes,
clearing them totally out of your body,
sending them back into space where they came from.
Watch it go to work for you.
It's marvelous to know that you have something
that's universal energy working for you.

Look at the cells of your body
in those areas that you want to release,
that you have made the decision to release,
Watch the vortex clearing your body.
It's the biggest vacuum cleaner you can have,
cleaning all the conditions out of the cells of your body.
See your cells begin to sparkle as they clear.
See your nerves begin to sparkle as they clear.
Feel the freedom from those pictures.
Feel the freedom from those conditions
as the vortex is cleaning up for you,
sending all those conditions and their causes
out of your body, back into space.
Feel the difference. . . . See the difference. . . .
See how clean your body is getting.
See how beautiful your nerves are revived,
how clean your glands and organs are — and any other area you want
to heal.

See how wonderful your ears can hear and your eyes can see.
And feel the joy of this release.
And know, *know* that you have done this,
you, *you*, you have done this.
It's your decision. . . . Know it. . . .

While you see it all clear, if there's any little segment left,
let the vortex clean it out for you.
Let the condition go back into space.
See it clear. . . . See it clear. . . .
Every cell in your body clear. . . .
Your blood clear. . . .
Your ears opened up to hear. . . .
Your eyes can see. . . .
Every organ in your body clear. . . .
Your blood is at a normal pressure. . . .
See it normal. . . . Feel it normal. . . .
Put the feeling there—a normal functioning of all your glands
and organs *now*.
See it clear. . . . Feel it clear. . . .
And *you* did it.
Know that you did it.
Put the knowing in there that you did it,
because everything you do the subconscious records,
the subconscious takes pictures of.
So put a knowing there, a knowing,
for you the superconscious mind is the knower.
And put in a joy with certainty, a joy with certainty.

Now that you have cleared your wonderful body,
now you can create and give your pictures to your body.
This is the first time on Earth
that this way is known to do this.
And this is a part of your evolution for the new era of planet Earth,
part of your Homo Novus—New Being—development.
So let's really get with it now.

In the room create an image of your body.
Select the space in the room and create an image,
a three-dimensional image of your body in color,
a three-dimensional image of your body in color.
You are creating this, using your imagination,
your fourth-dimensional ability, your imagination.
We do have gifts to use, such as visualization.
Let us use the gifts we have.
Keep putting that body there. . . .
Perfect it. . . . Perfect it. . . .
Now see that body that you've created.
Visualize it and see how perfect it is.
It's eyes are so sharp to see. . . .
It's ears are so sharp to hear. . . .
Blood is flowing throughout its body at a beautiful normal rate
of vibration. . . .
See all of this. . . . Feel it. . . . Know it. . . .
Take the picture. . . .
Take a good picture. . . .
Do not be skimpy about this.
This is your image for the New Age of Earth.
Be good to it. . . .
Feel the joy that now you can create your life.
You can create your body of perfect health,
your body of happiness and success.
You have that ability.
Know that you have that ability.
Put whatever it is you want in that body,
in that body and with that body,
whatever it is you want, whatever it is you want —
if it's money, if it's a home, a mate — whatever.
You create it and give it to your body.
This is your rightful heritage.
See how joyous your created body is.
Feel the joy. . . . Feel the joy. . . .
Feel the love you have for your newly created body.

Keep putting it there. . . .
Keep putting it there. . . .
Your own creation, as you want it.
Keep putting it there. . . .
Keep putting it there. . . .
You have the opportunity now
to have your body the way you want it,
the perfect body the way you want it to look and to feel,
and everything in it, and everything for it.
And that's a fact.
You don't have to believe in it.
You don't have to pray for it.
You don't have to have faith in it.
Just do it.
The technology's been given to us on how to do this.

Any time you want to add to your blueprint you can do it
but keep developing it, keep holding the picture.
Be good to it. . . .
You cannot afford not to.

Now move your blueprint, your picture
that you have visualized, into your body.
Turn it around. . . . Fit it into your body. . . .
That's right. . . . All the way in. . . .
Put it in there.
Feel it in there.
Enjoy it in there.
Move it in. . . . Move it in. . . .
Feel all of that wonderful stuff you've created going into your body.
Feel how wonderful it is.
It's like a soothing balm.
You're putting it there. . . .
You're giving it to the body. . . .
You're the creator.
You're Totality — a state of being whole and complete —

ninety-nine plus percent right here in your precious body.
You're Totality.
Feel the body all the way in. . . .
Get the difference. . . . Feel the difference. . . .
The ears can hear. . . . The eyes can see. . . .
The blood is operating at a beautiful, even tempo. . . .
Every organ in your body is just a gem, beautiful, alive, and healthy. . . .

All right, now that you've got it in there,
we address the subconscious mind, the photographer,
and tell it to take this picture.
It supersedes all former pictures.
It supersedes all past life pictures.
This is your own personal creation — for the first time on this planet.
And that is wonderful. . . . It's wonderful. . . .
Feel how wonderful it is. . . .
Love that body and that joy. . . .
Love it, cherish it, enjoy it, enjoy it. . . .
Let nothing interfere with that body.

Now be aware that there is a vortex in and around your body,
and in the astral body and the etheric body,
and give this information to the vortex,
going in from right to left, counterclockwise :
This is my new body!
This is my new body!
This perfect creation is mine!
Now watch that information turn into energy
and go rapidly from right to left,
down to the apex, the center, the power point.
Watch it. . . . Watch it. . . .
It does it for you.
All you have to do is to put it in there.
You're the creator.
The vortex is the worker.
See what it's doing for you,

putting your new image in there,
down to the apex, the powerhouse.
Make sure it gets to the apex,
down to the apex, down to the apex,
and then it explodes back out clockwise,
the tremendous energy of the vortex clockwise,
all the way through your body,
all the way through your astral and etheric bodies,
recording the new body you've put in there,
reacting it out for you,
reacting it out to cause persistence,
Let it develop. . . . Please let it develop. . . .
Don't interfere. . . .You have done a wonderful thing.
Let no other thought come in.
Just let the vortex react out this new body for you.
The photographer, the subconscious, has got the picture,
and the vortex is reacting it out for you.
You put it in there. . . .You see it. . . . .
It's a different body than you had before.
Recognize the difference!
Feel the difference!
Feel the goodies!
Feel the blood operating at a wonderful normal rate. . . .
And the vision is there, the hearing is there. . . .
Every gland and organ is perfect. . . .
Now we take this goodie,
this creation of the director,
the conscious mind that is in the fourth plane,
the conscious mind that can imagine —
and give it to yourself, your superconscious mind.
Give it to yourself. . . .
You are the producer.
Give it to yourself. . . . Give it to yourself. . . .
And be aware that you,
this white-light vortex energy,
is receiving this wonderful creation of the director.

And watch the producer take your creation
and put the thought and the picture into the time stream of Earth.
Watch it do that. . . .
Into the time stream of Earth.
Watch it. . . .
It becomes the moment from now that we call the future.

And from now on know this —

that you have followed a scientific principle of creation,
and you are determined to be true to it,
for you cannot afford to be otherwise in this New Evolutionary Era
of Earth.

Relax with joy at what you have achieved. . . .
Relax with joy and love. . . .
For this is the truth. . . .

PEACE ON EARTH

THE RIGHTFUL HERITAGE OF ALL UNIVERSES

PEACE ON EARTH - MEANS - FRESH AIR
NO BEING HAS THE RIGHT TO DEPRIVE HIMSELF
OR OTHERS OF THE BREATH OF LIFE.

PEACE ON EARTH - MEANS - CLEAN WATER
UNPOLLUTED WITH CHEMICALS OR WASTE PRODUCTS.

PEACE ON EARTH - MEANS - PURE FOODS
UNADULTERATED OR POISONED WITH PRESERVATIVES.

A NEW ERA IS DAWNING - THE AGE OF AQUARIUS IS TERMED THE
AGE OF ENLIGHTENMENT - THE TIME FOR KNOWING SPIRITUAL
VALUES AND EXPANDING AWARENESS ON PLANET EARTH.
THE ENVIRONMENTAL DESTRUCTION NOW OCCURRING CLEARLY
INDICATES WE STILL ARE BARBARIANS. IT IS ESSENTIAL TO
SURVIVAL THAT WE BECOME CIVILIZED - NOW.
WHAT IF YOU RETURN - NEXT LIFE-TIME? PRESENT SHORT-
SIGHTEDNESS COULD LEAD TO RESULTS UNMENTIONABLE HERE.

WE DO HAVE THE ABILITY TO DO SOMETHING ABOUT IT -
BE CAUSE:

SOME PART OF YOU KNOWS

T - TODAY I GRANT MYSELF THE RIGHT TO BE AWARE
    THAT - I - TOTALITY IS PRESENT -
    AS TOTALITY - NOW.
O - OF THIS I AM CERTAIN - AS TOTALITY THERE
    IS A TOTAL PRESENCE OF MYSELF WITHIN MY
    FAMILY AND MY LOVED ONES.
T - THEREFORE I - TOTALITY IS PRESENT, ALSO
    WITHIN GROUPS OF PEOPLE, CITIES,
    COMMUNITIES AND NATIONS.
A - AND THUS, I - TOTALITY IS PRESENT THROUGH-
    OUT ALL MANKIND. TRULY AM I THE "KEEPER"
    OF MY BROTHER.
L - LOVE I THEN, ALL LIVING THINGS WITHIN
    WHICH I DISCOVER THE TOTAL IMMORTAL
    PRESENCE OF MYSELF.
I - I - TOTALITY IS PRESENT THROUGHOUT ALL
    MATTER, ENERGY, SPACE AND CONSECUTIVE
    LOCATIONS KNOWN AS TIME.
T - TOTALLY AND INESCAPABLY I DISCOVER THAT
    ALL DIVINE BEINGS AND SPIRITS ARE
    MIRACULOUSLY WOVEN WITHIN THE MATRIX
    CREATED BY TOTALITY - MYSELF.
Y - YOU AND YOU AND I JOIN OUR AWARENESS AND
    CREATIVE THOUGHTS THIS DAY AND KNOW
    THAT I - TOTALITY IS -
    THE CREATIVE ETERNAL PRESENCE OF SELF.

    TOTALITY - A STATE OF BEING WHOLE
              AND COMPLETE.

TOTALITY - THE UNIVERSITY OF TOTOLOGY   701209
2544 WEST SEVENTH STREET LOS ANGELES, CALIFORNIA 213 - 388-7111

QUOTATION SOURCES

Because this book is mostly an oral history, quotations are given as remembered and spoken, some no more than fragments of song. Bible quotes are from the Revised Standard Version, even though oral memory is from the King James Version.

Throughout the book are quotations from *The Totality Concept — Beyond Immortality* by Hardin D. Walsh, PhD, HGA, TM, completed in 1976, used by permission of Totality Research and Development Corporation.

p. 35: Joe Miller— see *Great Song — The Life and Teachings of Joe Miller* edited by Richard Power, Maypop [Athens GA, 1993]

pp. 83, 289: "As Rumi says, '*Increase the necessity*'." — "Without need the Almighty God does not give anything to anyone. Need, then is the noose for (all) things that exist: Man has instruments in proportion to his need. Therefore quickly augment thy need, O needy one, in order that the Sea of Bounty may surge up in lovingkindness." — *The Mathnawi of Jalaluddin Rumi, Book II, 3274, 3279-3280*, translated by R. A. Nicholson, Luzac & Co. Ltd [London, 1972]

p. 115: "The love of money is the root of evil." — *1 Timothy 6:10:* "For the love of money is the root of all evils; it is through this craving that some have wandered away from the faith and pierced their hearts with many pangs."

p. 120: "Resist ye not evil." — *Matthew 5:39:* "But I say to you, Do not resist one who is evil. But if any one strikes you on the right cheek, turn to him the other also. . . ."

341

p. 181: Father William McNamara — see *The Art of Being Human*, Bruce [Milwaukee, 1962] and *The Human Adventure* — *Contemplation for Everyman*, Doubleday [Garden City NY, 1974]

p. 219, p. 232, p. 302: "... as Jesus said Be still and know."—*Psalms 46:10:* "Be still, and know that I am God."

p. 221: "Suffer the little children to come unto me." — *Matthew 9:14:* "... but Jesus said, 'Let the children come to me, and do not hinder them; for to such belongs the kingdom of heaven.'"

p. 230: "Our dear friend Dr. Einstein tells us, '*Imagination is greater than knowledge.*' And he said, '*I function from the fourth dimension.*' — The actual quote is: "Imagination is more important than knowledge." I have no source for the second quote.

p.232, p. 312: "Ask for that which you desire, knowing you already have it." — *Mark 11:23–24:* "Truly, I say to you, whoever says to this mountain, 'Be taken up and case into the sea,' and does not doubt in his heart, but believes that what he says will come to pass, it will be done for him. Therefore I tell you, whatever you ask in prayer, believe that you receive it, and you will."

p. 232, p. 312: "Know ye not that ye are gods? Know ye not?" — *John 10:34:* "Jesus answered them, 'Is it not written in your law, "I said, you are gods"?'" — which refers to *Psalms 82:6–7:* "I say, 'You are gods, sons of the Most High, all of you; nevertheless, you shall die like men and fall like any prince.'"

p. 259: Hazrat Inayat Khan — I cannot locate this quote in his published writings. It may be from his unpublished gathas.

p. 314: Frida Waterhouse — see *Why Me?* and *Tomorrow Never Comes*, Rainbow Bridge [San Francisco, 1974 and 1978]

p. 320: Nisargadatta Maharaj — p.381, *I Am That, Talks with Sri Nisargadatta Maharaj,* translated by Maurice Frydman, The Acorn Press [Durham NC, 1973]

ILLUSTRATION SOURCES

All cloud photographs by author.

All personal photographs used by permission of Totality Research and Development Corporation, with the exception of the photograph of Joanna on p. 224, which is by Sydney Brink and used by permission of the Santa Fe Reporter.

All drawings, diagrams, and charts by Hardin D. Walsh, used by permission of Totality Research and Development Corporation — with the exception of the diagram *Universal Vortex Energy — A Scientific Model* p. 59 (adapted from scientific diagrams whose source is unknown) and the diagram *Psychic Function and Use of Vortex Energy*, p. 60, both of which were created by the author.

Author photo by Roberta "Bird" Sharples.

Ahad Cobb is an accountant, astrologer, jyotishi, photographer, poet, musician, and leader of the Dances of Universal Peace. He was a long-term resident and is a continuing member of Lama Foundation, San Cristobal, New Mexico. He is the author of several books of poetry, the most recent being *Image Nation*. He lives in Santa Fe, New Mexico.